C-4999   CAREER EXAMINATION SERIES

This is your
PASSBOOK for...

NYC Bridge Exam

Test Preparation Study Guide
Questions & Answers

NATIONAL LEARNING CORPORATION®

COPYRIGHT NOTICE

This book is SOLELY intended for, is sold ONLY to, and its use is RESTRICTED to individual, bona fide applicants or candidates who qualify by virtue of having seriously filed applications for appropriate license, certificate, professional and/or promotional advancement, higher school matriculation, scholarship, or other legitimate requirements of education and/or governmental authorities.

This book is NOT intended for use, class instruction, tutoring, training, duplication, copying, reprinting, excerption, or adaptation, etc., by:

1) Other publishers
2) Proprietors and/or Instructors of "Coaching" and/or Preparatory Courses
3) Personnel and/or Training Divisions of commercial, industrial, and governmental organizations
4) Schools, colleges, or universities and/or their departments and staffs, including teachers and other personnel
5) Testing Agencies or Bureaus
6) Study groups which seek by the purchase of a single volume to copy and/or duplicate and/or adapt this material for use by the group as a whole without having purchased individual volumes for each of the members of the group
7) Et al.

Such persons would be in violation of appropriate Federal and State statutes.

PROVISION OF LICENSING AGREEMENTS – Recognized educational, commercial, industrial, and governmental institutions and organizations, and others legitimately engaged in educational pursuits, including training, testing, and measurement activities, may address request for a licensing agreement to the copyright owners, who will determine whether, and under what conditions, including fees and charges, the materials in this book may be used them. In other words, a licensing facility exists for the legitimate use of the material in this book on other than an individual basis. However, it is asseverated and affirmed here that the material in this book CANNOT be used without the receipt of the express permission of such a licensing agreement from the Publishers. Inquiries re licensing should be addressed to the company, attention rights and permissions department.

All rights reserved, including the right of reproduction in whole or in part, in any form or by any means, electronic or mechanical, including photocopying, recording, or by any information storage and retrieval system, without permission in writing from the Publisher.

Copyright © 2024 by
National Learning Corporation

212 Michael Drive, Syosset, NY 11791
(516) 921-8888 • www.passbooks.com
E-mail: info@passbooks.com

PUBLISHED IN THE UNITED STATES OF AMERICA

PASSBOOK® SERIES

THE *PASSBOOK® SERIES* has been created to prepare applicants and candidates for the ultimate academic battlefield – the examination room.

At some time in our lives, each and every one of us may be required to take an examination – for validation, matriculation, admission, qualification, registration, certification, or licensure.

Based on the assumption that every applicant or candidate has met the basic formal educational standards, has taken the required number of courses, and read the necessary texts, the *PASSBOOK® SERIES* furnishes the one special preparation which may assure passing with confidence, instead of failing with insecurity. Examination questions – together with answers – are furnished as the basic vehicle for study so that the mysteries of the examination and its compounding difficulties may be eliminated or diminished by a sure method.

This book is meant to help you pass your examination provided that you qualify and are serious in your objective.

The entire field is reviewed through the huge store of content information which is succinctly presented through a provocative and challenging approach – the question-and-answer method.

A climate of success is established by furnishing the correct answers at the end of each test.

You soon learn to recognize types of questions, forms of questions, and patterns of questioning. You may even begin to anticipate expected outcomes.

You perceive that many questions are repeated or adapted so that you can gain acute insights, which may enable you to score many sure points.

You learn how to confront new questions, or types of questions, and to attack them confidently and work out the correct answers.

You note objectives and emphases, and recognize pitfalls and dangers, so that you may make positive educational adjustments.

Moreover, you are kept fully informed in relation to new concepts, methods, practices, and directions in the field.

You discover that you are actually taking the examination all the time: you are preparing for the examination by "taking" an examination, not by reading extraneous and/or supererogatory textbooks.

In short, this PASSBOOK®, used directedly, should be an important factor in helping you to pass your test.

NYC BRIDGE EXAM

The New York City Bridge Exam is designed to offer you the opportunity to take one multiple-choice test for multiple titles and have your name appear on multiple civil service lists simultaneously if you meet the minimum qualification requirements.

With this new and innovative approach, during the application period, you will submit one application for the New York City Bridge Exam. On the day of the multiple-choice test, you will choose the title(s) that you wish to be considered for.

The current titles covered by this exam are:
- Bookkeeper
- Clerical Associate
- Computer Service Technician
- Maintenance Worker
- Secretary
- Staff Analyst Trainee

SCOPE OF THE EXAMINATION
You will be given an exam consisting of two parts: A Qualifying Education and Experience Exam for each title selected and a multiple-choice test at a computer terminal. Applicants must meet the minimum qualification requirements for each title selected. A civil service list will be established for each title separately.

The Qualifying Education and Experience Test:
The Qualifying Education and Experience test will be administered on the same date as the multiple-choice test. You will receive a rating of Qualified or Not Qualified on the Qualified Education and Experience Test for each title you selected.

The Multiple-Choice Test:
Your score on this test will be used to determine your place on each eligible list. You must achieve a score of at least 70% to pass the test. The multiple-choice test is designed to assess the extent to which candidates have certain abilities determined to be important to the performance of the tasks of each title. Task areas to be tested include: administrative duties, communication and correspondence, records management, and research and analysis.

The multiple-choice test may include questions requiring the use of any of the following abilities:

- **Deductive Reasoning**: the ability to apply general rules to specific problems to come up with logical answers. Example: A Bookkeeper, Clerical Associate, Clerical Associate (NYC H+H), Computer Service Technician, Maintenance Worker, Maintenance Worker (CUNY), Maintenance Worker (NYC H+H), Secretary, or Staff Analyst Trainee may use this ability when researching and cross-referencing discrepancies, irregularities, or fluctuations in reports, records, or statements in order to verify details.

- **Inductive Reasoning**: the ability to combine separate pieces of information or specific answers to problems to form general rules or conclusions; to think of possible reasons for why things go together. Example: A Bookkeeper, Clerical Associate, Clerical Associate (NYC H+H), Computer Service Technician, Maintenance Worker, Maintenance Worker (CUNY), Maintenance Worker (NYC H+H), Secretary, or Staff Analyst Trainee may use this ability when comparing, verifying, and reconciling data from multiple record sources in order to ensure accuracy of information and for conformity with established policy and procedures.
- **Information Ordering**: the ability to follow correctly a rule or set of rules or actions in a certain order. The rule or set of rules used must be given. The things or actions to be put in order can include numbers, letters, words, pictures, procedures, sentences and mathematical or logical operations. Example: A Bookkeeper, Clerical Associate, Clerical Associate (NYC H+H), Computer Service Technician, Maintenance Worker, Maintenance Worker (CUNY), Maintenance Worker (NYC H+H), Secretary, or Staff Analyst Trainee may use this ability when monitoring and updating records.
- **Memorization**: the ability to remember information, such as words, numbers, pictures & procedures. Pieces of information can be remembered by themselves or with other pieces of information. Example: A Bookkeeper, Clerical Associate, Clerical Associate (NYC H+H), Computer Service Technician, Maintenance Worker, Maintenance Worker (CUNY), Maintenance Worker (NYC H+H), Secretary, or Staff Analyst Trainee may use this ability when reading department guidelines and regulations, including general orders, operations orders, policies and procedures, computer messages and manuals, to stay informed and inform relevant parties of department procedural changes.
- **Problem Sensitivity**: the ability to tell when something is wrong or likely to go wrong. It includes being able to identify the whole problem, as well as elements of the problem. Example: A Bookkeeper, Clerical Associate, Clerical Associate (NYC H+H), Computer Service Technician, Maintenance Worker, Maintenance Worker (CUNY), Maintenance Worker (NYC H+H), Secretary, or Staff Analyst Trainee may use this ability when planning and collecting, organizing, analyzing, interpreting, and presenting data relative to the problems of the group or organization.
- **Time Sharing**: the ability to shift back and forth between two or more sources of information. Example: A Bookkeeper, Clerical Associate, Clerical Associate (NYC H+H), Computer Service Technician, Maintenance Worker, Maintenance Worker (CUNY), Maintenance Worker (NYC H+H), Secretary, or Staff Analyst Trainee may use this ability when searching for and retrieving information from computer records or files in order to compile information required to enter data on special reports and forms.
- **Written Comprehension**: the ability to understand written sentences and paragraphs. Example: A Bookkeeper, Clerical Associate, Clerical Associate (NYC H+H), Computer Service Technician, Maintenance Worker, Maintenance Worker (CUNY), Maintenance Worker (NYC H+H), Secretary, or Staff Analyst Trainee may use this ability when reviewing various requests for accuracy prior to processing.
- **Written Expression**: the ability to use English words or sentences in writing so that others will understand. Example: A Bookkeeper, Clerical Associate, Clerical Associate (NYC H+H), Computer Service Technician, Maintenance Worker, Maintenance Worker (CUNY), Maintenance Worker (NYC H+H), Secretary, or Staff Analyst Trainee may use this ability when contacting other internal work units or external organizations in writing to obtain necessary information.

HOW TO TAKE A TEST

I. YOU MUST PASS AN EXAMINATION

A. *WHAT EVERY CANDIDATE SHOULD KNOW*

Examination applicants often ask us for help in preparing for the written test. What can I study in advance? What kinds of questions will be asked? How will the test be given? How will the papers be graded?

As an applicant for a civil service examination, you may be wondering about some of these things. Our purpose here is to suggest effective methods of advance study and to describe civil service examinations.

Your chances for success on this examination can be increased if you know how to prepare. Those "pre-examination jitters" can be reduced if you know what to expect. You can even experience an adventure in good citizenship if you know why civil service exams are given.

B. *WHY ARE CIVIL SERVICE EXAMINATIONS GIVEN?*

Civil service examinations are important to you in two ways. As a citizen, you want public jobs filled by employees who know how to do their work. As a job seeker, you want a fair chance to compete for that job on an equal footing with other candidates. The best-known means of accomplishing this two-fold goal is the competitive examination.

Exams are widely publicized throughout the nation. They may be administered for jobs in federal, state, city, municipal, town or village governments or agencies.

Any citizen may apply, with some limitations, such as the age or residence of applicants. Your experience and education may be reviewed to see whether you meet the requirements for the particular examination. When these requirements exist, they are reasonable and applied consistently to all applicants. Thus, a competitive examination may cause you some uneasiness now, but it is your privilege and safeguard.

C. *HOW ARE CIVIL SERVICE EXAMS DEVELOPED?*

Examinations are carefully written by trained technicians who are specialists in the field known as "psychological measurement," in consultation with recognized authorities in the field of work that the test will cover. These experts recommend the subject matter areas or skills to be tested; only those knowledges or skills important to your success on the job are included. The most reliable books and source materials available are used as references. Together, the experts and technicians judge the difficulty level of the questions.

Test technicians know how to phrase questions so that the problem is clearly stated. Their ethics do not permit "trick" or "catch" questions. Questions may have been tried out on sample groups, or subjected to statistical analysis, to determine their usefulness.

Written tests are often used in combination with performance tests, ratings of training and experience, and oral interviews. All of these measures combine to form the best-known means of finding the right person for the right job.

II. HOW TO PASS THE WRITTEN TEST

A. NATURE OF THE EXAMINATION

To prepare intelligently for civil service examinations, you should know how they differ from school examinations you have taken. In school you were assigned certain definite pages to read or subjects to cover. The examination questions were quite detailed and usually emphasized memory. Civil service exams, on the other hand, try to discover your present ability to perform the duties of a position, plus your potentiality to learn these duties. In other words, a civil service exam attempts to predict how successful you will be. Questions cover such a broad area that they cannot be as minute and detailed as school exam questions.

In the public service similar kinds of work, or positions, are grouped together in one "class." This process is known as *position-classification*. All the positions in a class are paid according to the salary range for that class. One class title covers all of these positions, and they are all tested by the same examination.

B. FOUR BASIC STEPS

1) Study the announcement

How, then, can you know what subjects to study? Our best answer is: "Learn as much as possible about the class of positions for which you've applied." The exam will test the knowledge, skills and abilities needed to do the work.

Your most valuable source of information about the position you want is the official exam announcement. This announcement lists the training and experience qualifications. Check these standards and apply only if you come reasonably close to meeting them.

The brief description of the position in the examination announcement offers some clues to the subjects which will be tested. Think about the job itself. Review the duties in your mind. Can you perform them, or are there some in which you are rusty? Fill in the blank spots in your preparation.

Many jurisdictions preview the written test in the exam announcement by including a section called "Knowledge and Abilities Required," "Scope of the Examination," or some similar heading. Here you will find out specifically what fields will be tested.

2) Review your own background

Once you learn in general what the position is all about, and what you need to know to do the work, ask yourself which subjects you already know fairly well and which need improvement. You may wonder whether to concentrate on improving your strong areas or on building some background in your fields of weakness. When the announcement has specified "some knowledge" or "considerable knowledge," or has used adjectives like "beginning principles of..." or "advanced ... methods," you can get a clue as to the number and difficulty of questions to be asked in any given field. More questions, and hence broader coverage, would be included for those subjects which are more important in the work. Now weigh your strengths and weaknesses against the job requirements and prepare accordingly.

3) Determine the level of the position

Another way to tell how intensively you should prepare is to understand the level of the job for which you are applying. Is it the entering level? In other words, is this the position in which beginners in a field of work are hired? Or is it an intermediate or advanced level? Sometimes this is indicated by such words as "Junior" or "Senior" in the class title. Other jurisdictions use Roman numerals to designate the level – Clerk I, Clerk II, for example. The word "Supervisor" sometimes appears in the title. If the level is not indicated by the title, check the description of duties. Will you be working under very close supervision, or will you have responsibility for independent decisions in this work?

4) Choose appropriate study materials

Now that you know the subjects to be examined and the relative amount of each subject to be covered, you can choose suitable study materials. For beginning level jobs, or even advanced ones, if you have a pronounced weakness in some aspect of your training, read a modern, standard textbook in that field. Be sure it is up to date and has general coverage. Such books are normally available at your library, and the librarian will be glad to help you locate one. For entry-level positions, questions of appropriate difficulty are chosen – neither highly advanced questions, nor those too simple. Such questions require careful thought but not advanced training.

If the position for which you are applying is technical or advanced, you will read more advanced, specialized material. If you are already familiar with the basic principles of your field, elementary textbooks would waste your time. Concentrate on advanced textbooks and technical periodicals. Think through the concepts and review difficult problems in your field.

These are all general sources. You can get more ideas on your own initiative, following these leads. For example, training manuals and publications of the government agency which employs workers in your field can be useful, particularly for technical and professional positions. A letter or visit to the government department involved may result in more specific study suggestions, and certainly will provide you with a more definite idea of the exact nature of the position you are seeking.

III. KINDS OF TESTS

Tests are used for purposes other than measuring knowledge and ability to perform specified duties. For some positions, it is equally important to test ability to make adjustments to new situations or to profit from training. In others, basic mental abilities not dependent on information are essential. Questions which test these things may not appear as pertinent to the duties of the position as those which test for knowledge and information. Yet they are often highly important parts of a fair examination. For very general questions, it is almost impossible to help you direct your study efforts. What we can do is to point out some of the more common of these general abilities needed in public service positions and describe some typical questions.

1) General information

Broad, general information has been found useful for predicting job success in some kinds of work. This is tested in a variety of ways, from vocabulary lists to questions about current events. Basic background in some field of work, such as sociology or economics, may be sampled in a group of questions. Often these are principles which have become familiar to most persons through exposure rather than through formal training. It is difficult to advise you how to study for these questions; being alert to the world around you is our best suggestion.

2) Verbal ability

An example of an ability needed in many positions is verbal or language ability. Verbal ability is, in brief, the ability to use and understand words. Vocabulary and grammar tests are typical measures of this ability. Reading comprehension or paragraph interpretation questions are common in many kinds of civil service tests. You are given a paragraph of written material and asked to find its central meaning.

3) Numerical ability

Number skills can be tested by the familiar arithmetic problem, by checking paired lists of numbers to see which are alike and which are different, or by interpreting charts and graphs. In the latter test, a graph may be printed in the test booklet which you are asked to use as the basis for answering questions.

4) Observation

A popular test for law-enforcement positions is the observation test. A picture is shown to you for several minutes, then taken away. Questions about the picture test your ability to observe both details and larger elements.

5) Following directions

In many positions in the public service, the employee must be able to carry out written instructions dependably and accurately. You may be given a chart with several columns, each column listing a variety of information. The questions require you to carry out directions involving the information given in the chart.

6) Skills and aptitudes

Performance tests effectively measure some manual skills and aptitudes. When the skill is one in which you are trained, such as typing or shorthand, you can practice. These tests are often very much like those given in business school or high school courses. For many of the other skills and aptitudes, however, no short-time preparation can be made. Skills and abilities natural to you or that you have developed throughout your lifetime are being tested.

Many of the general questions just described provide all the data needed to answer the questions and ask you to use your reasoning ability to find the answers. Your best preparation for these tests, as well as for tests of facts and ideas, is to be at your physical and mental best. You, no doubt, have your own methods of getting into an exam-taking mood and keeping "in shape." The next section lists some ideas on this subject.

IV. KINDS OF QUESTIONS

Only rarely is the "essay" question, which you answer in narrative form, used in civil service tests. Civil service tests are usually of the short-answer type. Full instructions for answering these questions will be given to you at the examination. But in case this is your first experience with short-answer questions and separate answer sheets, here is what you need to know:

1) Multiple-choice Questions

Most popular of the short-answer questions is the "multiple choice" or "best answer" question. It can be used, for example, to test for factual knowledge, ability to solve problems or judgment in meeting situations found at work.

A multiple-choice question is normally one of three types—
- It can begin with an incomplete statement followed by several possible endings. You are to find the one ending which *best* completes the statement, although some of the others may not be entirely wrong.
- It can also be a complete statement in the form of a question which is answered by choosing one of the statements listed.

- It can be in the form of a problem – again you select the best answer.

Here is an example of a multiple-choice question with a discussion which should give you some clues as to the method for choosing the right answer:

When an employee has a complaint about his assignment, the action which will *best* help him overcome his difficulty is to
- A. discuss his difficulty with his coworkers
- B. take the problem to the head of the organization
- C. take the problem to the person who gave him the assignment
- D. say nothing to anyone about his complaint

In answering this question, you should study each of the choices to find which is best. Consider choice "A" – Certainly an employee may discuss his complaint with fellow employees, but no change or improvement can result, and the complaint remains unresolved. Choice "B" is a poor choice since the head of the organization probably does not know what assignment you have been given, and taking your problem to him is known as "going over the head" of the supervisor. The supervisor, or person who made the assignment, is the person who can clarify it or correct any injustice. Choice "C" is, therefore, correct. To say nothing, as in choice "D," is unwise. Supervisors have and interest in knowing the problems employees are facing, and the employee is seeking a solution to his problem.

2) True/False Questions

The "true/false" or "right/wrong" form of question is sometimes used. Here a complete statement is given. Your job is to decide whether the statement is right or wrong.

SAMPLE: A roaming cell-phone call to a nearby city costs less than a non-roaming call to a distant city.

This statement is wrong, or false, since roaming calls are more expensive.

This is not a complete list of all possible question forms, although most of the others are variations of these common types. You will always get complete directions for answering questions. Be sure you understand *how* to mark your answers – ask questions until you do.

V. RECORDING YOUR ANSWERS

Computer terminals are used more and more today for many different kinds of exams.

For an examination with very few applicants, you may be told to record your answers in the test booklet itself. Separate answer sheets are much more common. If this separate answer sheet is to be scored by machine – and this is often the case – it is highly important that you mark your answers correctly in order to get credit.

An electronic scoring machine is often used in civil service offices because of the speed with which papers can be scored. Machine-scored answer sheets must be marked with a pencil, which will be given to you. This pencil has a high graphite content which responds to the electronic scoring machine. As a matter of fact, stray dots may register as answers, so do not let your pencil rest on the answer sheet while you are pondering the correct answer. Also, if your pencil lead breaks or is otherwise defective, ask for another.

Since the answer sheet will be dropped in a slot in the scoring machine, be careful not to bend the corners or get the paper crumpled.

The answer sheet normally has five vertical columns of numbers, with 30 numbers to a column. These numbers correspond to the question numbers in your test booklet. After each number, going across the page are four or five pairs of dotted lines. These short dotted lines have small letters or numbers above them. The first two pairs may also have a "T" or "F" above the letters. This indicates that the first two pairs only are to be used if the questions are of the true-false type. If the questions are multiple choice, disregard the "T" and "F" and pay attention only to the small letters or numbers.

Answer your questions in the manner of the sample that follows:

    32. The largest city in the United States is
        A. Washington, D.C.
        B. New York City
        C. Chicago
        D. Detroit
        E. San Francisco

1) Choose the answer you think is best. (New York City is the largest, so "B" is correct.)
2) Find the row of dotted lines numbered the same as the question you are answering. (Find row number 32)
3) Find the pair of dotted lines corresponding to the answer. (Find the pair of lines under the mark "B.")
4) Make a solid black mark between the dotted lines.

VI. BEFORE THE TEST

Common sense will help you find procedures to follow to get ready for an examination. Too many of us, however, overlook these sensible measures. Indeed, nervousness and fatigue have been found to be the most serious reasons why applicants fail to do their best on civil service tests. Here is a list of reminders:

- Begin your preparation early – Don't wait until the last minute to go scurrying around for books and materials or to find out what the position is all about.
- Prepare continuously – An hour a night for a week is better than an all-night cram session. This has been definitely established. What is more, a night a week for a month will return better dividends than crowding your study into a shorter period of time.
- Locate the place of the exam – You have been sent a notice telling you when and where to report for the examination. If the location is in a different town or otherwise unfamiliar to you, it would be well to inquire the best route and learn something about the building.
- Relax the night before the test – Allow your mind to rest. Do not study at all that night. Plan some mild recreation or diversion; then go to bed early and get a good night's sleep.
- Get up early enough to make a leisurely trip to the place for the test – This way unforeseen events, traffic snarls, unfamiliar buildings, etc. will not upset you.
- Dress comfortably – A written test is not a fashion show. You will be known by number and not by name, so wear something comfortable.

- Leave excess paraphernalia at home – Shopping bags and odd bundles will get in your way. You need bring only the items mentioned in the official notice you received; usually everything you need is provided. Do not bring reference books to the exam. They will only confuse those last minutes and be taken away from you when in the test room.
- Arrive somewhat ahead of time – If because of transportation schedules you must get there very early, bring a newspaper or magazine to take your mind off yourself while waiting.
- Locate the examination room – When you have found the proper room, you will be directed to the seat or part of the room where you will sit. Sometimes you are given a sheet of instructions to read while you are waiting. Do not fill out any forms until you are told to do so; just read them and be prepared.
- Relax and prepare to listen to the instructions
- If you have any physical problem that may keep you from doing your best, be sure to tell the test administrator. If you are sick or in poor health, you really cannot do your best on the exam. You can come back and take the test some other time.

VII. AT THE TEST

The day of the test is here and you have the test booklet in your hand. The temptation to get going is very strong. Caution! There is more to success than knowing the right answers. You must know how to identify your papers and understand variations in the type of short-answer question used in this particular examination. Follow these suggestions for maximum results from your efforts:

1) Cooperate with the monitor

The test administrator has a duty to create a situation in which you can be as much at ease as possible. He will give instructions, tell you when to begin, check to see that you are marking your answer sheet correctly, and so on. He is not there to guard you, although he will see that your competitors do not take unfair advantage. He wants to help you do your best.

2) Listen to all instructions

Don't jump the gun! Wait until you understand all directions. In most civil service tests you get more time than you need to answer the questions. So don't be in a hurry. Read each word of instructions until you clearly understand the meaning. Study the examples, listen to all announcements and follow directions. Ask questions if you do not understand what to do.

3) Identify your papers

Civil service exams are usually identified by number only. You will be assigned a number; you must not put your name on your test papers. Be sure to copy your number correctly. Since more than one exam may be given, copy your exact examination title.

4) Plan your time

Unless you are told that a test is a "speed" or "rate of work" test, speed itself is usually not important. Time enough to answer all the questions will be provided, but this does not mean that you have all day. An overall time limit has been set. Divide the total time (in minutes) by the number of questions to determine the approximate time you have for each question.

5) Do not linger over difficult questions

If you come across a difficult question, mark it with a paper clip (useful to have along) and come back to it when you have been through the booklet. One caution if you do this – be sure to skip a number on your answer sheet as well. Check often to be sure that you have not lost your place and that you are marking in the row numbered the same as the question you are answering.

6) Read the questions

Be sure you know what the question asks! Many capable people are unsuccessful because they failed to *read* the questions correctly.

7) Answer all questions

Unless you have been instructed that a penalty will be deducted for incorrect answers, it is better to guess than to omit a question.

8) Speed tests

It is often better NOT to guess on speed tests. It has been found that on timed tests people are tempted to spend the last few seconds before time is called in marking answers at random – without even reading them – in the hope of picking up a few extra points. To discourage this practice, the instructions may warn you that your score will be "corrected" for guessing. That is, a penalty will be applied. The incorrect answers will be deducted from the correct ones, or some other penalty formula will be used.

9) Review your answers

If you finish before time is called, go back to the questions you guessed or omitted to give them further thought. Review other answers if you have time.

10) Return your test materials

If you are ready to leave before others have finished or time is called, take ALL your materials to the monitor and leave quietly. Never take any test material with you. The monitor can discover whose papers are not complete, and taking a test booklet may be grounds for disqualification.

VIII. EXAMINATION TECHNIQUES

1) Read the general instructions carefully. These are usually printed on the first page of the exam booklet. As a rule, these instructions refer to the timing of the examination; the fact that you should not start work until the signal and must stop work at a signal, etc. If there are any *special* instructions, such as a choice of questions to be answered, make sure that you note this instruction carefully.

2) When you are ready to start work on the examination, that is as soon as the signal has been given, read the instructions to each question booklet, underline any key words or phrases, such as *least, best, outline, describe* and the like. In this way you will tend to answer as requested rather than discover on reviewing your paper that you *listed without describing*, that you selected the *worst* choice rather than the *best* choice, etc.

3) If the examination is of the objective or multiple-choice type – that is, each question will also give a series of possible answers: A, B, C or D, and you are called upon to select the best answer and write the letter next to that answer on your answer paper – it is advisable to start answering each question in turn. There may be anywhere from 50 to 100 such questions in the three or four hours allotted and you can see how much time would be taken if you read through all the questions before beginning to answer any. Furthermore, if you come across a question or group of questions which you know would be difficult to answer, it would undoubtedly affect your handling of all the other questions.

4) If the examination is of the essay type and contains but a few questions, it is a moot point as to whether you should read all the questions before starting to answer any one. Of course, if you are given a choice – say five out of seven and the like – then it is essential to read all the questions so you can eliminate the two that are most difficult. If, however, you are asked to answer all the questions, there may be danger in trying to answer the easiest one first because you may find that you will spend too much time on it. The best technique is to answer the first question, then proceed to the second, etc.

5) Time your answers. Before the exam begins, write down the time it started, then add the time allowed for the examination and write down the time it must be completed, then divide the time available somewhat as follows:
    - If 3-1/2 hours are allowed, that would be 210 minutes. If you have 80 objective-type questions, that would be an average of 2-1/2 minutes per question. Allow yourself no more than 2 minutes per question, or a total of 160 minutes, which will permit about 50 minutes to review.
    - If for the time allotment of 210 minutes there are 7 essay questions to answer, that would average about 30 minutes a question. Give yourself only 25 minutes per question so that you have about 35 minutes to review.

6) The most important instruction is to *read each question* and make sure you know what is wanted. The second most important instruction is to *time yourself properly* so that you answer every question. The third most important instruction is to *answer every question*. Guess if you have to but include something for each question. Remember that you will receive no credit for a blank and will probably receive some credit if you write something in answer to an essay question. If you guess a letter – say "B" for a multiple-choice question – you may have guessed right. If you leave a blank as an answer to a multiple-choice question, the examiners may respect your feelings but it will not add a point to your score. Some exams may penalize you for wrong answers, so in such cases *only*, you may not want to guess unless you have some basis for your answer.

7) Suggestions
   a. Objective-type questions
      1. Examine the question booklet for proper sequence of pages and questions
      2. Read all instructions carefully
      3. Skip any question which seems too difficult; return to it after all other questions have been answered
      4. Apportion your time properly; do not spend too much time on any single question or group of questions

5. Note and underline key words – *all, most, fewest, least, best, worst, same, opposite,* etc.
6. Pay particular attention to negatives
7. Note unusual option, e.g., unduly long, short, complex, different or similar in content to the body of the question
8. Observe the use of "hedging" words – *probably, may, most likely,* etc.
9. Make sure that your answer is put next to the same number as the question
10. Do not second-guess unless you have good reason to believe the second answer is definitely more correct
11. Cross out original answer if you decide another answer is more accurate; do not erase until you are ready to hand your paper in
12. Answer all questions; guess unless instructed otherwise
13. Leave time for review

b. Essay questions
1. Read each question carefully
2. Determine exactly what is wanted. Underline key words or phrases.
3. Decide on outline or paragraph answer
4. Include many different points and elements unless asked to develop any one or two points or elements
5. Show impartiality by giving pros and cons unless directed to select one side only
6. Make and write down any assumptions you find necessary to answer the questions
7. Watch your English, grammar, punctuation and choice of words
8. Time your answers; don't crowd material

8) Answering the essay question

Most essay questions can be answered by framing the specific response around several key words or ideas. Here are a few such key words or ideas:

M's: manpower, materials, methods, money, management
P's: purpose, program, policy, plan, procedure, practice, problems, pitfalls, personnel, public relations

a. Six basic steps in handling problems:
1. Preliminary plan and background development
2. Collect information, data and facts
3. Analyze and interpret information, data and facts
4. Analyze and develop solutions as well as make recommendations
5. Prepare report and sell recommendations
6. Install recommendations and follow up effectiveness

b. Pitfalls to avoid
1. *Taking things for granted* – A statement of the situation does not necessarily imply that each of the elements is necessarily true; for example, a complaint may be invalid and biased so that all that can be taken for granted is that a complaint has been registered

2. *Considering only one side of a situation* – Wherever possible, indicate several alternatives and then point out the reasons you selected the best one
3. *Failing to indicate follow up* – Whenever your answer indicates action on your part, make certain that you will take proper follow-up action to see how successful your recommendations, procedures or actions turn out to be
4. *Taking too long in answering any single question* – Remember to time your answers properly

IX. AFTER THE TEST

Scoring procedures differ in detail among civil service jurisdictions although the general principles are the same. Whether the papers are hand-scored or graded by machine we have described, they are nearly always graded by number. That is, the person who marks the paper knows only the number – never the name – of the applicant. Not until all the papers have been graded will they be matched with names. If other tests, such as training and experience or oral interview ratings have been given, scores will be combined. Different parts of the examination usually have different weights. For example, the written test might count 60 percent of the final grade, and a rating of training and experience 40 percent. In many jurisdictions, veterans will have a certain number of points added to their grades.

After the final grade has been determined, the names are placed in grade order and an eligible list is established. There are various methods for resolving ties between those who get the same final grade – probably the most common is to place first the name of the person whose application was received first. Job offers are made from the eligible list in the order the names appear on it. You will be notified of your grade and your rank as soon as all these computations have been made. This will be done as rapidly as possible.

People who are found to meet the requirements in the announcement are called "eligibles." Their names are put on a list of eligible candidates. An eligible's chances of getting a job depend on how high he stands on this list and how fast agencies are filling jobs from the list.

When a job is to be filled from a list of eligibles, the agency asks for the names of people on the list of eligibles for that job. When the civil service commission receives this request, it sends to the agency the names of the three people highest on this list. Or, if the job to be filled has specialized requirements, the office sends the agency the names of the top three persons who meet these requirements from the general list.

The appointing officer makes a choice from among the three people whose names were sent to him. If the selected person accepts the appointment, the names of the others are put back on the list to be considered for future openings.

That is the rule in hiring from all kinds of eligible lists, whether they are for typist, carpenter, chemist, or something else. For every vacancy, the appointing officer has his choice of any one of the top three eligibles on the list. This explains why the person whose name is on top of the list sometimes does not get an appointment when some of the persons lower on the list do. If the appointing officer chooses the second or third eligible, the No. 1 eligible does not get a job at once, but stays on the list until he is appointed or the list is terminated.

X. HOW TO PASS THE INTERVIEW TEST

The examination for which you applied requires an oral interview test. You have already taken the written test and you are now being called for the interview test – the final part of the formal examination.

You may think that it is not possible to prepare for an interview test and that there are no procedures to follow during an interview. Our purpose is to point out some things you can do in advance that will help you and some good rules to follow and pitfalls to avoid while you are being interviewed.

What is an interview supposed to test?

The written examination is designed to test the technical knowledge and competence of the candidate; the oral is designed to evaluate intangible qualities, not readily measured otherwise, and to establish a list showing the relative fitness of each candidate – as measured against his competitors – for the position sought. Scoring is not on the basis of "right" and "wrong," but on a sliding scale of values ranging from "not passable" to "outstanding." As a matter of fact, it is possible to achieve a relatively low score without a single "incorrect" answer because of evident weakness in the qualities being measured.

Occasionally, an examination may consist entirely of an oral test – either an individual or a group oral. In such cases, information is sought concerning the technical knowledges and abilities of the candidate, since there has been no written examination for this purpose. More commonly, however, an oral test is used to supplement a written examination.

Who conducts interviews?

The composition of oral boards varies among different jurisdictions. In nearly all, a representative of the personnel department serves as chairman. One of the members of the board may be a representative of the department in which the candidate would work. In some cases, "outside experts" are used, and, frequently, a businessman or some other representative of the general public is asked to serve. Labor and management or other special groups may be represented. The aim is to secure the services of experts in the appropriate field.

However the board is composed, it is a good idea (and not at all improper or unethical) to ascertain in advance of the interview who the members are and what groups they represent. When you are introduced to them, you will have some idea of their backgrounds and interests, and at least you will not stutter and stammer over their names.

What should be done before the interview?

While knowledge about the board members is useful and takes some of the surprise element out of the interview, there is other preparation which is more substantive. It *is* possible to prepare for an oral interview – in several ways:

1) Keep a copy of your application and review it carefully before the interview

This may be the only document before the oral board, and the starting point of the interview. Know what education and experience you have listed there, and the sequence and dates of all of it. Sometimes the board will ask you to review the highlights of your experience for them; you should not have to hem and haw doing it.

2) Study the class specification and the examination announcement

Usually, the oral board has one or both of these to guide them. The qualities, characteristics or knowledges required by the position sought are stated in these documents. They offer valuable clues as to the nature of the oral interview. For example, if the job involves supervisory responsibilities, the announcement will usually indicate that knowledge of modern supervisory methods and the qualifications of the candidate as a supervisor will be tested. If so, you can expect such questions, frequently in the form of a hypothetical situation which you are expected to solve. NEVER go into an oral without knowledge of the duties and responsibilities of the job you seek.

3) Think through each qualification required

Try to visualize the kind of questions you would ask if you were a board member. How well could you answer them? Try especially to appraise your own knowledge and background in each area, *measured against the job sought*, and identify any areas in which you are weak. Be critical and realistic – do not flatter yourself.

4) Do some general reading in areas in which you feel you may be weak

For example, if the job involves supervision and your past experience has NOT, some general reading in supervisory methods and practices, particularly in the field of human relations, might be useful. Do NOT study agency procedures or detailed manuals. The oral board will be testing your understanding and capacity, not your memory.

5) Get a good night's sleep and watch your general health and mental attitude

You will want a clear head at the interview. Take care of a cold or any other minor ailment, and of course, no hangovers.

What should be done on the day of the interview?

Now comes the day of the interview itself. Give yourself plenty of time to get there. Plan to arrive somewhat ahead of the scheduled time, particularly if your appointment is in the fore part of the day. If a previous candidate fails to appear, the board might be ready for you a bit early. By early afternoon an oral board is almost invariably behind schedule if there are many candidates, and you may have to wait. Take along a book or magazine to read, or your application to review, but leave any extraneous material in the waiting room when you go in for your interview. In any event, relax and compose yourself.

The matter of dress is important. The board is forming impressions about you – from your experience, your manners, your attitude, and your appearance. Give your personal appearance careful attention. Dress your best, but not your flashiest. Choose conservative, appropriate clothing, and be sure it is immaculate. This is a business interview, and your appearance should indicate that you regard it as such. Besides, being well groomed and properly dressed will help boost your confidence.

Sooner or later, someone will call your name and escort you into the interview room. *This is it.* From here on you are on your own. It is too late for any more preparation. But remember, you asked for this opportunity to prove your fitness, and you are here because your request was granted.

What happens when you go in?

The usual sequence of events will be as follows: The clerk (who is often the board stenographer) will introduce you to the chairman of the oral board, who will introduce you to the other members of the board. Acknowledge the introductions before you sit down. Do not be surprised if you find a microphone facing you or a stenotypist sitting by. Oral interviews are usually recorded in the event of an appeal or other review.

Usually the chairman of the board will open the interview by reviewing the highlights of your education and work experience from your application – primarily for the benefit of the other members of the board, as well as to get the material into the record. Do not interrupt or comment unless there is an error or significant misinterpretation; if that is the case, do not hesitate. But do not quibble about insignificant matters. Also, he will usually ask you some question about your education, experience or your present job – partly to get you to start talking and to establish the interviewing "rapport." He may start the actual questioning, or turn it over to one of the other members. Frequently, each member undertakes the questioning on a particular area, one in which he is perhaps most competent, so you can expect each member to participate in the examination. Because time is limited, you may also expect some rather abrupt switches in the direction the questioning takes, so do not be upset by it. Normally, a board member will not pursue a single line of questioning unless he discovers a particular strength or weakness.

After each member has participated, the chairman will usually ask whether any member has any further questions, then will ask you if you have anything you wish to add. Unless you are expecting this question, it may floor you. Worse, it may start you off on an extended, extemporaneous speech. The board is not usually seeking more information. The question is principally to offer you a last opportunity to present further qualifications or to indicate that you have nothing to add. So, if you feel that a significant qualification or characteristic has been overlooked, it is proper to point it out in a sentence or so. Do not compliment the board on the thoroughness of their examination – they have been sketchy, and you know it. If you wish, merely say, "No thank you, I have nothing further to add." This is a point where you can "talk yourself out" of a good impression or fail to present an important bit of information. Remember, *you close the interview yourself.*

The chairman will then say, "That is all, Mr. _____, thank you." Do not be startled; the interview is over, and quicker than you think. Thank him, gather your belongings and take your leave. Save your sigh of relief for the other side of the door.

How to put your best foot forward

Throughout this entire process, you may feel that the board individually and collectively is trying to pierce your defenses, seek out your hidden weaknesses and embarrass and confuse you. Actually, this is not true. They are obliged to make an appraisal of your qualifications for the job you are seeking, and they want to see you in your best light. Remember, they must interview all candidates and a non-cooperative candidate may become a failure in spite of their best efforts to bring out his qualifications. Here are 15 suggestions that will help you:

1) Be natural – Keep your attitude confident, not cocky

If you are not confident that you can do the job, do not expect the board to be. Do not apologize for your weaknesses, try to bring out your strong points. The board is interested in a positive, not negative, presentation. Cockiness will antagonize any board member and make him wonder if you are covering up a weakness by a false show of strength.

2) Get comfortable, but don't lounge or sprawl

Sit erectly but not stiffly. A careless posture may lead the board to conclude that you are careless in other things, or at least that you are not impressed by the importance of the occasion. Either conclusion is natural, even if incorrect. Do not fuss with your clothing, a pencil or an ashtray. Your hands may occasionally be useful to emphasize a point; do not let them become a point of distraction.

3) Do not wisecrack or make small talk

This is a serious situation, and your attitude should show that you consider it as such. Further, the time of the board is limited – they do not want to waste it, and neither should you.

4) Do not exaggerate your experience or abilities

In the first place, from information in the application or other interviews and sources, the board may know more about you than you think. Secondly, you probably will not get away with it. An experienced board is rather adept at spotting such a situation, so do not take the chance.

5) If you know a board member, do not make a point of it, yet do not hide it

Certainly you are not fooling him, and probably not the other members of the board. Do not try to take advantage of your acquaintanceship – it will probably do you little good.

6) Do not dominate the interview

Let the board do that. They will give you the clues – do not assume that you have to do all the talking. Realize that the board has a number of questions to ask you, and do not try to take up all the interview time by showing off your extensive knowledge of the answer to the first one.

7) Be attentive

You only have 20 minutes or so, and you should keep your attention at its sharpest throughout. When a member is addressing a problem or question to you, give him your undivided attention. Address your reply principally to him, but do not exclude the other board members.

8) Do not interrupt

A board member may be stating a problem for you to analyze. He will ask you a question when the time comes. Let him state the problem, and wait for the question.

9) Make sure you understand the question

Do not try to answer until you are sure what the question is. If it is not clear, restate it in your own words or ask the board member to clarify it for you. However, do not haggle about minor elements.

10) Reply promptly but not hastily

A common entry on oral board rating sheets is "candidate responded readily," or "candidate hesitated in replies." Respond as promptly and quickly as you can, but do not jump to a hasty, ill-considered answer.

11) Do not be peremptory in your answers

A brief answer is proper – but do not fire your answer back. That is a losing game from your point of view. The board member can probably ask questions much faster than you can answer them.

12) Do not try to create the answer you think the board member wants

He is interested in what kind of mind you have and how it works – not in playing games. Furthermore, he can usually spot this practice and will actually grade you down on it.

13) Do not switch sides in your reply merely to agree with a board member

Frequently, a member will take a contrary position merely to draw you out and to see if you are willing and able to defend your point of view. Do not start a debate, yet do not surrender a good position. If a position is worth taking, it is worth defending.

14) Do not be afraid to admit an error in judgment if you are shown to be wrong

The board knows that you are forced to reply without any opportunity for careful consideration. Your answer may be demonstrably wrong. If so, admit it and get on with the interview.

15) Do not dwell at length on your present job

The opening question may relate to your present assignment. Answer the question but do not go into an extended discussion. You are being examined for a *new* job, not your present one. As a matter of fact, try to phrase ALL your answers in terms of the job for which you are being examined.

Basis of Rating

Probably you will forget most of these "do's" and "don'ts" when you walk into the oral interview room. Even remembering them all will not ensure you a passing grade. Perhaps you did not have the qualifications in the first place. But remembering them will help you to put your best foot forward, without treading on the toes of the board members.

Rumor and popular opinion to the contrary notwithstanding, an oral board wants you to make the best appearance possible. They know you are under pressure – but they also want to see how you respond to it as a guide to what your reaction would be under the pressures of the job you seek. They will be influenced by the degree of poise you display, the personal traits you show and the manner in which you respond.

ABOUT THIS BOOK

This book contains tests divided into Examination Sections. Go through each test, answering every question in the margin. We have also attached a sample answer sheet at the back of the book that can be removed and used. At the end of each test look at the answer key and check your answers. On the ones you got wrong, look at the right answer choice and learn. Do not fill in the answers first. Do not memorize the questions and answers, but understand the answer and principles involved. On your test, the questions will likely be different from the samples. Questions are changed and new ones added. If you understand these past questions you should have success with any changes that arise. Tests may consist of several types of questions. We have additional books on each subject should more study be advisable or necessary for you. Finally, the more you study, the better prepared you will be. This book is intended to be the last thing you study before you walk into the examination room. Prior study of relevant texts is also recommended. NLC publishes some of these in our Fundamental Series. Knowledge and good sense are important factors in passing your exam. Good luck also helps. So now study this Passbook, absorb the material contained within and take that knowledge into the examination. Then do your best to pass that exam.

EXAMINATION SECTION

EXAMINATION SECTION
TEST 1

DIRECTIONS: Each question or incomplete statement is followed by several suggested answers or completions. Select the one that BEST answers the question or completes the statement. *PRINT THE LETTER OF THE CORRECT ANSWER IN THE SPACE AT THE RIGHT.*

1. If you can't come to work in the morning because you do not feel well, you should   1.____

    A. call your supervisor and let him know that you are sick
    B. try to get someone else to take your place
    C. have your doctor call your office as proof that you are sick
    D. come to work anyway so that you won't lose your job

2. Many machines have certain safety devices for the operators.   2.____
   The MOST important reason for having these safety devices is to

    A. increase the amount of work that the machines can do
    B. permit repairs to be made on the machines without shutting them down
    C. help prevent accidents to people who use the machines
    D. reduce the cost of electric power needed to run the machines

3. While working on the job, you accidentally break a window pane. No one is around, and   3.____
   you are able to clean up the broken pieces of glass.
   It would then be BEST for you to

    A. leave a note near the window that a new glass has to be put in because it was accidentally broken
    B. forget about the whole thing because the window was not broken on purpose
    C. write a report to your supervisor telling him that you saw a broken window pane that has to be fixed
    D. tell your supervisor that you accidentally broke the window pane while working

4. There is a two-light fixture in the room where you are working. One of the light bulbs goes   4.____
   out, and you need more light to work by.
   You should

    A. change the fuse in the fuse box
    B. have a new bulb put in
    C. call for an electrician and stop work until he comes
    D. find out what is causing the short circuit

5. The BEST way to remove some small pieces of broken glass from a floor is to   5.____

    A. use a brush and dust pan
    B. pick up the pieces carefully with your hands
    C. use a wet mop and a wringer
    D. sweep the pieces into the corner of the room

6. When you are not sure about some instructions that your supervisor has given you on how to do a certain job, it would be BEST for you to

   A. start doing the work and stop when you come to the part that you do not understand
   B. ask the supervisor to go over the instructions which are not clear to you
   C. do the job immediately from beginning to the end, leaving out the part that you are not sure of
   D. wait until the supervisor leaves and then ask a more experienced worker to explain the job to you

7. When an employee first comes on the job, he is given a period of training by his supervisor.
   The MAIN reason for this training period is to

   A. make sure that the employee will learn to do his work correctly and safely
   B. give the employee a chance to show the supervisor that he can learn quickly
   C. allow the supervisor and the employee a chance to become friendly with each other
   D. find out which employees will make good supervisors later on

8. After you open a sealed box of supplies, you find that the box is not full and that some of the supplies are missing.
   You should

   A. use fewer supplies than you intended to
   B. seal the box and take it back to the storeroom
   C. get signed statements from other employees that when you opened the box, it was not full
   D. tell your supervisor about it

9. Suppose that after you have been on the job a few months, your supervisor shows you some small mistakes you are making in your work.
   You should

   A. tell your supervisor that these mistakes don't keep you from finishing your work
   B. ask your supervisor how you can avoid these mistakes
   C. try to show your supervisor that your way of doing the work is just as good as his way of doing it
   D. check with the other workers to find out if your supervisor is also finding fault with them

10. If your supervisor gives you an order to do a special job which you do not like to do, you should

    A. take a long time to do the job so that you won't get this job again
    B. do the job the best way you know how even though you don't like it
    C. make believe that you didn't hear your supervisor and do your regular work
    D. say nothing but tell another employee that the supervisor wants him to do this special job

11. If two employees who are working together on a job do not agree on how to do the job, it would be BEST

    A. for each worker to do the job in his own way until it is finished
    B. to put off doing the job until both workers agree to do it the same way
    C. to ask the supervisor to decide on the way the job is to be done
    D. for each worker to ask for a transfer to another assignment because they can't get along with each other

12. Suppose that in order to finish your work, you have to lift a heavy box off the floor onto an empty desk.
    You should

    A. leave the box where it is and tell your supervisor that you have finished your work
    B. lift the box by yourself very quickly so that your supervisor will see that you are a strong, willing worker
    C. ask another employee to give you a hand to lift the box off the floor
    D. complain to your supervisor that he should check a job before giving you such a tough assignment

13. Bulletin boards for the posting of official notices are usually put up near the place where employees check in and out each day.
    For an employee to spend a few minutes each day to read the new notices is

    A. *good;* these notices give him information about the Department and his own work
    B. *bad;* all important information is given to employees by their supervisors
    C. *good;* this is a way to "take a break" during the day
    D. *bad;* the notices can't help him in his work

14. Suppose that your supervisor gives you a job to do and tells you that he wants you to finish it in three hours.
    If you finish the work at the end of 2 hours, you should

    A. wait until the three hours are up and then tell your supervisor that you are finished
    B. go to your supervisor and tell him that you finished a half-hour ahead of time
    C. spend the next half-hour getting ready for the next job you think your supervisor may give you
    D. take a half-hour rest period because good work deserves a reward

15. Which one of the following is it LEAST important to include in an accident report?

    A. Name and address of the injured person
    B. Date, time, and place where the accident happened
    C. Name and address of the injured person's family doctor
    D. An explanation of how the accident happened

16. If, near the end of the day, you realize that you made a mistake in your work and you can't do the work over, you should

    A. forget about it because there is only a small chance that the mistake can be traced back to you
    B. wait a few days and take the blame for the mistake if it is caught
    C. ask the other employees to keep the mistake a secret so that no one can be blamed
    D. tell your supervisor about the mistake right away

17. Employees should wipe up water spilled on floors immediately.
The BEST reason for this is that water on a floor

   A. is a sign that employees are sloppy
   B. makes for a slippery condition that could cause an accident
   C. will eat into the wax protecting the floor
   D. is against health regulations

18. Another worker, who is a good friend of yours, leaves work an hour before quitting time to take care of a personal matter. When you leave later, you find that your friend did not sign out on the timesheet.
For you to sign out for your friend would be

   A. *good,* because he will do the same for you some day when you want to leave early
   B. *bad,* because other employees will also want you to do the same favor for them on other days
   C. *good,* because the timesheet should not have any empty spaces on it
   D. *bad,* because timesheets are official records which employees should keep honestly and accurately

19. While you are working, a person asks you how to get to an office which you know is one floor above you in the building where you work.
It would be BEST for you to tell this person that

   A. you can't answer any questions because you have to finish your work
   B. he should go back to the lobby and check the list of offices
   C. the office he is looking for is on the next floor
   D. he should call the office he is looking for to get exact instructions on how to get there

20. While you are at work, you find a sealed brown envelope under a desk. The envelope is marked *Personal - Hand Delivery* and is addressed to an official who has an office in the building where you are working.
You should

   A. drop the envelope into the nearest mailbox so that it can be delivered the next day
   B. look up the telephone number of the official and call him up to tell him what you have found
   C. put the envelope in your pocket and come in early the next day to deliver it personally to the official
   D. give the envelope to your supervisor right away and tell him where you found it

21. A messenger delivered 32 letters on Monday, 47 on Tuesday, 29 on Wednesday, 36 on Thursday, and 41 on Friday.
How many letters did he deliver altogether?

   A. 157   B. 185   C. 218   D. 229

22. Mr. White paid 4% sales tax on a $95 television set.
The amount of sales tax that he paid was

   A. $9.50   B. $4.00   C. $3.80   D. $.95

23. How many square feet are there in a room which is 25 feet long and 35 feet wide? _____ square feet.   23.____

    A. 600   B. 750   C. 875   D. 925

24. How much would it cost to send a 34 pound package by parcel post if the postage is $1.60 for the first 20 pounds and 7 for each additional pound?   24.____

    A. $2.34   B. $2.58   C. $2.66   D. $2.80

25. Adding together 1/2, 3/4, and 1/8, the total is   25.____

    A. 1 1/4   B. 1 1/2   C. 1 3/8   D. 1 3/4

26. If a piece of wood 40 inches long is cut into two pieces so that the larger piece is three times as long as the, smaller piece, the smaller piece is _____ inches.   26.____

    A. 4   B. 5   C. 8   D. 10

27. Two friends, Smith and Jones, together spend $1,800 to buy a car. If Smith put up twice as much money as Jones, then Jones' share of the cost of the car was   27.____

    A. $300   B. $600   C. $900   D. $1,200

28. In a certain agency, two-thirds of the employees are clerks and the remainder are typists. If there are 180 clerks, then the number of typists in this agency is   28.____

    A. 270   B. 90   C. 240   D. 60

Questions 29-35.

DIRECTIONS: Answer Questions 29 through 35 ONLY according to the information given in the chart below.

EMPLOYEE RECORD

Name of Employee	Where Assigned	Number of Days Absent Vacation	Sick Leave	Yearly Salary
Carey	Laundry	18	4	$18,650
Hayes	Mortuary	24	8	$17,930
Irwin	Buildings	20	17	$18,290
King	Supply	12	10	$17,930
Lane	Mortuary	17	8	$17,750
Martin	Buildings	13	12	$17,750
Prince	Buildings	5	7	$17,750
Quinn	Supply	19	0	$17,250
Sands	Buildings	23	10	$18,470
Victor	Laundry	21	2	$18,150

29. The *only* employee who was NOT absent because of sickness is 29._____

    A. Hayes   B. Lane   C. Victor   D. Quinn

30. The employee with the HIGHEST salary is 30._____

    A. Carey   B. Irwin   C. Sands   D. Victor

31. The employee with the LOWEST salary is assigned to the _____ Bureau. 31._____

    A. Laundry   B. Mortuary   C. Building   D. Supply

32. Which one of these was absent or on vacation more than 20 days? 32._____

    A. Irwin   B. Lane   C. Quinn   D. Victor

33. The number of employees whose salary is LESS than $18,100 a year is 33._____

    A. 4   B. 5   C. 6   D. 7

34. MOST employees are assigned to 34._____

    A. Laundry   B. Mortuary   C. Buildings   D. Supply

35. From the chart, you can figure out for each employee 35._____

    A. how long he has worked in his present assignment
    B. how many days vacation he has left
    C. how many times he has been late
    D. how much he earns a month

KEY (CORRECT ANSWERS)

1.	A	16.	D
2.	C	17.	B
3.	D	18.	D
4.	B	19.	C
5.	A	20.	D
6.	B	21.	B
7.	A	22.	C
8.	D	23.	C
9.	B	24.	B
10.	B	25.	C
11.	C	26.	D
12.	C	27.	B
13.	A	28.	B
14.	B	29.	D
15.	C	30.	A

31. D
32. D
33. C
34. C
35. D

TEST 2

DIRECTIONS: Each question or incomplete statement is followed by several suggested answers or completions. Select the one that BEST answers the question or completes the statement. *PRINT THE LETTER OF THE CORRECT ANSWER IN THE SPACE AT THE RIGHT.*

Questions 1-5.

DIRECTIONS: Answer Questions 1 to 5 ONLY according to the information given in the following passage.

EMPLOYEE LEAVE REGULATIONS

Peter Smith, as a full-time permanent City employee under the Career and Salary Plan, earns an "annual leave allowance" This consists of a certain number of days off a year with pay and may be used for vacation, personal business, and for observing religious holidays. As a newly appointed employee, during his first eight years of City service, he will earn an "annual leave allowance" of twenty days off a year (an average of 1 2/3 days off a month). After he has finished eight full years of working for the City, he will begin earning an additional five days off a year. His "annual leave allowance," therefore, will then be twenty-five days a year and will remain at this amount for seven full years. He will begin earning an additional two days off a year after he has completed a total of fifteen years of City employment. Therefore, in his sixteenth year of working for the City, Mr. Smith will be earning twenty-seven days off a year as his "annual leave allowance" (an average of 2 1/4 days off a month).

A "sick leave allowance" of one day a month is also given to Mr. Smith, but it can be used only in case of actual illness. When Mr. Smith returns to work after using "sick leave allowance," he must have a doctor's note if the absence is for a total of more than three days, but he may also be required to show a doctor's note for absences of one, two, or three days.

1. According to the above passage, Mr. Smith's *annual leave allowance* consists of a certain number of days off a year which he   1.____

   A. does not get paid for
   B. gets paid for at time and a half
   C. may use for personal business
   D. may not use for observing religious holidays

2. According to the above passage, after Mr. Smith has been working for the City for nine years, his *annual leave allowance* will be _____ days a year.   2.____

   A. 20   B. 25   C. 27   D. 37

3. According to the above passage, Mr. Smith will begin earning an average of 2 1/4 days off a month as his *annual leave allowance* after he has worked for the City for _____ full years.   3.____

   A. 7   B. 8   C. 15   D. 17

4. According to the above passage, Mr. Smith is given a *sick leave allowance* of   4.____

   A. 1 day every 2 months   B. 1 day per month
   C. 1 2/3 days per month   D. 2 1/4 days a month

5. According to the above passage, when he uses *sick leave allowance,* Mr. Smith may be required to show a doctor's note

   A. even if his absence is for only 1 day
   B. only if his absence is for more than 2 days
   C. only if his absence is for more than 3 days
   D. only if his absence is for 3 days or more

Questions 6-9.

DIRECTIONS: Answer Questions 6 to 9 ONLY according to the information given in the following passag

MOPPING FLOORS

When mopping hardened cement floors, either painted or unpainted, a soap and water mixture should be used. This should be made by dissolving 1/2 a cup of soft soap in a pail of hot water. It is not desirable, however, under any circumstances, to use a soap and water mixture on cement floors that are not hardened. For mopping this type of floor, it is recommended that the cleaning agent be made up of two ounces of laundry soda mixed in a pail of water.

Soaps are not generally used on hard tile floors because slippery films may build up on the floor. It is generally recommended that these floors be mopped using a pail of hot water in which has been mixed two ounces of washing powder for each gallon of water. The floors should then be rinsed thoroughly.

After the mopping is finished, proper care should be taken of the mop. This is done by first cleaning the mop in clear, warm water. Then, it should be wrung out, after which the strands of the mop should be untangled. Finally, the mop should be hung by its handle to dry.

6. According to the above passage, you should NEVER use a soap and water mixture when mopping _____ floors.

   A. hardened cement   B. painted
   C. unhardened cement   D. unpainted

7. According to the above passage, using laundry soda mixed in a pail of water as a cleaning agent is recommended for

   A. all floors
   B. all floors except hard tile floors
   C. some cement floors
   D. lineoleum floor coverings only

8. According to the above passage, the generally recommended mixture for mopping hard tile floors is

   A. 1/2 a cup of soft soap for each gallon of hot water
   B. 1/2 a cup of soft soap in a pail of hot water
   C. 2 ounces of washing powder in a pail of hot water
   D. 2 ounces of washing powder for each gallon of hot water

9. According to the above passage, the proper care of a mop after it is used includes

   A. cleaning it in clear cold water and hanging it by its handle to dry
   B. wringing it out, untangling and drying it
   C. untangling its strands before wringing it out
   D. untangling its strands while cleaning it in clear water

Questions 10-13.

DIRECTIONS: Answer Questions 10 to 13 ONLY according to the information given in the following passage.

HANDLING HOSPITAL LAUNDRY

In a hospital, care must be taken when handling laundry in order to reduce the chance of germs spreading. There is always the possibility that dirty laundry will be carrying dangerous germs. To avoid catching germs when they are working with dirty laundry, laundry workers should be sure that any cuts or wounds they have are bandaged before they touch the dirty laundry. They should also be careful when handling this laundry not to rub their eyes, nose, or mout. Just like all other hospital workers, laundry workers should also protect themselves against germs by washing and rinsing their hands thoroughly before eating meals and before leaving work at the end of the day.

To be sure that germs from dirty laundry do not pass onto clean laundry and thereby increase the danger to patients, clean and dirty laundry should not be handled near each other or by the same person. Special care also has to be taken with laundry that comes from a patient who has a dangerous, highly contagious disease so that as few people as possible come in direct contact with this laundry. Laundry from this patient, therefore, should be kept separate from other dirty laundry at all times.

10. According to the above passage, when working with dirty laundry, laundry workers should

    A. destroy laundry carrying dangerous germs
    B. have any cuts bandaged before touching the dirty laundry
    C. never touch the dirty laundry directly
    D. rub their eyes, nose, and mouth to protect them from germs

11. According to the above passage, all hospital workers should wash their hands thoroughly

    A. after eating meals to remove any trace of food from their hands
    B. at every opportunity to show good example to the patients
    C. before eating meals to protect themselves against germs
    D. before starting work in the morning to feel fresh and ready to do a good day's work

12. According to the above passage, the danger to patients will increase

    A. unless a worker handles dirty and clean laundry at the same time
    B. unless clean and dirty laundry are handled near each other
    C. when clean laundry is ironed frequently
    D. when germs pass from dirty laundry to clean laundry

13. According to the above passage, laundry from a patient with a dangerous, highly contagious disease should be

   A. given special care so that as few people as possible come in direct contact with it
   B. handled in the same way as any other dirty laundry
   C. washed by hand
   D. separated from the other dirty laundry just before it is washed

Questions 14-17.

DIRECTIONS: Answer Questions 14 to 17 ONLY according to the information given in the following passage.

EMPLOYEE SUGGESTIONS

To increase the effectiveness of the New York City governments the City asks its employees to offer suggestions when they feel an improvement could be made in some government operation. The Employees' Suggestions Program was started to encourage City employees to do this. Through this Program, which is only for City employees, cash awards may be given to those whose suggestions are submitted and approve Suggestions are looked for not only from supervisors but from all City employees as any City employee may get an idea which might be approved and contribute greatly to the solution of some problem of City government.

Therefore, all suggestions for improvement are welcome, whether they be suggestions on how to improve working conditions, or on how to increase the speed with which work is done, or on how to reduce or eliminate such things as waste, time losses, accidents, or fire hazards. There are, however, a few types of suggestions for which cash awards can not be given. An example of this type would be a suggestion to increase salaries or a suggestion to change the regulations about annual leave or about sick leave. The number of suggestions sent in has increased sharply during the past few years. It is hoped that it will keep increasing in the future in order to meet the City's needs for more ideas for improved ways of doing things.

14. According to the above passage, the main reason why the City asks its employees for suggestions about government operations is to

   A. increase the effectiveness of the City government
   B. show that the Employees' Suggestion Program is working well
   C. show that everybody helps run the City government
   D. have the employee win a prize

15. According to the above passage, the Employees' Suggestion Program can approve awards only for those suggestions that come from

   A. City employees
   B. City employees who are supervisors
   C. City employees who are not supervisors
   D. experienced employees of the City

16. According to the above passage, a cash award can not be given through the Employees' Suggestion Program for a suggestion about

   A. getting work done faster
   B. helping prevent accidents on the job
   C. increasing the amount of annual leave for City employees
   D. reducing the chance of fire where City employees work

17. According to the above passage, the suggestions sent in during the past few years have

   A. all been approved
   B. generally been well written
   C. been mostly about reducing or eliminating waste
   D. been greater in number than before

Questions 18-21.

DIRECTIONS: Answer Questions 18 to 21 ONLY according to the information given in the following passage.

ACCIDENT PREVENTION

Many accidents and injuries can be prevented if employees learn to be more careful. The wearing of shoes with thin or badly worn soles or open toes can easily lead to foot injuries from tacks, nails, and chair and desk legs. Loose or torn clothing should not be worn near moving machinery. This is especially true of neckties which can very easily become caught in the machine. You should not place objects so that they block or partly block hallways, corridors, or other passageways. Even when they are stored in the proper place, tools, supplies, and equipment should be carefully placed or piled so as not to fall, nor have anything stick out from a pile. Before cabinets, lockers, or ladders are moved, the tops should be cleared of anything which might injure someone or fall of If necessary, use a dolly to move these or other bulky objects.

Despite all efforts to avoid accidents and injuries, however, some will happen. If an employee is injured, no matter how small the injury, he should report it to his supervisor and have the injury treated. A small cut that is not attended to can easily become infected and can cause more trouble than some injuries which at first seem more serious. It never pays to take chances.

18. According to the above passage, the one statement that is NOT true is that

   A. by being more careful, employees can reduce the number of accidents that happen
   B. women should wear shoes with open toes for comfort when working
   C. supplies should be piled so that nothing is sticking out from the pile
   D. if an employee sprains his wrist at work, he should tell his supervisor about it

19. According to the above passage, you should NOT wear loose clothing when you are

   A. in a corridor
   B. storing tools
   C. opening cabinets
   D. near moving machinery

20. According to the above passage, before moving a ladder, you should 20.___

    A. test all the rungs
    B. get a dolly to carry the ladder at all times
    C. remove everything from the top of the ladder which might fall off
    D. remove your necktie

21. According to the above passage, an employee who gets a slight cut should 21.___

    A. have it treated to help prevent infection
    B. know that a slight cut becomes more easily infected than a big cut
    C. pay no attention to it as it can't become serious
    D. realize that it is more serious than any other type of injury

Questions 22-24.

DIRECTIONS: Answer Questions 22 to 24 ONLY according to the information given in the following passage.

GOOD EMPLOYEE PRACTICES

As a City employee, you will be expected to take an interest in your work and perform the duties of your job to the best of your ability and in a spirit of cooperation. Nothing shows an interest in your work more than coming to work on time, not only at the start of the day but also when returning from lunch. If it is necessary for you to keep a personal appointment at lunch hour which might cause a delay in getting back to work on time, you should explain the situation to your supervisor and get his approval to come back a little late before you leave for lunch.

You should do everything that is asked of you willingly and consider important even the small jobs that your supervisor gives you. Although these jobs may seem unimportant, if you forget to do them or if you don't do them right, trouble may develop later.

Getting along well with your fellow workers will add much to the enjoyment of your work. You should respect your fellow workers and try to see their side when a disagreement arises. The better you get along with your fellow workers and your supervisor, the better you will like your job and the better you will be able to do it.

22. According to the above passage, in your job as a City employee, you are expected to 22.___

    A. show a willingness to cooperate on the job
    B. get your supervisor's approval before keeping any personal appointments at lunch hour
    C. avoid doing small jobs that seem unimportant
    D. do the easier jobs at the start of the day and the more difficult ones later on

23. According to the above passage, getting to work on time shows that you 23.___

    A. need the job
    B. have an interest in your work
    C. get along well with your fellow workers
    D. like your supervisor

24. According to the above passage, the one of the following statements that is NOT true is   24.____
    A. if you do a small job wrong, trouble may develop
    B. you should respect your fellow workers
    C. if you disagree with a fellow worker, you should try to see his side of the story
    D. the less you get along with your supervisor, the better you will be able to do your job

Questions 25-35.   VOCABULARY

25. The porter cleaned the VACANT room.   25.____
    In this sentence, the word VACANT means nearly the same as
    A. empty   B. large   C. main   D. crowded

26. The supervisor gave a BRIEF report to his men.   26.____
    In this sentence, the word BRIEF means nearly the same as
    A. long   B. safety   C. complete   D. short

27. The supervisor told him to CONNECT the two pieces.   27.____
    In this sentence, the word CONNECT means nearly the same as
    A. join   B. paint   C. return   D. weigh

28. Standing on the top of a ladder is RISKY.   28.____
    In this sentence, the word RISKY means nearly the same as
    A. dangerous   B. sensible   C. safe   D. foolish

29. He RAISED the cover of the machine.   29.____
    In this sentence, the word RAISED means nearly the same as
    A. broke   B. lifted   C. lost   D. found

30. The form used for reporting the finished work was REVISED.   30.____
    In this sentence, the word REVISED means nearly the same as
    A. printed   B. ordered   C. dropped   D. changed

31. He did his work RAPIDLY.   31.____
    In this sentence, the word RAPIDLY means nearly the same as
    A. carefully   B. quickly   C. slowly   D. quietly

32. The worker was OCCASIONALLY late   32.____
    In this sentence, the word OCCASIONALLY means nearly the same as
    A. sometimes   B. often   C. never   D. always

33. He SELECTED the best tool for the job.   33.____
    In this sentence, the word SELECTED means nearly the same as
    A. bought   B. picked   C. lost   D. broke

34. He needed ASSISTANCE to lift the package.
    In this sentence, the word ASSISTANCE means nearly the same as

    A. strength B. time C. help D. instructions

35. The tools were ISSUED by the supervisor.
    In this sentence, the word ISSUED means nearly the same as

    A. collected B. cleaned up
    C. given out D. examined

KEY (CORRECT ANSWERS)

1. C	16. C
2. B	17. D
3. C	18. B
4. B	19. D
5. A	20. C
6. C	21. A
7. C	22. A
8. D	23. B
9. B	24. D
10. B	25. A
11. C	26. D
12. D	27. A
13. A	28. A
14. A	29. B
15. A	30. D

31. B
32. A
33. B
34. C
35. C

EXAMINATION SECTION
TEST 1

DIRECTIONS: Below are 10 groups of statements and conclusions, numbered 1 through 10. For each group of statements, select the one conclusion lettered A, B, C, which is fully supported by and is based SOLELY on the statements. *PRINT THE LETTER OF THE CORRECT ANSWER IN THE SPACE AT THE RIGHT.*

1. He is either approved or disapproved for this examination. But, he is not approved. Therefore, he is

   A. qualified   B. disapproved   C. a taxpayer

   1.____

2. In planning the itinerary for Mr. Kane, his secretary told him: Route 20 runs parallel to Route 6. Route 6 runs parallel to Route 18.
   Mr. Kane concluded that,
   Therefore, Route

   A. 20 is north of Route 6
   B. 18 intersects Route 20
   C. 20 is parallel to Route 18

   2.____

3. Either the valedictorian is more intelligent than the salutatorian, or as intelligent, or less intelligent.
   But the valedictorian is not more intelligent, nor is she less intelligent.
   Therefore, the valedictorian is

   A. less intelligent than the salutatorian
   B. as intelligent as the salutatorian
   C. more intelligent than the salutatorian

   3.____

4. If the date for the examination is changed, it will be held July 28, or it will be postponed until October 15.
   The date is not changed.
   Therefore, the examination

   A. will probably be held July 28
   B. date is uncertain
   C. will be held July 28, or it will be postponed until October 15

   4.____

5. Joan transcribes faster than Nancy.
   Nancy transcribes faster than Anne.
   Therefore,

   A. Nancy transcribes faster than Joan
   B. Joan transcribes faster than Anne
   C. Nancy has had longer experience than Anne in taking dictation

   5.____

6. The files in Division D contain either pending matter, completed case records, or dead material.
   They do not contain pending matter.
   Therefore, they contain

   6.____

A. completed case records
B. completed case records and dead material
C. either completed case records or dead material

7. Either stenographer B in pool C types faster than stenographer A in pool D, or she types at the same rate as stenographer A, or she types slower than stenographer A. But, she does not type faster than stenographer A, nor does she type slower than stenographer Therefore, stenographer

   A. B does not type as fast as stenographer A
   B. B is more efficient than stenographer A
   C. A types as fast as stenographer B

8. Miss Andre can be eligible for retirement when she has been in city service 35 years, or if she is 55 years of age. She is fifty-four years old and has been in city service 36 years. Therefore, she

   A. is not eligible for retirement now
   B. is eligible for retirement now
   C. will be eligible for retirement only if she stays in city service for another year

9. If K is L, O is P; if M is N, Q is R.
   Either K is L, or M is N.
   Therefore,

   A. K is P or M is R
   B. either O is P or Q is R
   C. the conclusion is uncertain

10. If the employee is in error, the supervisor's refusal to listen to his side is unreasonable. If he is not in error, the supervisor's refusal is unjust. But the employee is in error or he is not.
    Therefore, the supervisor's refusal

    A. may be considered later
    B. is either unreasonable or it is unjust
    C. is justifiable

KEY (CORRECT ANSWERS)

1. B   6. C
2. C   7. C
3. B   8. B
4. B   9. B
5. B   10. B

TEST 2

Questions 1-5

DIRECTIONS: Below are 5 groups of statements and conclusions, numbered 1 through 5. For each group of statements, select the one conclusion lettered A, B, C, which is fully supported by and is based SOLELY on the statements. *PRINT THE LETTER OF THE CORRECT ANSWER IN THE SPACE AT THE RIGHT.*

1. Three desks are placed in a straight row just inside the door in our office. Desk 1 is farther from the door than Desk 2. Desk 3 is farther from the door than Desk 1. Which desk is in the middle position from the door? Desk

   A. 1 B. 2 C. 3

2. The problem is either correct or incorrect or is unsolvable.
   The problem is not correct.
   Therefore, the

   A. problem is incorrect
   B. problem is either incorrect or is unsolvable
   C. conclusion is uncertain

3. Village E is situated between City F and Village G.
   City F is situated between Village G and Town H.
   Therefore, Village E is

   A. not situated between Village G and Town H
   B. situated between City F and Town H
   C. situated nearer to City F than to Town H

4. Jurisdiction No. 1 is between Jurisdictions No. 2 and No. 3.
   Jurisdiction No. 2 is between Jurisdictions No. 3 and No. 4.
   Therefore, Jurisdiction No. 1 is

   A. not between Jurisdictions No. 3 and No. 4
   B. between Jurisdictions No. 2 and No. 4
   C. nearer to Jurisdiction No. 2 than to No. 4

5. Five candidates (A, B, C, D, and E) are seated in the same room. D is between A and B, E is between A and D; C is the same distance from A and E, and D is the same distance from A and B.
   Therefore,

   A. E is nearer to B than to A
   B. C is nearer to E than to D
   C. B is nearer to E than to D

Questions 6-10.

DIRECTIONS: Each question or incomplete statement is followed by several suggested answers or completions. Select the one that BEST answers the question or completes the statement. *PRINT THE LETTER OF THE CORRECT ANSWER IN THE SPACE AT THE RIGHT.*

6. If John is older than Mary and Mary is younger than Jane, then

   A. twice Mary's age is less than the sum of the ages of John and Jane
   B. the sum of the ages of John and Mary exceeds the age of Jane
   C. the ages of John and Jane are equal
   D. three times Mary's age equals the sum of the ages of John and Jane

7. John is older than Mary, Henry is older than Mary.
   It follows, therefore, that

   A. John and Henry are the same age
   B. the sum of the ages of John and Mary exceeds the age of Henry
   C. Mary's age is less than half of the sum of John's and Henry's ages
   D. none of the preceding three statements is true

8. The average of 9 numbers is 70.
   It follows that

   A. the sum of the numbers is 630
   B. the median of the numbers is 70
   C. the median of the numbers cannot be 70
   D. no two of the numbers can be equal

9. John is twice as old as Mary.
   The only statement about their ages which is NOT true is

   A. in five years, John will be twice as old as Mary
   B. in five years, the sum of their ages will be 10 more than the present sum of their ages
   C. Mary's present age is one-third of the sum of their present ages
   D. two years ago, the difference between their ages was the same as it will be two years hence

10. A is taller than B; C is 2 inches shorter than B.
    The one statement of the following four statements which is NOT necessarily true is

    A. B is taller than C
    B. A is taller than C
    C. A is taller than C by more than 2 inches
    D. B's height is the average of the heights of A and C

KEY (CORRECT ANSWERS)

1. A
2. B
3. C
4. C
5. B

6. A
7. C
8. D
9. A
10. D

TEST 3

DIRECTIONS: Each question or incomplete statement is followed by several suggested answers or completions. Select the one that BEST answers the question or completes the statement. *PRINT THE LETTER OF THE CORRECT ANSWER IN THE SPACE AT THE RIGHT.*

1. A stenographer can BEST deal with the situation which arises when her pencil breaks during dictation by   1.____

    A. asking the person dictating to lend her one
    B. being equipped at every dictation with several pencils
    C. going back to her desk to secure another one
    D. making a call to the supply room for some pencils

2. Accuracy is of greater importance than speed in filing CHIEFLY because   2.____

    A. city offices have a tremendous amount of filing to do
    B. fast workers are usually inferior workers
    C. there is considerable difficulty in locating materials which have been filed incorrectly
    D. there are many varieties of filing systems which may be used

3. Many persons dictate so rapidly that they pay little attention to matters of punctuation and English, but they expect their stenographers to correct errors.
   This statement implies MOST clearly that stenographers should be   3.____

    A. able to write acceptable original reports when required
    B. good citizens as well as good stenographers
    C. efficient clerks as well as good stenographers
    D. efficient in language usage

4. A typed letter should resemble a picture properly framed.
   This statement MOST emphasizes   4.____

    A. accuracy   B. speed
    C. convenience   D. neatness

5. Of the following, the CHIEF advantage of the use of a mechanical check is that it   5.____

    A. guards against tearing in handling the check
    B. decreases the possibility of alteration in the amount of the check
    C. tends to prevent the mislaying and loss of checks
    D. facilitates keeping checks in proper order for mailing

6. Of the following, the CHIEF advantage of the use of a dictating machine is that the   6.____

    A. stenographer must be able to take rapid dictation
    B. person dictating tends to make few errors
    C. dictator may be dictating letters while the stenographer is busy at some other task
    D. usual noise in an office is lessened

7. The CHIEF value of indicating enclosures beneath the identification marks on the lower left side of a letter is that it

    A. acts as a check upon the contents before mailing and upon receiving a letter
    B. helps determine the weight for mailing
    C. is useful in checking the accuracy of typed matter
    D. requires an efficient mailing clerk

8. The one of the following which is NOT an advantage of the window envelope is that it

    A. saves time since the inside address serves also as an outside address
    B. gives protection to the address from wear and tear of the mails
    C. lessens the possibility of mistakes since the address is written only once
    D. tends to be much easier to seal than the plain envelope

9. A question as to proper syllabication of a word at the end of a line may BEST be settled by consulting

    A. the person who dictated the letter
    B. a shorthand manual
    C. a dictionary
    D. a file of letters

10. Mailing a letter which contains many erasures is undesirable CHIEFLY because

    A. paper should not be wasted
    B. some stenographers are able to carry on some of the correspondence in an office without consulting their superiors
    C. correspondence should be neat
    D. erasures indicate that the dictator was not certain of what he intended to say in the letter

KEY (CORRECT ANSWERS)

1. B
2. C
3. D
4. D
5. B
6. C
7. A
8. D
9. C
10. C

TEST 4

DIRECTIONS: Each question or incomplete statement is followed by several suggested answers or completions. Select the one that BEST answers the question or completes the statement. *PRINT THE LETTER OF THE CORRECT ANSWER IN THE SPACE AT THE RIGHT.*

1. A charter operates for a city in somewhat the same fashion as

    A. the United States Supreme Court functions with regard to federal legislation
    B. the United States Constitution operates for the entire country
    C. the Governor functions for New York State
    D. a lease for a landlord

2. All civil employees should be especially interested in the activities of the United States Supreme Court PRIMARILY because

    A. its decisions provide certain kinds of important general rules
    B. the Supreme Court consists of nine persons appointed by the President
    C. the American Constitution is the finest document which man has ever produced
    D. the President's plan for reorganization of the court may be revived

3. Of the following, it is most frequently argued that labor problems are of concern to the civil employee PRIMARILY because

    A. the problems of labor are the same as the problems of government
    B. newspapers carry considerable information about labor problems
    C. the civil employee is a wage or salary earner
    D. a government is of the people, for the people, and by the people

4. Warfare in any part of the world should be of interest to the civil employee PRIMARILY as a result of the fact that

    A. strict American neutrality is secured by not permitting the sale of munitions to any country at war
    B. war has not been declared though warfare is raging
    C. the United States participates in the meetings of the UN
    D. facilities for transportation and communication have produced a "smaller" world

5. Cities regulate certain aspects of housing CHIEFLY because

    A. the city is the largest municipality in the country
    B. zoning is the concern of all residents of the city
    C. housing affects health
    D. the state constitution makes regulation optional

6. In general, it is PROBABLY true that the functions which a city administers are those

    A. most necessary to the preservation of the well-being of its residents
    B. of little or no interest to private business
    C. forbidden to the state
    D. not capable of being financed by private business

1.____

2.____

3.____

4.____

5.____

6.____

7. There is no more convincing mark of a cultured speaker or writer than accuracy of statement.
   This statement stresses the importance of

   A. new ideas
   B. facts
   C. acquiring a pleasing speaking voice
   D. poise

8. When a department is called, the voice which answers the telephone is, to the person calling, the department itself.
   This statement implies *most clearly* that

   A. only one person should answer the telephone in each office
   B. a clerk with a pleasing, courteous telephone manner is an asset to an office
   C. an efficient clerk will terminate all telephone conversations as quickly as possible
   D. making personal telephone calls is looked upon with disfavor in some offices

9. Probably the CHIEF advantage of filling higher vacancies by promotion is that this procedure

   A. stimulates the worker to improve his work and general knowledge and technique
   B. provides an easy check on the work of the individual
   C. eliminates personnel problems in a department
   D. harmonizes the work of one department with that of all other departments

10. Greatest efficiency is reached when filing method and filing clerk are harmoniously adjusted to the needs of an office.
    This statement means *most nearly* that

    A. the filing method is more important than the clerk in securing the successful handling of valuable papers
    B. almost any clerk can do office filing well
    C. a good clerk using a good filing system assures good filing
    D. every office needs a filing system

KEY (CORRECT ANSWERS)

1. B
2. A
3. C
4. D
5. C

6. A
7. B
8. B
9. A
10. C

TEST 5

DIRECTIONS: Each question or incomplete statement is followed by several suggested answers or completions. Select the one that BEST answers the question or completes the statement. *PRINT THE LETTER OF THE CORRECT ANSWER IN THE SPACE AT THE RIGHT.*

1. Your superior, Mr. Hotchkiss, is in conference and has requested that he not be disturbed.
   The condition under which you would MOST probably disturb the conference is:

   A. A Mr. Smith, whom you have not seen before, says he has important business with Mr, Hotchkiss
   B. Mrs. Hotchkiss telephones, saying there has been a serious accident at home
   C. You do not know how a certain letter should be filed and wish to ask the advice of Mr. Hotchkiss
   D. A fellow clerk wishes to ask Mr. Hotchkiss whether a particular city department handles certain matters

   1.____

2. Your superior directs you to find certain papers. You know the purpose for which the papers are to be used. In the course of your search for the papers, you come across certain material which would be very useful for the purpose to be served by the papers. You should

   A. bring the papers to your superior and ask whether he wants the other materials
   B. go to your superior immediately and ask whether he wishes both the materials and the papers or only one of the two
   C. bring to your superior the other materials, together with the papers you were directed to find
   D. bring only the other materials to your superior and point out the manner in which these materials are of greater value than the papers

   2.____

3. If a fellow employee asks you a question to which you do not know the answer, you should say,

   A. "I don't know. What's the difference?"
   B. "The answer to that question forms no part of my duties here."
   C. "My dear sir, the thing for you to do is to look the matter up yourself because it is your responsibility, not mine."
   D. "I'm sorry. I don't know."

   3.____

4. In general, it is PROBABLY true that MOST people are

   A. so self-seeking that they pay no attention to the wants, needs, or behavior of others
   B. so changeable that one never knows what his fellow employee is likely to do next
   C. not worth the trouble to bother about
   D. quite ready to help others

   4.____

5. Of the following, the one which is NOT a reason for avoiding clerical errors is that

   A. time is lost
   B. money is wasted
   C. many clerks are very intelligent
   D. serious consequences may follow

   5.____

6. Of the following, the MAIN reason for keeping a careful record of incoming mail is that

    A. some people are less industrious than others
    B. this record helps to speed up outgoing mail
    C. this record is a kind of legal evidence
    D. this information may be useful in answering questions which may arise

7. Of the following, the MAIN reason for using a calculating machine is that

    A. a lesser knowledge of arithmetic is needed
    B. a more attractive product is obtained
    C. greater speed and accuracy are obtained
    D. it is not difficult to learn how to operate a calculating machine

8. Of the following, the MAIN reason for being polite over the telephone is that

    A. persons who are speaking over the telephone cannot see each other
    B. politeness makes for pleasant business relationships
    C. it is not at all difficult or costly to be courteous
    D. one's voice is of great importance because voice reflects mood

9. Because telephone directories contain printed pages, they are called books.
   This statement assumes *most nearly* that

    A. some books do not contain printed pages
    B. not all telephone directories are books which contain printed pages
    C. material which contains printed pages is called a book
    D. all books which contain printed pages are called telephone directories

10. Mr. Cross must be using a budget because he has been able to reduce his unnecessary expenses.
    On the basis of only the material included in this statement, it may MOST accurately be said that this statement assumes that

    A. all people who use budgets lower certain types of expenses
    B. some people who do not use budgets reduce unnecessary expenses
    C. some people who use budgets do not reduce unnecessary expenses
    D. all types of expenses are reduced by the use of a budget

---

KEY (CORRECT ANSWERS)

1.	B	6.	D
2.	C	7.	C
3.	D	8.	B
4.	D	9.	C
5.	C	10.	A

EXAMINATION SECTION
TEST 1

DIRECTIONS: Each question or incomplete statement is followed by several suggested answers or completions. Select the one that BEST answers the question or completes the statement. *PRINT THE LETTER OF THE CORRECT ANSWER IN THE SPACE AT THE RIGHT.*

1. Tom wanted to cut six inches off the end of the board, so he went to the tool chest and took out a 1.____

    A. wrench   B. screwdriver   C. hammer   D. saw

2. Last year, American industry lost a quarter of a billion dollars more from crime than from fire. Any industrialist who feels that fire insurance is a necessary protection cannot afford to overlook the possibility that he also needs protection against 2.____

    A. insurance agencies   B. labor
    C. government   D. crime

3. Jimmie was a little boy who did not want to help his mother or father. Jimmie was 3.____

    A. lazy   B. strong   C. stupid   D. kind

4. In areas where wood is widely used for building, there is plenty of work for 4.____

    A. architects   B. carpenters   C. masons   D. electricians

5. The two boys had played together for six years. They did not fight. They were 5.____

    A. friends   B. cousins   C. boys   D. enemies

6. Saws driven by gasoline engines cannot be used in areas where a spark or backfire might set off an explosion. Recently, however, power saws operated by compressed air have been designed by German engineers to work in places threatened by 6.____

    A. manpower shortages   B. enemy attacks
    C. fire hazards   D. power cutoffs

7. The speaker's talk was long and dull. It seemed that it would never end. How glad we were when he finally 7.____

    A. spoke   B. died   C. stopped   D. clapped

8. I gave the girl twenty cents to buy apples. On the way to the store, she lost the money, so she could not buy the 8.____

    A. oranges   B. fruit   C. candy   D. bread

9. The road was built only a few months ago. Already there are cracks in its surface. It is too bad that this new road needs to be 9.____

    A. built   B. sold   C. widened   D. repaired

10. As cities become larger, it is necessary for engineers to seek new sources of water to meet the demands of growing

   A. populations   B. children   C. gardens   D. lakes

11. These mountain peaks will not be conquered easily by a person who lacks climbing experience.
    The Mountain Club advises climbers not to try to scale these until they have

   A. become club members   B. climbed other mountains
   C. read about climbers   D. joined a party of climbers

12. A girl is reading a book. The book has pictures in it. She shows the pictures to the baby, but all he wants to do is tear the

   A. pages   B. rags   C. dress   D. cloth

13. Jane's favorite TV program is the weekly circus. She likes to watch the

   A. airplanes   B. books   C. cars   D. clowns

14. In comic strips, people and animals do things that they cannot do in real life. Some people can fly without airplanes and some animals can

   A. play   B. run   C. bark   D. talk

15. It would be easier to plan the monthly expenses both of business firms and of households is all the months had the same number of

   A. workers   B. days   C. holidays   D. sales

16. It is not only necessary but also enlightening to merely sit, listen, and observe on some occasions. Often it has been said that spectators see more of any athletic contest than anyone else.
    In many situations, in fact, a spectator can usually take note of what is happening as well as, if not better than, one who is

   A. paying attention   B. actually present
   C. involved in the fray   D. on the winning team

17. His athletic interests are strong. He enjoys not only baseball and football but almost all

   A. sports   B. books   C. food   D. people

18. Dan got very dirty playing in the yard. Then he went into the house and took a nice warm bath.
    When he stepped out of the tub, he said, *"My, it feels good to be*

   A. rich."   B. clean."   C. tired."   D. hungry."

19. The angle that a bomb makes with the horizontal area at the point of impact is called the angle of fall. The degree of penetration of the bomb increases with the size of the angle of fall.
    Thus, given an angle of 90 degrees, the amount of penetration will be

   A. 25% of maximum   B. maximum
   C. unpredictable   D. 50% of maximum

20. The greater part of the world's creative work is done by those who subsist by some other occupation. Science today is vigorous partly because research and teaching go well together. In the fine arts, it is not easy to make a living by really good work, and it is equally as hard to find an occupation that leaves leisure time for creation. Quite likely, this is one reason why art

    A. appeals to the lazy man
    B. is less flourishing than science
    C. makes such great contributions to our society
    D. is not appreciated by the majority of the people

21. When the driver of the car saw the tree blocking the road, he

    A. opened the hood
    B. went faster
    C. stopped
    D. passed it

22. Furniture that is to be left outdoors should be made of materials that will not be ruined by bad

    A. meals
    B. backyards
    C. weather
    D. children

23. Jane's little kitten cried because it was hungry. It wanted to

    A. sleep
    B. play
    C. eat
    D. run

24. All the crew bailed out of the plane.
    The plane crashed and burned but no lives were

    A. saved
    B. lost
    C. rescued
    D. parachuted

25. The Chinese philosopher Lao-tse taught his followers to believe in feng-shui, a mystical spirit connected with the land and giving continuity to the labors of successive generations. The concept of feng-shui carries with it an admonition to the Chinese farmers that they are merely trustees of the soil that they till, since it belongs not only to them but to all their ancestors and descendants. One practical outcome of this agrarian philosophy is the centuries-old Chinese practice of

    A. fêng-shuiism
    B. soil conservation
    C. feudalism
    D. rice cultivation

KEY (CORRECT ANSWERS)

1. D
2. D
3. A
4. B
5. A

6. C
7. C
8. B
9. D
10. A

11. B
12. A
13. D
14. D
15. B

16. C
17. A
18. B
19. B
20. B

21. C
22. C
23. C
24. B
25. B

TEST 2

DIRECTIONS: Each question or incomplete statement is followed by several suggested answers or completions. Select the one that BEST answers the question or completes the statement. *PRINT THE LETTER OF THE CORRECT ANSWER IN THE SPACE AT THE RIGHT.*

1. It seems likely that the word *Gothic* was originally used to describe a type of architecture that suggested barbaric qualities in the nation producing it. It did not indicate that the people of the nation were really descendants of the Goths or that the architecture was originated by the Goths.
It only implied that the people and their structures showed

   A. signs of Gothic influence
   B. a new type of architectural design
   C. trends found only in the art of the Goths
   D. a degree of sternness and rudeness

1._____

2. Compulsory retirement provisions in industry give younger men added assurance that new opportunities

   A. will open up to them
   B. must be sought in new work
   C. are fairly distributed
   D. will help the older workers

2._____

3. We planned to drive from New York to Detroit. To decide which highway to follow, we looked at a road

   A. lane   B. builder   C. surface   D. map

3._____

4. Instead of using one word over and over again, a person who has a good vocabulary uses different words with the same

   A. spelling   B. length   C. sound   D. meaning

4._____

5. He could never remember Bill's telephone number. He always had to look it up in the

   A. almanac   B. encyclopedia
   C. telephone directory D. dictionary

5._____

6. It is hard to speak properly upon a subject where it is even difficult to convince your hearers that you are speaking the truth. On the one hand, the friend who is familiar with every facet of the story may think that some point has not been set forth with that fullness he wishes and knows it to deserve. On the other hand, he who is a stranger to the matter may be led by envy to suspect exaggeration if he hears anything above his own nature. For men can endure to hear others praised only so long as they can severally persuade themselves of their own ability to equal the actions recounted: when this point is passed, envy comes in and with it

   A. exaggeration   B. false pride
   C. incredulity   D. deceit

6._____

7. The Spanish settlers of the New World, eager for gold, had little interest in agriculture. For many decades, potentially valuable farmland was

   A. expensive   B. neglected   C. demanded   D. explored

7._____

29

8. The term *specialization* refers to the system in which each person performs a particular and perhaps different task. This person receives money for his work and with it buys goods and services that others have produced. Specialization has thus led to a(n)

   A. lower standard of living
   B. money economy
   C. immobile social structure
   D. barter economy

9. The car was stuck in the mud.
   Three men pushed as hard as they could, still the car did not

   A. stop   B. start   C. c. move   D. stall

10. According to T.S. Eliot, "When a poet's mind is perfectly equipped for its work, it is constantly amalgamating disparate experience: the ordinary man's experience is chaotic., irregular, fragmentary. The latter falls in love, or reads Spinoza, and these two experiences have nothing to do with each other, or with the noise of the typewriter or the smell of cooking; in the mind of the poet, these experiences are

    A. separately considered."
    B. always forming new wholes."
    C. contradictory to his philosophy."
    D. the bases of artistic work."

11. There were few people at his funeral.
    He had outlived his hundreds of true friends who would have been at the funeral if they

    A. had not been so old
    B. had known about it
    C. could have sent flowers
    D. had been alive

12. For expository purposes, the Utopias that have been set up '. thus far may be classified according to their placement on two continua: first, on the continuum extending from chaos to complete harmony, and second, on the continuum extending from behavior ruled by reason to behavior controlled by strict religious axioms. Most Utopias that could be classified as showing harmony have been those ruled by fixed precepts.
    There appears to be a(n)

    A. direct relationship between chaos and rule by axiom
    B. direct relationship between harmony and rule by reason
    C. inverse relationship between chaos and rule by axiom
    D. circular relationship between chaos and rule by reason

13. Thousands of persons watched the automobile race. Newspapers carried stories and pictures for those who could not

    A. hear   B. bet   C. go   D. drive

14. Fish live in water. They swim and swim all day. They cannot live on land.
    If you take them out of water, they will soon

    A. walk   B. die   C. run away   D. get lost

15. In the arena, two gladiators fought each other with short swords. Occasionally, one of the gladiators would be knocked down and would raise a finger to the audience, asking them for mercy. The spectators waved clenched fists to signal that they wished a particular gladiator put to death.
Other spectators, who favored this fighter, waved open hands, asking that the gladiator be given

    A. a defeat
    B. a new sword
    C. mercy
    D. to the lions

    15.____

16. If the quantity with which a person is concerned is finite, one and one thousand are quite different. But if the quantity under consideration is infinite, one and one thousand are the same.
Finite quantities can be thought of as equal when

    A. compared with each other
    B. compared with an infinite quantity
    C. regarded as individual cases
    D. mathematical principles are ignored

    16.____

17. Plans for the wolf hunt were being made. The farmers had lost sheep and chickens. The wolves killed their pigs. Even cattle were not

    A. attacked   B. safe   C. butchered   D. hunted

    17.____

18. The man took his boat out on the lake.
Black clouds came up in the sky so he had to hurry home before the

    A. sun came out
    B. lake dried up
    C. rain came
    D. boat sank

    18.____

19. Honeybees make honey. They make it from nectar that they get from flowers.
If there were no flowers, we could not get

    A. honey   B. roses   C. water   D. perfume

    19.____

20. Any proposition that does not involve a contradiction in terms may possibly be true; and if all the circumstances that raise a probability in its favor be stated and enforced, and those which lead to an opposite conclusion be omitted or lightly passed over, it may

    A. properly be declared true
    B. be rightly evaluated as false
    C. appear to be demonstrated
    D. appear ridiculous when actually true

    20.____

21. Acetylene, a colorless gas, produces a flame whose light penetrates fog and darkness remarkably well.
This property, along with the capacity of the acetylene generator to operate without attention for long periods of time, makes the gas valuable for use in

    A. industrial heating
    B. mining
    C. lighthouses
    D. blowtorches

    21.____

22. Surety bonds covering acceptable completion of the contracts involved in public projects are required by law. One function of these bonds is to insure that the project will be

    A. finished   B. practical   C. popular   D. inexpensive

23. The mystery writer unfolds his plot in a logical, inexorable sequence. After the first event happens, it seems that the next could not fail to happen.
    We feel that the incidents follow each other as they do, not because the author planned it so, but because

    A. we desired it so
    B. it had to be so
    C. the plot was unique
    D. it is so in our own lives

24. We didn't have any milk for breakfast because the milkman didn't

    A. stay   B. come   C. write   D. phone

25. From a purely selfish point of view, it is not advisable to let a person know that you think he is stupid.
    You might be wrong, in which case he will quite justifiably

    A. continually ask you for advice
    B. defer to your ability to judge others
    C. concur in your opinion
    D. form the same opinion of you

KEY (CORRECT ANSWERS)

1. D
2. A
3. D
4. D
5. C
6. C
7. B
8. B
9. C
10. B
11. D
12. C
13. C
14. B
15. C
16. B
17. B
18. C
19. A
20. C
21. C
22. A
23. B
24. B
25. D

TEST 3

DIRECTIONS: Each question or incomplete statement is followed by several suggested answers or completions. Select the one that BEST answers the question or completes the statement. *PRINT THE LETTER OF THE CORRECT ANSWER IN THE SPACE AT THE RIGHT.*

1. Whether or not this historian will subsist as a standard supreme authority is a question. Wherever and whenever read, he will be read with fascination, with delight, with wonder. And with copious instruction too; but also with copious reserve, with questioning scrutiny, with liberty to reject, and with much exercise of that liberty. The contemporary mind may in rare cases be taken by storm; but posterity, never.
   The tribunal of the present is accessible to influence, that of the future is

   A. incorrupt B. unsympathetic
   C. prejudiced D. predictable

   1.____

2. Jim knew that morning had not come, for outside it was quite

   A. dark   B. bright   C. foggy   D. cool

   2.____

3. In his travels about China as a representative of Kublai Khan, Marco Polo observed that the Chinese were extremely honest.
   They left their doors open at night without fear of

   A. rain   B. insects   C. cold   D. thieves

   3.____

4. One must be careful about keeping matches out of the reach of

   A. ladies B. men
   C. young children D. pockets

   4.____

5. Billy and his friends loved to play cowboys, so his mother bought him a

   A. tool chest B. cowboy suit
   C. bicycle D. dog

   5.____

6. A person who enjoys golf will derive more benefit from that sport than from setting-up exercises that he would do with more of a sense of duty than of

   A. accomplishment B. pleasure
   C. benefit D. determination

   6.____

7. When we finally reached the cabin, we were very tired.
   The three-mile walk up the side of the mountain had not been

   A. interesting   B. long   C. slow   D. easy

   7.____

8. So numerous, indeed, and so powerful are the causes that serve to give a false bias to the judgment that we, upon many occasions, see wise and good men on the wrong as well as on the right side of questions of the first importance to society.
   This circumstance, if duly attended to by those who are ever so much persuaded of their being in the right in any controversy, would furnish

   A. an argument for the opposition
   B. a lesson of moderation
   C. a change of heart
   D. justification of their position

   8.____

33

9. The polar bear's sense of smell is very good. Though food may be hidden, he is able to

   A. want it   B. hide it   C. see it   D. find it

10. At nine o'clock, the school bell rang.
    All the children left the playground and went into the

    A. classroom   B. office   C. park   D. store

11. We have solved one long-standing economic problem only to meet another sort of difficulty. For centuries, men tried vainly to supply in sufficient quantity the things that they needed and wanted. Because of recent advances in technology, more goods are available now than are purchased, and this situation will last.
    The new problem is that of

    A. reducing production below the desirable level
    B. making men want more than enough things
    C. equalizing consumption among social classes
    D. decreasing the number of luxuries that men want

12. The thermostat is an instrument for automatically adjusting the temperature produced by a heating system. In one type, when the temperature rises to a certain point, it causes a fluid within the thermostat to expand. This expansion activates a mechanism that decreases the amount of fuel supplied.
    When the temperature falls to a certain point, the fluid contracts and activates a mechanism that

    A. decreases the temperature
    B. restores the system to manual control
    C. causes the fluid to expand again
    D. supplies more fuel

13. Experts generally agree that the primary cause of war is international competition for economic superiority. Each nation desires to achieve economic advantages equal to those enjoyed by its neighbors, and to attain these a nation may be compelled to add to its territory. Many believe that this struggle for territory is frequently the major cause of war, but I believe that it is only a minor aspect of the greater economic competition.
    Dispute over territory by rival nations is

    A. necessary for economic survival
    B. the cause of economic struggle
    C. the major cause of war
    D. necessary for economic survival

14. Long ago in ancient Babylonia, each schoolboy was given a tablet covered with soft clay on which he wrote.
    When the tablet was filled, he could smooth out the marks with a flat stick, or make himself a new tablet with

    A. bullrushes   B. birch bark
    C. a fresh ball of clay   D. paper

15. The Board of Health is responsible for matters of public health policy and for drafting the city's

    A. traffic regulations
    B. house numbers
    C. tax laws
    D. sanitary code

16. When he looked at his watch, he began to walk faster. He was afraid he would be

    A. on time   B. caught   C. late   D. slow

17. Until a century or so ago, man was almost immune to scientific investigation. I think that the modern trend is rather clearly revealed by a consideration of the order in which certain natural sciences have become a standard part of most college curricula: first came geology, followed by botany, zoology, and finally psychology.
    This series seems to suggest an advance by natural science

    A. in usefulness
    B. in general
    C. on man
    D. on physical science

18. The fat woman tourist sat astride the camel.
    She tried to smile and look as if she were enjoying her ride, but she really wasn't very

    A. heavy
    B. foreign
    C. rich
    D. comfortable

19. The shrill note of the referee's whistle told the team that they had broken a

    A. rule   B. habit   C. record   D. leg

20. When life was first coming onto land from the sea, it was washed ashore by one tide and carried back by another.
    In this way, it could grow used to the land without a

    A. sudden change
    B. tide
    C. success
    D. gradual change

21. Summer visitors to Niagara Falls cannot imagine that the endless roar of the torrent of rushing water could cease. Were they to return in winter, however, they would find that Nature had silenced the waters by

    A. rechanneling them
    B. subduing them
    C. freezing them
    D. reducing their volume

22. The couple wanted to dance, but they were so far from the orchestra that they could not

    A. leave the party
    B. see their friends
    C. hear the music
    D. call the waiter

23. When it began to rain, the children ran into the house so that they would not be

    A. cold   B. late   C. tired   D. wet

24. There was baseball at the Polo Grounds that night. Eight banks of 120 lights, with each light 1500 watts, turned night into

    A. pleasure   B. sport   C. day   D. suspense

25. From the beginning of this self-governing republic, military chieftains have had to lay down their swords before assuming civil offices. Victorious generals in this country, contrary to experience elsewhere in the world, have not used military power to seize

    A. the army and navy
    B. valuable documents
    C. the country's treasury
    D. political authority

25.____

KEY (CORRECT ANSWERS)

1.	A	11.	B
2.	A	12.	D
3.	D	13.	D
4.	C	14.	C
5.	B	15.	B
6.	B	16.	C
7.	D	17.	C
8.	B	18.	D
9.	D	19.	A
10.	A	20.	A

21. C
22. C
23. D
24. C
25. D

TEST 4

DIRECTIONS: Each question or incomplete statement is followed by several suggested answers or completions. Select the one that BEST answers the question or completes the statement. *PRINT THE LETTER OF THE CORRECT ANSWER IN THE SPACE AT THE RIGHT.*

1. Plants are entirely satisfied with mere existence; lower animals are almost so. Man, as a rule, demands a great deal more from life than sheer being. In fact, one might say that to the degree that a man is content with mere existence, he

    A. realizes his ambitions
    B. reflects on his state
    C. is dull and obtuse
    D. is a sedentary being

    1.____

2. Many people are killed in automobile accidents by being thrown from the automobile. This could sometimes be prevented if the automobile doors were kept

    A. greased   B. locked   C. open   D. clean

    2.____

3. Before the Industrial Revolution, each craftsman was forced to keep in his small shop many different kinds of equipment, although he could use only one piece of equipment at a time.
Now, in a modern factory, each man is assigned to a machine, and all equipment is

    A. kept repaired
    B. constantly used
    C. skillfully operated
    D. elaborately designed

    3.____

4. Voltaire, probably as much as any other person, popularized Newton's scientific discoveries. It is highly unlikely today that an eminent literary figure would disseminate scientific findings, for the accumulation and complexity of knowledge is such that, to achieve any real understanding, a man must resign himself to

    A. specificity of inquiry
    B. knowing nothing
    C. taking a graduate degree
    D. lack of scientific knowledge

    4.____

5. Since the queen bee is an autocrat, there is room in each hive for only one queen. When a strange queen bee wanders into a hive that already has a queen, there is

    A. room for her
    B. no disturbance in the hive
    C. a royal reception
    D. a battle for power

    5.____

6. I am amazed, therefore, that none have yet found out the secret of flattering the worthless, and yet of preserving a safe conscience.
I have often wished for some method by which a man might do himself and his deceased patron justice without being under the hateful reproach of

    A. self-conviction
    B. sincere flattery
    C. his admiring friends
    D. envious rivals

    6.____

7. Even primitive man found it necessary to have a home of some kind to protect himself from changes in the weather. Since he had no tools for constructing such a shelter, he had to live in

    A. caves   B. cabins   C. cottages   D. houses

    7.____

8. Fire irons do not rust when they are used constantly. They are kept dry by the

   A. light B. danger C. heat D. color

9. According to modern modes of thought, elements of nature are not to be considered resources until there is some use for them in our technology.
   Thus, if, for some reason, zinc were no longer necessary in our civilization, no matter how little there was in the country, we would say that

   A. there could never be a scarcity of zinc
   B. there was a scarcity of the natural resource mentioned
   C. as far as technology is concerned, there was a scarcity of zinc
   D. there was not a scarcity of the natural resource zinc

10. The boxer lay on the floor of the ring while the referee counted to ten. His fans were disappointed. Now he would no longer be

    A. champion B. tired C. alive D. out

11. The art of executing a design in color on textiles, or batik, is as difficult as etching or painting. It is practically impossible to correct a mistake in drawing or color after it has been made on cloth.
    Truly, this is no art for those who work by

    A. dependence on vision alone
    B. dim illumination
    C. trial-and-error methods
    D. hand rather than with tools

12. There are several types of human blood. The blood given in a transfusion must match the patient's blood. If the transfused blood is of a different type from the patient's blood, blood clotting and death will result.
    When a patient is given a transfusion, his very life is dependent on the

    A. amount of blood available
    B. anesthetic administered
    C. surgical skill of the doctor
    D. type of the transfused blood

13. The wolf's footsteps showed that it had been prowling around outside the hut during the night, and the broken-down door showed that it had found an

    A. escape B. entrance C. animal D. enemy

14. The atmosphere is saturated with change. It has the lightheaded going around in fantastic circles, and even the most level-headed are filled with a sense of

    A. optimism B. satisfaction C. permanency D. insecurity

15. Although installation of dial phones has replaced many thousands of telephone operators, the total number of persons employed in this industry has continued to rise. This fact should help destroy the myth that

   A. dial phones can never entirely replace switchboards
   B. employment depends upon machinery
   C. machinery increases unemployment
   D. employment and mechanization go hand in hand

16. The public imagination was stirred by the effrontery of this colorful swindler whom the newspapers referred to as a modern

   A. prophet   B. pirate   C. kidnaper   D. knight

17. Death, other conditions remaining the same, is more profoundly affecting in summer than in other parts -of the year. There is an antagonism between the tropical redundancy of life in summer and the frozen sterilities of the grave.
   The summer we see, the grave we haunt with our thoughts; the glory is around us, the darkness is within us; and, summer and death coming into collision,

   A. we comprehend the inevitable pattern of life and death
   B. each exalts the other into stronger relief
   C. the summer becomes meaningless and is forgotten
   D. the beauty of one eases the pain of the other

18. They had to wade across the stream, for at the point where they wished to cross there was no

   A. ford   B. water   C. bridge   D. bank

19. Man is inconsistent in his likes and dislikes. What he loves at twenty, he hates at forty, but this inconsistency speaks well of his ability to profit from experience.
   If he never changed his attitudes, he would be marked as

   A. a wise man   B. true to himself
   C. unable to learn   D. preferring simple things

20. One of the great needs of Utopias, which usually have inefficient methods of obtaining food and other necessities, is a large percentage of workers per number of members. This might be achieved, in the very short run, by

   A. outlawing marriage and children
   B. modernizing farming techniques
   C. encouraging marriage
   D. adopting infants

21. Leaders seem to operate on the theory that pity is a powerful force that can overcome even the jealousy of their followers.
   Leaders loudly complain about pressure and overwork merely to

   A. deplore the suffering of the great
   B. abate the edge of envy
   C. increase their range of sentiments
   D. make their prestige more obvious

22. Most of the prehistoric reptiles were unable either to adapt to the ice that eventually covered their accustomed habitat or to migrate to

    A. warmer zones
    B. Canada
    C. modern countries
    D. frozen lands

23. Serfs were not bought and sold; rather, they were transferred with the land upon which they worked.
    The essential economic characteristic of serfdom was bondage to

    A. labor   B. masters   C. soil   D. chains

24. In India, actors in the early days of the theater were among the lower class of a rigid society.
    Parents feared that their children might take up dramatic careers, for the theater through the years had supported only

    A. drama critics
    B. trained performers
    C. vagabonds and profligates
    D. amateurs

25. The Indians had eaten little for many months.
    Only the strongest people of the tribe remained alive, and now they were weak from

    A. war   B. cold   C. hunger   D. sorrow

KEY (CORRECT ANSWERS)

1. C
2. B
3. B
4. A
5. D

6. A
7. A
8. C
9. D
10. A

11. C
12. D
13. B
14. D
15. C

16. B
17. B
18. C
19. C
20. A

21. B
22. A
23. C
24. C
25. C

REASONING AND JUDGMENT

EXAMINATION SECTION
TEST 1

DIRECTIONS: Each question or incomplete statement is followed by several suggested answers or completions. Select the one that BEST answers the question or completes the statement. *PRINT THE LETTER OF THE CORRECT ANSWER IN THE SPACE AT THE RIGHT.*

1. Lapland consists of the most northern parts of Norway, Sweden, and Finland, and the Kola Peninsula in Russia. The inhabitants, called Lapps, are very hardy people who farm and fish for a livelihood. Their meat, milk, and furs come from the reindeer, which is their only domestic animal.
   There is no country named Lapland, so we cannot ask,

   A. "Who is president of Lapland?"
   B. "What kind of education is there in Lapland?"
   C. "What is the climate in Lapland?"
   D. "Are any of the Lapps wealthy?"

1._____

2. Induction is a method of reasoning by which general laws are inferred from the observation of a large number of individual cases. The laws thus derived are based not upon logical necessity but upon consistency among observations.
   Since any new observation conceivably could fail to follow the inductive law which it would be predicted to follow, an inductive law is never

   A. sought in scientific research
   B. as useful as a deductive law
   C. used as a basis for action
   D. more than probably true

2._____

3. A lion, finding a hare asleep, was about to devour it when he saw a deer passing. He left the hare and chased the deer, which was so swift that it escaped him. When the lion returned to eat the hare, he found that it had been awakened by the noise and had escaped.
   This story was told to make the point that men often lose moderate gains by trying for

   A. easier ones   B. larger ones
   C. sure profit   D. great losses

3._____

4. In Norse mythology, no god was better loved than Balder, the god of light and peace. He was slain by the trickery of Loki, a jealous god.
   When the dark winter comes to the Norseland, the people say, "All nature grieves for Balder," and when the spring comes again, they say,

   A. "Summer is here again."
   B. "Balder has never lived."
   C. "Loki will never return to earth."
   D. "The spirit of Balder has returned."

4._____

5. Living organisms are able to exist at great ocean depths in spite of the tremendous pressure of the water so long as their, body spaces are not filled with air or any other gas. This is possible because the pressure is equally applied on all sides of the organism and the same pressure is maintained inside and outside. Similarly, man does not feel the effects of pressure in the atmosphere exerted on him at 14.7 pounds per square inch, but he cannot withstand the great pressure of water below depths of 100 feet because his body contains spaces filled with _____ pressure.

   A. water at low   B. air at the same
   C. water at high D. air at low

6. The oak tree has long been a symbol of strength and bravery. Mindful of this symbolism, the Romans, who were a hardy people, decorated their war heroes with crowns of _____ leaves.

   A. maple   B. olive   C. laurel   D. oak

7. In aviation, the ceiling is the distance from the ground to the bottom of the clouds when the sky is more than half-covered. When there is heavy fog on the ground, the ceiling is said to be zero. When the sky is clear or there are only scattered clouds, the ceiling is unlimited. An airplane pilot must know what the ceiling is before takeoff so that he can determine the proper flight

   A. altitude   B. direction   C. instruments   D. speed

8. In THE RIGHTS OF MAN, Thomas Paine wrote, "Every age and generation must be as free to act for itself in all oases as the ages and generations which preceded it. The vanity and presumption of governing beyond the grave is the most ridiculous and insolent of ail tyrannies. Man has no property in man; neither has any generation a property in the generations which are to follow."
   According to this, citizens of the United States should respect the Constitution because they believe it is right and not because it is

   A. debatable   B. old   C. English   D. misunderstood

9. Before newspapers were common, a man called a town crier was appointed to make public announcements. The town crier was an important person in England and in the British North American colonies, but he disappeared when newspapers became more widely distributed. Nowadays we often hear news before we read it in the paper.
   We hear it from an electronic town crier -

   A. the theater   B. a radio or a television set
   C. a town meeting   D. a phonograph

10. The opal is a gem that reflects a number of beautiful colors. For a long time, opals were unpopular because of a superstition that it was bad luck to wear them unless they were one's birthstone.
    Few people believe this superstition anymore, and opals have become more

    A. transparent   B. colorful   C. popular   D. beautiful

11. Newton's third law of motion states that for every action there is an equal and opposite reaction. When a gun is fired, the force that pushes the bullet forward is equal to the force with which the gun recoils.
    Space vehicles, having left the earth's atmosphere, can maneuver by firing small rockets in the direction

    A. of the earth
    B. in which they wish to go
    C. opposite to their destination
    D. at right angles to their destination

11.____

12. When the purchasing power of the dollar steadily declines over a period of time, we speak of *inflation*. The reverse situation, in which a dollar buys more than formerly, is called deflation.
    Inflation and deflation, then, are defined by changes in the relation between

    A. borrowing and lending   B. money and goods
    C. supply and demand   D. decrease and increase

12.____

13. The seed gatherers were a group of Indians who lived in the arid region between the Rocky Mountains and the Sierra Nevada. They were called seed gatherers because of the way in which they got most of their food. Seeds and berries suitable to eat grew in different regions at different times of the year.
    For this reason, the seed gatherers

    A. were skilled archers   B. changed homes often
    C. fished in the sea   D. made fancy baskets

13.____

14. The men of the Coast Guard rescue many people from disasters at sea. Their work is often dangerous because they sometimes have to go out on a rescue mission under very bad conditions.
    The men have excellent equipment, and they are well-trained, but their duties involve great

    A. speed   B. preparation   C. risks   D. thrills

14.____

15. A crocodile can snap a wooden plank in two with its powerful jaws. But a man can hold the jaws of a crocodile together with very little effort.
    The crocodile exerts the greatest amount of power when

    A. snapping at wood   B. opening its mouth
    C. C. lashing its tail   D. closing its jaws

15.____

16. All of Alaska is farther west than the westernmost part of the continental United States. Juneau, the capital of Alaska, is in the same time zone as California, although its longitude should place it in the Yukon time zone. Some of the Aleutian Islands, a part of Alaska, are on one side of the 180 meridian and some are on the other, but the date line does not follow the 180 meridian and does not cut the Aleutians.
    The result is that although there are four time zones in the United States, they are all

    A. on the same side of the date line
    B. on standard time
    C. really west of Greenwich
    D. in the Western Hemisphere

16.____

17. In Greek mythology, a chimera was a fire-breathing female monster with the head of a lion, the body of a goat, and the tail of a dragon. Of course, there really was no such animal, but the idea was so fantastic that we use the name chimera now for any

    A. deliberate falsehood
    B. figment of the imagination
    C. strange animal
    D. hybrid animal

18. The German shepherd is intelligent, alert, loyal, highly trainable, and has a good disposition. It is frequently used as a guide dog for the blind.
    It is sometimes called *German police dog* because so many of this breed have been trained for

    A. seeing eye dogs   B. police work
    C. army scouts   D. rescue work

19. Unless an adequate supply of protein is included in a person's diet, loss of weight and even death may result. The problem of determining the amount of protein needed is important in rationing food in war or in famine. The minimal requirement of protein to maintain the body in health is less when the protein consumed is animal protein than when it is vegetable protein.
    In some parts of the world, protein deficiency is a problem because the diet of the people is almost completely made up of

    A. animal proteins   B. fish
    C. solids   D. cereals

20. Emerson said, "Character is adroitness to keep the old and trodden 'round, and power and courage to make new roads to new and better goals."
    This means that the person of high character is both

    A. conformist and creator   B. friendly and aloof
    C. student and laborer   D. popular and unpopular

KEY (CORRECT ANSWERS)

1.	A	11.	C
2.	D	12.	B
3.	B	13.	B
4.	D	14.	C
5.	D	15.	D
6.	D	16.	A
7.	A	17.	B
8.	B	18.	B
9.	B	19.	D
10.	C	20.	A

TEST 2

DIRECTIONS: Each question or incomplete statement is followed by several suggested answers or completions. Select the one that BEST answers the question or completes the statement. *PRINT THE LETTER OF THE CORRECT ANSWER IN THE SPACE AT THE RIGHT.*

1. The small Boston terrier has a dark coat with white chest, neck, and feet. Many people are drawn to this dog because of its neat appearance and large brown eyes. The Boston terrier is a popular pet because it likes people and

   A. grows so large
   B. bites postmen
   C. is hard to train
   D. makes friends easily

   1.____

2. The gradations of the moral faculties in the higher animals and man are so imperceptible that to deny to the first a certain sense of responsibility and consciousness would certainly be an exaggeration of the difference between animals and man.
   When animals fight with one another, when they associate for a common purpose, when they warn one another of danger, when they come to the rescue of another, when they display pain and joy, they manifest impulses of the same kind as are considered among the

   A. most general in the animal kingdom
   B. animal instincts of man
   C. divine provisions for man
   D. moral attributes of man

   2.____

3. In ancient times, a country guaranteed its treaty promises by giving hostages to the other party. The hostages were often important people in their own country. They were held as prisoners and could be killed if their country failed to keep its treaty promises.
   Today, most countries rely on the good faith of other countries and on public opinion to ensure that they will keep their treaties, and the hostage system

   A. is strictly observed
   B. is no longer used
   C. protects treaty makers
   D. has grown in effectiveness

   3.____

4. The Pekingese was held in great esteem by Chinese royalty. The dog was bred to accentuate marks that were related in various ways to the upper classes of society. A white spot on the forehead of a Pekingese was admired, for this mark was associated with the Buddha.
   A mark round the dog's body resembling a sash was quite admirable, for during the time when the Pekingese breed was so much admired,

   A. sashes were used to hold the outer garments together
   B. only high-ranking officials could wear sashes
   C. it was difficult to breed a dog with a sash mark
   D. sash marks signified royal blood

   4.____

5. A recent U.S. study showed that of 100 high school seniors who received national academic scholarships, nine out of ten read at least one book a month, while of 100 high school seniors accepted by various colleges but not awarded scholarships, only six out of ten read at least one book a month.
   This shows that those who read more are MOST likely to

   A. waste time
   B. achieve more
   C. become librarians
   D. spend less money

6. Turbines in motor vehicles cannot be operated on gasoline containing lead. Diesel fuel, on which turbines can be operated, is available only on major turnpikes and on roads that trucks use.
   Thus, if regular cars are to utilize turbines,

   A. highways must be rerouted
   B. the turbines must be small
   C. diesel fuel distribution must be expanded
   D. filling stations must stop selling regular gasoline

7. A gun collector of my acquaintance owns an old rifle that sold for about $35 twenty years ago and would now bring a price of $400 to $450. But it isn't always easy to make money on antiques. Experts warn that people who have never dabbled in antiques should study the market carefully, choose a few specialties, read every available book in those fields, and consult reliable dealers before buying. They say that few pieces will be acquired cheaply by the

   A. inexperienced seller
   B. gun collector
   C. novice collector
   D. country tourist

8. Dinosaurs were the largest land animals ever known. They were sixty to ninety feet long. These figures are not guesses; they are based on measurements of bones that have been

   A. found   B. painted   C. reproduced   D. molded

9. Painting goes back at least as far as the time of cavemen. Wall paintings have been found inside some of their caves. It is believed that these pictures were not drawn primarily for decoration because most of them are

   A. pictures of animals rather than of people
   B. far back in the cave away from all light
   C. unrelated to the cavemen's lives
   D. intricate drawings that have beauty

10. The ermine, a native of northern countries, is a weasel with valuable fur. In the summer the fur is brown, but as the weather gets cooler, the fur gets lighter until it is pure white during the coldest part of the year. Since most people prefer the white ermine pelts, most ermine trapping is done

    A. with specialized traps
    B. in early fall
    C. after the snow disappears
    D. during the winter

11. The pilot of an airplane is dependent upon the plane's radio for communication from the ground concerning takeoff, landing, the movements of other planes, and the weather. The safety of the passengers in the plane is dependent upon this communication. In case the radio is out of order, a pilot may use other signals, such as lights, but the radio is very important.
    Even small planes are usually equipped with.

    A. radios   B. landing gear   C. horns   D. pilots

12. Although more men than women play golf, women have played the game for many years. Mary, Queen of Scots, who lived in the sixteenth century, may have been the first woman golfer. She used the term *cadet* (pupil) for the boy who carried her clubs around the course.
    This term is still used today, but the spelling has been changed to

    A. Scotsman   B. cadet   C. caddy   D. golfer

13. According to Emerson, *"A man is a center for nature, running out threads of relation through everything, fluid and solid, material and elemental... How few materials are yet used by our arts! It would seem as if each waited like the enchanted princes in fairy tales, for a destined human deliverer. All that is yet inanimate will one day speak and reason. Unpublished nature will have its whole secret told."*
    If Emerson were to come to life in the twentieth century, he would

    A. lose his faith in fairy tales
    B. not be surprised by man's advancement in outer space
    C. feel compelled to use more materials in his arts
    D. be frightened by this industrial age

14. At one time, California had to ship its products around Cape Horn, which is at the southern tip of South America, to get them to the eastern part of the United States. This route was long, but the land routes were worse because of the mountains, deserts, and plains. It is not surprising that California planned a big celebration in 1914 to emphasize the importance of the opening of

    A. the Panama Canal   B. eastern harbors
    C. European routes   D. Chinese trade

15. Gordius, mythical king of Phrygia, tied an intricate knot in the thong that held the pole of his chariot to the yoke. An oracle had declared that he who untied the knot should be master of Asia. Many tried and failed. Alexander the Great looked at the knot and quickly cut it with his sword. We use the expression *to cut the Gordian knot* to mean to

    A. do the impossible
    B. use your head instead of your hands
    C. solve a difficult problem by bold action
    D. become an oracle

16. Many millions of dollars worth of gold, silver, and jewels have gone down with ships in numerous ship disasters. These treasures lie at the bottom of almost every major body of water in the world.
    It is not surprising that divers spend a great deal of time and money looking for

    A. treasure islands   B. sunken treasure
    C. scientific data   D. new oceans

17. The following quotation is from Thomas Hobbes: *"Nature has made men so equal in the faculties of body and mind* as that though there be found one man sometimes manifestly stronger in body, or of quicker mind than another, yet when all is reckoned together, the difference between man and man is not so considerable as that one man can thereupon claim to himself any benefit to which another

    A. has already attained."
    B. is capable of attaining."
    C. may not reach as well as he."
    D. would deny him."

17.____

18. The Louvre in Paris has the restoration of a stone found in 1868 at Dhiban in what was ancient Moab. The stone is believed to have been carved by a scribe about 800 B.C. and is of interest to scholars of ancient languages. When the French tried to buy the stone, the Arabs broke it into many pieces, hoping to get more money for it.
    The French bought some of the larger pieces and were able to make the restoration of the entire stone because a French embassy official at Constantinople (now Istanbul) had

    A. made a paper cast of the stone
    B. hidden the original from the Turks
    C. had the writing deciphered
    D. handled the financial arrangements

18.____

19. There are many primitive countries in the world that have never taken a census, an official count of the population. Population figures from these countries are

    A. accurate   B. too high   C. estimates   D. lost

19.____

20. The National Audubon Society reported that their 1962 census of bald eagles in the United States, excluding Alaska, was 3807, as compared to 3642 in 1961. Of 118 dead eagles reported to the society in 1962, 91 had been shot. There is great concern that the bald eagle, which is the national bird, may completely disappear.
    The Audubon Society urges a nationwide campaign to educate the public not to _____ eagles.

    A. protect   B. feed   C. harm   D. count

20.____

KEY (CORRECT ANSWERS)

1.	D	11.	A
2.	D	12.	C
3.	B	13.	B
4.	B	14.	A
5.	B	15.	C
6.	C	16.	B
7.	C	17.	C
8.	A	18.	A
9.	B	19.	C
10.	D	20.	C

TEST 3

DIRECTIONS: Each question or incomplete statement is followed by several suggested answers or completions. Select the one that BEST answers the question or completes the statement. *PRINT THE LETTER OF THE CORRECT ANSWER IN THE SPACE AT THE RIGHT.*

1. A library may be very large, but if it is in disorder, it is not as useful as one that is small but

   A. disordered
   B. closed to the public
   C. nearby
   D. well arranged

2. It is no great wonder if in the long process of time, while fortune takes her course hither and thither, numerous coincidences should spontaneously occur.
   If the number of subjects to be wrought upon be infinite, it is all the more easy for fortune, with such an abundance of material, to

   A. effect this similarity of results
   B. fill all men with wonder
   C. prevent spontaneous coincidences
   D. effect a man's success

3. Clearinghouses are useful in reducing the volume of concrete interbank transactions. Each member bank sends to the clearinghouse a record of the money it has paid out on checks drawn on each other member.
   When the lists are compared, equal reciprocal debts are

   A. reduced   B. collected   C. recorded   D. canceled

4. Many citizens of other nations deposit their money in banks in Switzerland. The Swiss banks carefully protect the identities of their depositors, a matter of some importance to certain depositors. An agent trying to determine if someone has money in a particular Swiss bank sometimes tries to make a deposit in the name of that person.
   Since the acceptance of such a deposit would imply that the account did exist, Swiss banks will not

   A. cash large checks for depositors
   B. accept deposits that have been mailed in
   C. allow foreigners to open checking accounts
   D. accept deposits from unidentified persons

5. Very few states have done anything to ensure that untrained people are not allowed to carry guns. Safe gun loading can be taught, and if people had to pass a test before they could obtain a hunting license, the number of shooting accidents would probably

   A. pass laws   B. fail   C. increase   D. decrease

6. In a Dutch auction, so called because it originated in the Netherlands, the auctioneer offers an object for sale at a price above its value. He gradually reduces the price until someone accepts it. In a regular auction, the auctioneer asks for an opening bid, which is always low. Then the auctioneer tries to get people to make higher bids and sells when no one will raise the bid.
   These two methods, though opposite in procedure, may both reach a sale at the highest price

   A. anyone is willing to pay
   B. that is fair to the buyer
   C. that the object is worth
   D. the seller can demand

7. Optical glass is used in cameras, telescopes, eyeglasses, and many kinds of scientific equipment. The glass is almost flawless; it must be made with great care and only from the finest materials.
   For these reasons, optical glass is

   A. expensive   B. scientific   C. brittle   D. unavailable

8. It was quite understandable that it was the policy of the old priest-nobles of Egypt and India to divert their peoples from becoming familiar with the seas and to represent the occupation of a seaman as incompatible with the purity of the highest caste.
   The sea deserved to be hated by those who wished to maintain the old aristocracies, inasmuch as

   A. the sea has been the mightiest instrument in the leveling of mankind
   B. the life of a sailor was quite dangerous
   C. many of the sailors lost their lives while on voyages
   D. the priest-nobles were trying to further the spread of education

9. Six cities of ancient Palestine were set aside as places of refuge for people who had killed any person unawares. In these cities, the accused could receive a fair trial. If he was found guilty of intentional murder, he was returned for punishment to the place from which he had escaped.
   But if the killing was found to be accidental or not willful, the accused was allowed to remain safely in

   A. his boyhood home   B. a country of exile
   C. the city of refuge   D. the original prison

10. The average density of a cubic foot of earth is about 5.5 times that of a cubic foot of water. This is determined by dividing the earth mass by its volume. However, rocks on the earth's surface have an average density of approximately 2.7.
    Therefore, in order to offset the lighter weight of the surface materials, the interior of the earth MUST have a density

    A. of 5.5   B. greater than 5.5
    C. less than 5.5   D. less than 2.7

11. Our opinions and actions are influenced to a great extent by words - the words we read and the words we hear. Yet we do not carefully attend to the subtle implications, good or bad, conveyed by these words through association.
    Some words are slippery: they gloss over the actual attributes of the thing to which they refer. For example, the supporters of a favored point of view are *progressive* while those who hold an opinion less to our liking are *radical*.
    The words that are chosen imply

    A. only one interpretation   B. precisely what they state
    C. no subtle connotation   D. more than they state

12. When the Mormons who settled in the Valley of the Great Salt Lake applied for statehood in 1849, they wanted the name of the state to be Deseret. Deseret is the Mormon word for honeybee, which the Mormons had taken as a symbol of the work they all had to do to make the desert productive. They were refused statehood and remained the Territory of Utah until 1896, when Utah became the forty-fifth state. The state seal has a beehive on it, and the official motto of the state is *Industry*. These are tributes to Utah's

    A. acceptance as a state
    B. principal occupation
    C. Ute Indians
    D. early Mormon settlers

    12.____

13. Pythagoras, an ancient Greek, discovered the true nature of the harmonic series by observing the vibration of a single taut string stretched over a resonator. When a movable bridge was placed at the string's midpoint, the string vibrated in two segments at twice the speed at which it vibrated without a bridge. When moved to a third of the string's length, the string would vibrate in three segments at three times the speed. This phenomenon was repeated with each successive position of the bridge. Thus, Pythagoras was able to express the pitch relationships of the harmonic series in terms of

    A. mathematical ratios
    B. string lengths
    C. musical notation
    D. chemical formulas

    13.____

14. Not only were the Romans undemocratic, but at no period of its history did Rome love equality. In the Republic, rank was determined by wealth. The census was the basis of the social system. Every citizen had to declare his fortune before a magistrate, and his grade was then assigned him.
    Poverty and wealth established the

    A. legal differences between men
    B. democratic system of the Republic
    C. need for a strong judicial system
    D. social equality among men

    14.____

15. A surveyor's chain has 100 links, each 792 inches long. The chain is a unit of measurement that for most purposes would be very awkward, but it is particularly useful in surveying land because ten square chains made on acre. The original measuring instrument was actually made of chains. A surveyor's chain has 100 links, each 792 inches long. The chain is a unit of measurement that for most purposes would be very awkward, but it is particularly useful in surveying land because ten square chains made on acre.
    The original measuring instrument was actually made of chains.

    A. numerical   B. accurate   C. awkward   D. easy

    15.____

16. Millions of people in the world spend as much as one-third of their days by hauling water. Their diets are determined by a water shortage that restricts the variety of their agricultural products.
    If the scientists of the United States can increase the water supply of arid regions by removing the salt from sea-water, they will gain

    A. new travel opportunities abroad
    B. new export articles
    C. the gratitude of millions
    D. great profits from friends

    16.____

17. *"A friend stands at the door,*
    In either tight-closed hand
    Hiding rich gifts, three hundred
    And three score."
    These lines are from a poem titled

    A. EASTER MORNING   B. CHRISTMAS EVE
    C. NEW YEAR'S EVE   D. THANKSGIVING DAY

18. Our repugnance to death increases in proportion to our consciousness of having lived in vain - to the

    A. usefulness of our lives
    B. keenness of our disappointments
    C. intensity of our physical suffering
    D. greatness of our vanity

19. The ripeness or unripeness of the occasion must ever be well weighed; and generally it is good to commit the beginnings of all great actions to Argus with his hundred eyes, and the ends to Briareus with his hundred hands; first to watch, and then to

    A. consider   B. decide   C. begin   D. speed

20. Benjamin Franklin said, "We may perhaps learn to deprive large masses of their Gravity, and give them absolute Levity for the sake of easy Transport. Agriculture may diminish its Labour and double its Produce; all Diseases may by sure means be prevented or cured, not excepting even that of old Age, and our Lives lengthened at pleasure even beyond the antediluvian Standard. O that moral science were in as fair a way of

    A. Acceptance   B. Cure   C. Religion   D. Study

KEY (CORRECT ANSWERS)

1. D
2. A
3. D
4. D
5. D
6. A
7. A
8. C
9. C
10. B
11. D
12. D
13. A
14. A
15. D
16. C
17. C
18. B
19. D
20. D

VISUAL RECALL

EXAMINATION SECTION
TEST 1

DIRECTIONS: Each question or incomplete statement is followed by several suggested answers or completions. Select the one that BEST answers the question or completes the statement. *PRINT THE LETTER OF THE CORRECT ANSWER IN THE SPACE AT THE RIGHT.* This test consists of four(4) pictures with questions following each picture. Study each picture for three (3) minutes. Then answer the questions based upon what you remember without looking back at the pictures.

Questions 1-5

DIRECTIONS: Questions 1 through 5 are based on the drawing below showing a view of a waiting area in a public building.

1. A desk is shown in the drawing. Which of the following is on the desk? 1.____
    A(n)

    A. plant   B. telephone
    C. in-out file   D. *Information* sign

2. On which floor is the waiting area? 2.____

    A. Basement   B. Main floor
    C. Second floor   D. Third floor

3. The door <u>immediately to the right</u> of the desk is a(n) 3.____

    A. door to the Personnel Office
    B. elevator door
    C. door to another corridor
    D. door to the stairs

4. Among the magazines on the tables in the waiting area are 4.____

    A. TIME and NEWSWEEK
    B. READER'S DIGEST and T.V. GUIDE
    C. NEW YORK and READER'S DIGEST
    D. TIME and T.V. GUIDE

5. One door is partly open. 5.____
    This is the door to

    A. the Director's office
    B. the Personnel Manager's office
    C. the stairs
    D. an unmarked office

Questions 6-9.

DIRECTIONS: Questions 6 through 9 are based on the drawing below showing the contents of a male suspect's pockets.

6. The suspect had a slip in his pockets showing an appointment at an out-patient clinic on 6.____

   A. February 9, 2009
   B. September 2, 2008
   C. February 19, 2008
   D. September 12, 2009

7. The transistor radio that was found on the suspect was made by 7.____

   A. RCA B. GE C. Sony D. Zenith

8. The coins found in the suspect's pockets have a TOTAL value of 8.____

   A. 56¢ B. 77¢ C. $1.05 D. $1.26

9. All except one of the following were found in the suspect's pockets. 9.____
   Which was NOT found?
   A

   A. ticket stub   B. comb
   C. subway token   D. pen

Questions 10-13.

DIRECTIONS: Questions 10 through 13 are based on the picture showing the contents of a woman's handbag. Assume that all of the contents are shown in the picture.

4 (#1)

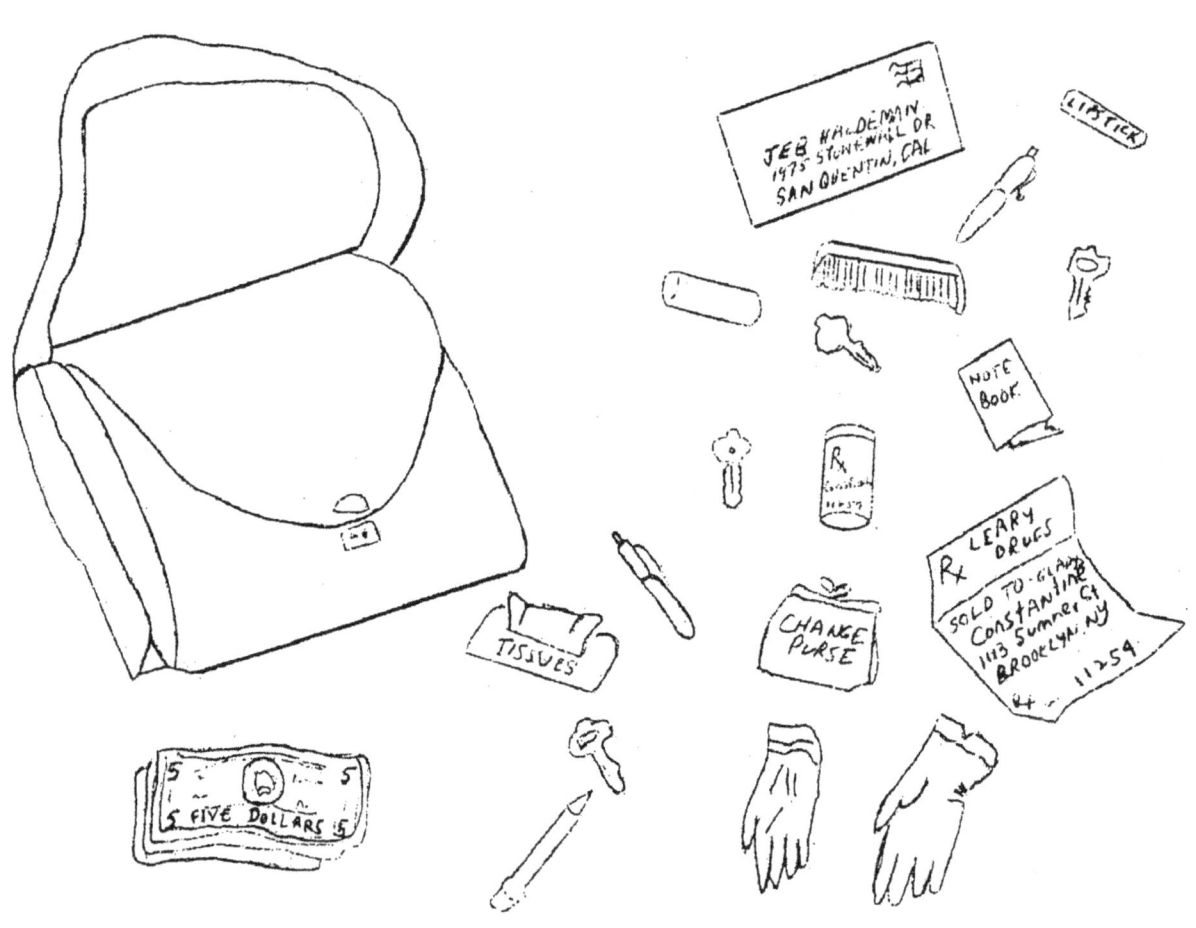

10. Where does Gladys Constantine live?
    _____ Street in _____.

    A. Chalmers; Manhattan
    B. Summer; Manhattan
    C. Summer; Brooklyn
    D. Chalmers; Brooklyn

11. How many keys were in the handbag?

    A. 2   B. 3   C. 4   D. 5

12. How much money was in the handbag?
    _____ dollar(s).

    A. Exactly five
    B. More than five
    C. Exactly ten
    D. Less than one

13. The sales slip found in the handbag shows the purchase of which of the following?

    A. The handbag
    B. Lipstick
    C. Tissues
    D. Prescription medicine

Questions 14-18.

DIRECTIONS: Questions 14 through 18 are based on the street scene on the following page. A robbery may be in progress down the block from where you are standing. Study and memorize the details before answering these questions.

14. The man carrying the two shopping bags is wearing   14._____

    A. khaki shorts and work boots
    B. a hat and black jacket
    C. a zip-up fleece and glasses
    D. a casual shirt and jeans

15. The building at the center of the photo is a(n)   15._____

    A. hotel   B. bank   C. restaurant   D. office building

16. The sidewalk is lined on the street side with   16._____

    A. parking meters   B. safety pillars
    C. street vendors   D. flower beds

17. Among the people standing in front of the center building is a   17._____

    A. man wearing khaki pants
    B. woman wearing knee-high boots
    C. young boy chasing another young boy
    D. man wearing a sports jersey

18. Reflections in the store windows indicate that   18._____

    A. there are food carts parked in the street
    B. a white truck is driving nearby
    C. it is a very sunny day
    D. a man is sitting on a curb nearby

KEY (CORRECT ANSWERS)

1.	D	11.	C
2.	C	12.	B
3.	B	13.	D
4.	D	14.	C
5.	B	15.	A
6.	A	16.	D
7.	C	17.	A
8.	D	18.	B
9.	D		
10.	C		

EXAMINATION SECTION

TEST 1

DIRECTIONS: Each question or incomplete statement is followed by several suggested answers or completions. Select the one that BEST answers the question or completes the statement. *PRINT THE LETTER OF THE CORRECT ANSWER IN THE SPACE AT THE RIGHT.*

Questions 1-4.

DIRECTIONS: Questions 1 through 4 measure your ability to recognize objects, people, events, parts of maps, or crime, accident, or other scenes to which you have been exposed.

Below and on the following pages are twenty illustrations. Study them carefully. In the test, you will be shown pairs of drawings. For each pair, you will be asked which is or are from the twenty illustrations in this part.

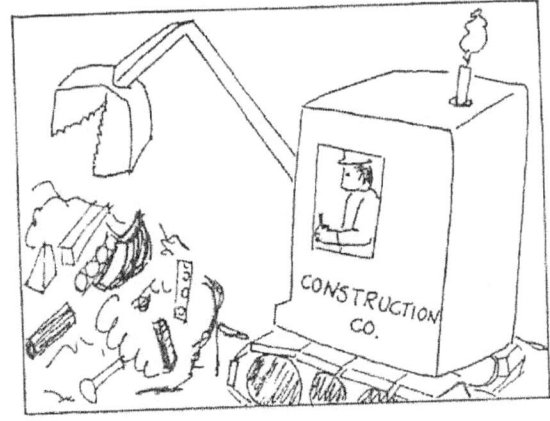
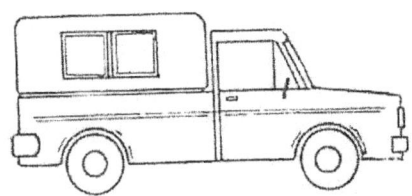

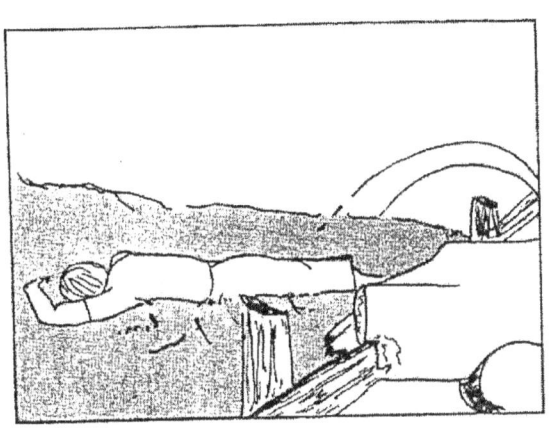

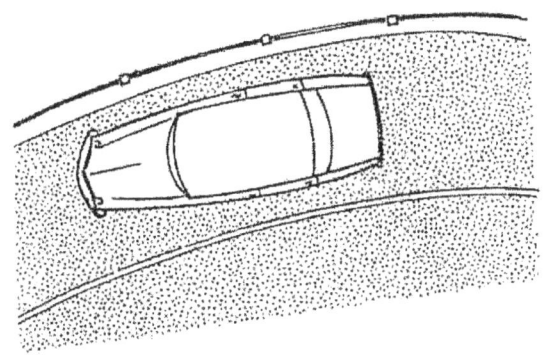

4 (#1)

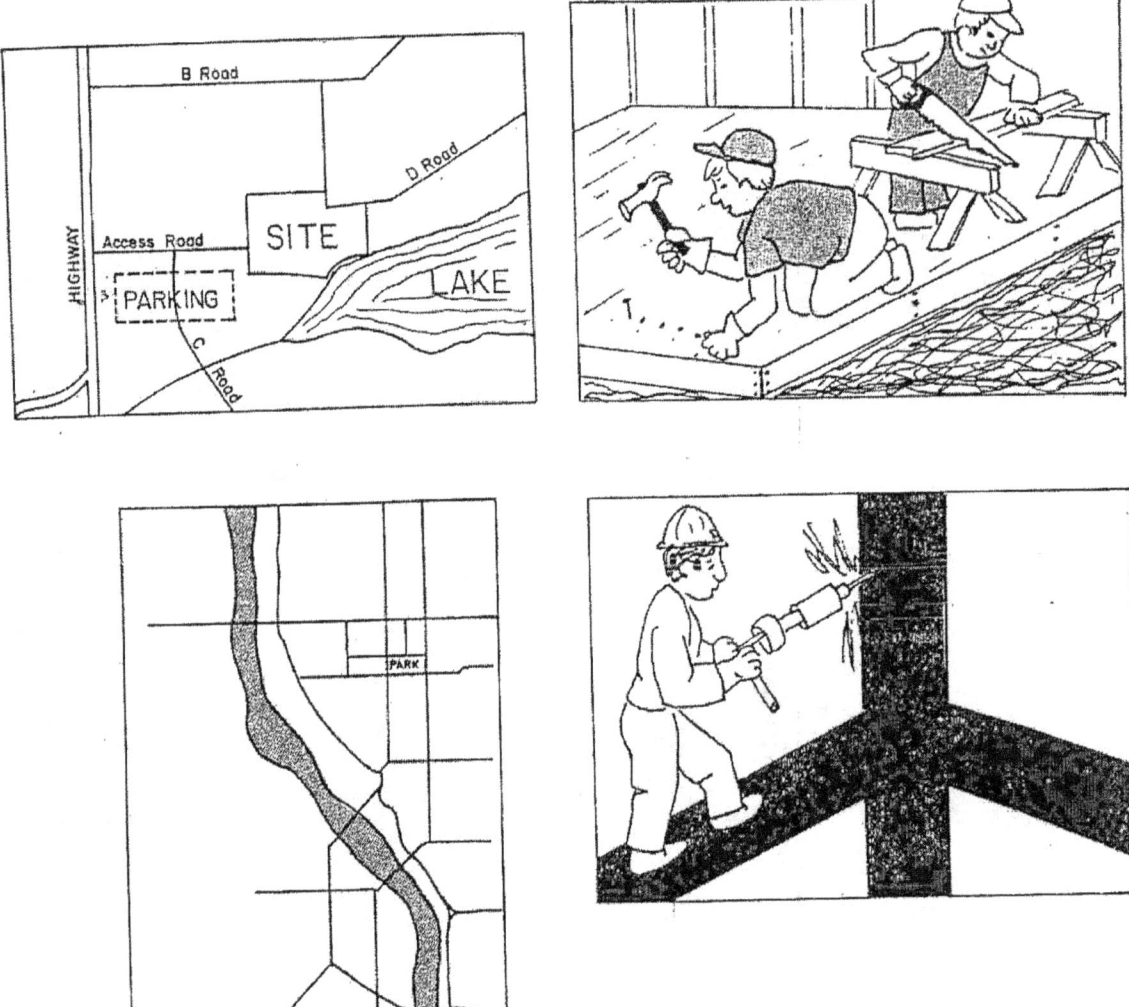

Questions 1-4.

DIRECTIONS: In Questions 1 through 4, select the choice that corresponds to the scene(s) that is(are) from the illustrations for this section. *PRINT THE LETTER OF THE CORRECT ANSWER IN THE SPACE AT THE RIGHT.*

1.   I   II   2.____

A. I only
B. II only
C. Both I and II
D. Neither I nor II

2.   I   II   2.____

A. I only
B. II only
C. Both I and II
D. Neither I nor II

3.

A. I only
C. Both I and II
B. II only
D. Neither I nor II

4.

A. I only
C. Both I and II
B. II only
D. Neither I nor II

Questions 5-6.

DIRECTIONS: Questions 5 and 6 measure your ability to notice and interpret details accurately. You will be shown a picture, below, and then asked a set of questions about the picture. You do NOT need to memorize this picture. You may look at the picture when answering the questions.

5.

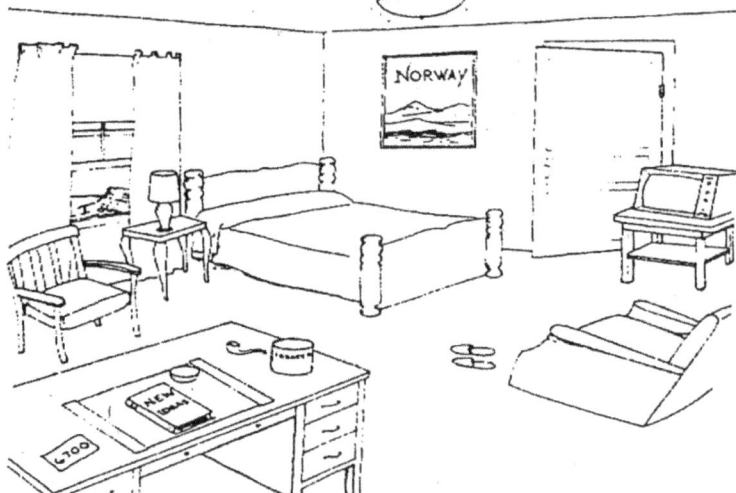

Details in the picture lend some support to or do NOT tend to contradict which of the following statements about the person who occupies the room?
 I. The person is very careless.
 II. The person smokes.
The CORRECT answer is:
   A. I only
   B. II only
   C. Both I and II
   D. Neither I nor II

6. The number on the piece of paper on the desk is MOST likely a
   A. ZIP code
   B. street number
   C. social security number
   D. telephone area code

Questions 7-10.

DIRECTIONS: Questions 7 through 10 measure your ability to recognize objects or people in differing views, contexts, or situations. Each question consists of three pictures; one labeled I and one labeled II. In each question, you are to determine whether A – I only, B – II only, C – Both I and II, and D – Neither I nor II COULD be the subject.

The Subject is *always* ONE person or ONE object. The Subject picture shows the object or person as it, he, or she appeared at the time of initial contact. Pictures I and II show objects from a different viewpoint than that of the Subject picture. For example, if the Subject picture presents a front view, I and II may present back views, side views, or a back and a side view. Also, art objects may be displayed differently, may have a different base or frame or method of hanging.

When the subject is a person, I or II will be a picture of a different person or will be a picture of the same person after some change has taken place. The person may have made a deliberate attempt to alter his or her appearance, such as wearing (or taking off a wig, growing (or shaving off) a beard or mustache, or dressing as a member of the opposite sex. The change may also be a natural one, such as changing a hair style, changing from work clothes to play clothes, or from play clothes to work clothes, or growing older, thinner, or fatter. None has had cosmetic surgery.

7. Subject   I   II   7.____

A. I only
C. Both I and II
B. II only
D. Neither I nor II

8. Subject   I   II   8.____

A. I only
C. Both I and II
B. II only
D. Neither I nor II

9. Subject   I   II   9.____

A. I only
C. Both I and II
B. II only
D. Neither I nor II

10. Subject

I

II

A. I only
B. II only
C. Both I and II
D. Neither I nor II

10.____

KEY (CORRECT ANSWERS)

1.	B	6.	B
2.	D	7.	D
3.	A	8.	A
4.	A	9.	D
5.	B	10.	D

MEMORY FOR FACTS AND INFORMATION

EXAMINATION SECTION
TEST 1

DIRECTIONS: Questions 1 through 15 test your ability to remember key facts and details. You are given a rather long reading passage, which you will have approximately ten minutes to read. The reading selection should then be turned over. Then immediately answer the fifteen questions that refer to this passage. Please do NOT refer back to the reading passage at any time while you are answering the questions. Select the letter that represents the BEST of the four possible choices.

THE CASE OF THE MISSING OVERTIME WAGES

Melba Tolliber is a new Labor Standards Investigator assigned to investigate a complaint of nonpayment of some overtime wages. The complaint came in the form of a telephone call from Albert Brater, employed by the Whizzer Audio and Video Store in Dorchester. Whizzer Audio and Video, Inc. is a fast-growing and very successful chain in the Northeast. Their headquarters is in Dorchester.

Melba Tolliber drives the eight miles to Dorchester on a breezy Monday morning. She meets with Albert Brater, the employee who called. He is employed in the warehouse unit.

Hello, Mr. Brater, my name is Melba Tolliber, and I'm here to investigate whether you've been paid the proper amount of overtime wages.

Nice to meet you, Ms. Tolliber. I'm not the only one with this problem. Two salesclerks in the Dorchester store, Mary and Martin, have also gotten less for overtime than they should have.

Can I talk with them, too? Melba asks.

Well, the problem is, we're worried about getting into a lot of trouble with, the company. We were hoping you could talk just to me. I'm a little worried about talking with you myself.

This is a confidential interview; don't worry. It would be very helpful, however, if I could at least get copies of their pay stubs.

Albert hesitates and then says, *Gee, I hope I can find my last paystub. Anyway, we've been working forty-six hours a week the last four weeks, but only getting paid our usual rate of $5.25 an hour.*

Melba says, *But that's below the minimum wage.*

Maybe it's $5.35; I get confused; I'll have to check. I think it's $5.35. Yeah, I'm pretty sure it's $5.35. But you know what else? I was promised a raise of $.50 per hour after eight months of working here, and that's up next week. We'll see if I get it or not.

Have the other employees here gotten the raises they were promised?

Yeah, I think they have. But I know of at least one person, a truckdriver, who hasn't gotten his raise yet.

Do you know his name?

Just his first name. But the next time I see him, I'll ask him if he's gotten the raise yet. I'll let you know if he hasn't.

What day would be good for you to drop off the paystubs and have a second interview?

Well, you have to give me some time to get them from Mary and Martin, too. How about this Thursday afternoon at one?

Fine, heres my card. I'll see you this Thursday at one.

At the beginning of their next meeting, Albert gives Melba the paystubs for the last month's work for all three employees.

Let's do you first, Albert. What have your hours been each week for the last four weeks?

I've worked the same schedule for the past month, my usual forty hours - 8 to 5 with an hour for lunch, which I don't like, on Mondays, Tuesdays, and Thursdays. Wednesdays and Fridays I've worked from 8 A.M. to 9 P.M. because those are the days we do our most shipping. They give us from 5 to 6 P.M. as a dinner break on those days.

So that adds up to forty-six hours. Give me a few minutes to go over these figures with my calculator.

That's a great calculator; it's so small. Looks like a credit card.

Thanks, but I have to be careful how I hit the numbers; there's not much room.... Well, according to my calculations, you're owed $48.15 in overtime pay for the last four weeks. But there's something else wrong, too. It looks like they've been taking out a little too much money for Social Security. Let me recheck this.

1. In the passage, Melba Tolliber visited 1.____

    A. Midwood B. Dorchester
    C. Midale D. Midville

2. In the passage, Melba talked with 2.____

    A. Albert who works in the warehouse unit
    B. Albert who works in the warehouse unit and in the store
    C. Robert who works in the warehouse
    D. Robert, Martin, and Mary who work in the warehouse and the store

3. The organization whose payment of overtime wages is in question 3._____

   A. is struggling to succeed
   B. is the most successful of the new audio-visual store chains in the Northeast
   C. has its headquarters in the town that Melba travels to
   D. has successfully switched from selling just records to selling records, tapes, and video equipment

4. During their initial discussion, how sure of his rate of pay was the employee to whom Melba spoke? 4._____

   A. Not sure at all
   B. Very sure
   C. Pretty sure
   D. Totally unsure

5. What day of the week did Melba conduct the initial interview? 5._____

   A. Monday
   B. Wednesday
   C. Tuesday
   D. Thursday

6. When did Melba conduct the second interview? 6._____

   A. Monday at 1 P.M.
   B. Thursday at 1 P.M.
   C. Wednesday at 1 P.M.
   D. Friday at 1 P.M.

7. In order to calculate how much money the employee should have received, Melba used a 7._____

   A. credit card
   B. calculator
   C. credit card/calculator/watch combination
   D. desk top personal computer

8. According to the passage, what did Melba do to try to make the employee feel more at ease? 8._____
   She

   A. gave him time to collect his thoughts
   B. assured him that she believed what he said
   C. assured him that the interview was confidential
   D. asked if she could speak with the other two employees affected

9. The initial complaint from the employee 9._____

   A. resulted in his receiving back pay
   B. came in the form of a phone call
   C. was anonymous
   D. resulted in a large-scale investigation

10. The name of the establishment the employee works for is the 10._____

    A. Whizzer
    B. Genuine Article
    C. Electronic Era
    D. Gizmos etcetera

11. The other two employees who have questions about their overtime pay

    A. are truckdrivers
    B. work in the warehouse
    C. are salesclerks
    D. work in maintenance

12. The organization told the employee he would receive a

    A. $.60 per hour raise after eight months
    B. $.60 per hour raise after five months
    C. $.50 per hour raise after six months
    D. $.50 per hour raise after eight months

13. How many hours a week have the employees who are questioning their pay been working for the last month?

    A. Forty-four
    B. Forty-five
    C. Forty-six
    D. Forty-eight

14. In the last month, what hours did the employee Melba interviewed work on Wednesdays?

    A. 8 A.M. to 5 P.M.
    B. 9 A.M. to 10 P.M.
    C. 9 A.M. to 5 P.M.
    D. 8 A.M. to 9 P.M.

15. At the start of the second interview,

    A. the employee gives Melba the paystubs for the last month for all three workers involved
    B. the employee gives Melba the paystubs for the last month for all three workers involved, with the exception of his last paystub
    C. the employee gives Melba only his paystubs from the last month
    D. it cannot be determined if the employee gives Melba any paystubs

KEY (CORRECT ANSWERS)

1. B
2. A
3. C
4. C
5. A
6. B
7. B
8. C
9. B
10. A
11. C
12. D
13. C
14. D
15. A

TEST 2

DIRECTIONS: Questions 1 through 15 test your ability to remember key facts and details. You are given a rather long reading passage, which you will have approximately ten minutes to read. The reading selection should then be turned over. Then immediately answer the fifteen questions that refer to this passage. Please do NOT refer back to the reading passage at any time while you are answering these questions. Select the letter that represents the BEST of the four possible choices.

THE CASE OF THE DELINQUENT TAXPAYER

David Owens has been a Tax Investigator for five years. His unit has received another anonymous tip about possible sales tax abuse, and David's supervisor, William, has assigned David to conduct the investigation. The organization in question is Bob's News, a 24-hour newsstand and variety store. The store is located in Hillsdell, five miles away. The anonymous caller did not provide details, but stated that she was an employee, and that there was widespread abuse in the collection and reporting of sales tax by the store. The agency has had a series of crank calls regarding sales tax abuse in Hillsdell.

For this investigation, David has been instructed not to work undercover, but to go in, identify himself, and discuss the situation with the owner and some employees without divulging the reason for the visit. On Wednesday, David drives to the store in a government car, a 2004 Plymouth.

David arrives at the store and buys a magazine for which he is properly not charged sales tax. He speaks to the employee whose name tag says Susan.

Hello, Susan, my name is David Owens, and I'm from the State Tax Department. Here's my identification. We're doing a routine check-up to see if things are in order with regard to sales tax collection and reporting. Is the owner around?

No, Bob is out of town today. He'll be back tomorrow. You seem surprised that his name is Bob. Some people think he must not exist, sort of like a Betty Crocker or something. Can I help you with anything? I'm the Assistant Manager.

Well, it would be helpful if you could answer a few questions for me.

As long as it doesn't get me in trouble with my boss, I'd be glad to, Susan replied.

Don't worry, I won't ask you anything that could, get you in trouble.

OK, then.

Did someone tell employees how to go about collecting sales tax on items?

Bob has a list of items we're not allowed to collect tax on. It's right next to the cash register. Would you like to see it?

If you don't mind. Thanks. It says here not to collect tax on magazines, but there's no mention of newspapers.

I guess that's because he probably assumes we know better than that. I'll ask him to add it to the list.

This is a pretty good list, but what's this written on the bottom here about toilet paper? That's a taxable item.

Oh, I know. Henry who works nights put that in as a joke because he says toilet paper is a necessity, not a luxury, and shouldn't be taxed. I agree. So does Bob. But don't worry, we collect sales tax on it. Nine percent, right?

No, the rate is eight percent.

Just kidding, David. We know that. I guess I shouldn't joke about something like that; I don't want to end up in jail. What else do you need to know?

Who keeps the records and submits the sales tax money to Metro City every quarter?

Bob does that himself, but I'd rather you come back tomorrow to talk with him about that end of it....I think that would be best. I don't know much about it, except that he yells if I don't have everything - the records and stuff - ready for him when he wants it.

What time do you think Bob will be in tomorrow?

I think the morning would be best, you'll be sure to catch him then.

OK, I'll drop by tomorrow around nine. See you then. Thanks again.

The next day, David drives back to the store to meet with Bob at the time stated earlier. When he arrives, Susan immediately introduces him to Bob.

It's nice to meet you, Bob. Nice store you have here. How long have you been in business?

We've been open for five years. Time really flies, doesn't it?

It sure does. As Susan probably mentioned, I'm here on a routine type check-up about sales tax collection.

Sure thing.

Well, I just noticed you're not displaying the Sales Tax Certificate of Authority, that you need to show in order to collect sales tax.

That's strange; it was there yesterday. Here it is. It fell under the counter. We're off to a great start. Let me tape this thing back up.

How many employees work here. Bob?

We have six full-time and three part-time employees, plus myself. I understand you'd like to see our books. Come on in to my office. Stay in here as long as you need. I've got it all laid out for you.

Thanks.

Several hours later, David finishes looking through the books.

Well, Bob, things look in order. The only question I have is why your receipts for 2004 were so much lower than in other years?

A chain store moved in about eight blocks away, and we initially lost a lot of business. But eventually our customers started coming back. We do the little things - save them the Boston papers, things like that. The chain moved downtown in early 2005.

Well, listen, thanks very much for all of your time. I really appreciate it.

No problem. Anytime. Well, I wouldn't go that far, but it's been nice meeting you.

1. What was the name of the Tax Investigator in the above passage?

    A. David Allen
    B. Bob Williams
    C. Derwin Williams
    D. David Owens

2. What was the name of the city the investigator visited?

    A. Hillsville
    B. Hillsdale
    C. Hicksville
    D. Hillsdell

3. The store under investigation is a

    A. department store
    B. 24-hour massage parlor
    C. newsstand and variety store
    D. sporting goods store

4. The phone call received by the agency was

    A. placed by an anonymous employee of the store being accused of sales tax fraud
    B. received by the investigator handling the case
    C. placed by an anonymous caller
    D. received by the investigator's supervisor

5. The investigator on this case

    A. did not work undercover
    B. was instructed to work undercover, but refused because of the nature of the case
    C. worked undercover
    D. pretended to his supervisor that he worked undercover

6. According to the above passage, it is

    A. not correct to charge sales tax for a magazine
    B. correct to charge sales tax for pet food

C. correct to charge sales tax for a newspaper
D. correct to charge sales tax for a magazine

7. The Assistant Manager of the store is

   A. Susan
   B. David
   C. Bob
   D. Betty Crocker

8. What day was the initial investigation conducted?

   A. Monday
   B. Wednesday
   C. Tuesday
   D. Thursday

9. The list the investigator was shown contained

   A. a list of sales taxable items
   B. a list of non-taxable items
   C. a list of products on which sales tax was mistakenly charged
   D. the Certificate of Authority

10. According to the above passage, sales tax was to be charged on

    A. pet food
    B. cigarettes
    C. gasoline
    D. toilet paper

11. According to the above passage, the sales tax was _____%.

    A. seven
    B. nine
    C. eight
    D. ten

12. According to the passage, how often was the sales tax submitted?

    A. Every month
    B. Quarterly
    C. Twice a year
    D. Once every six months

13. According to the passage, where are the sales tax monies sent?

    A. River City
    B. Metro City
    C. Metropolis
    D. Hillswood

14. According to the passage, which of the following is TRUE? Bob's business, called Bob's

    A. News and Variety, has been open for five years
    B. Department Store, has been open for six years
    C. Variety, has been open for six years
    D. News, has been open for five years

15. The only question the investigator had about Bob's books was why receipts for _____ than in other years.

    A. 2005 were so much lower
    B. 2004 were so much lower
    C. 2005 were so much higher
    D. 2004 were so much higher

KEY (CORRECT ANSWERS)

1. D
2. D
3. C
4. C
5. A

6. A
7. A
8. B
9. B
10. D

11. C
12. B
13. B
14. D
15. B

READING COMPREHENSION
UNDERSTANDING AND INTERPRETING WRITTEN MATERIAL
EXAMINATION SECTION
TEST 1

DIRECTIONS: Each question has five suggested answers, lettered A to E. Decide which one is the BEST answer. *PRINT THE LETTER OF THE CORRECT ANSWER IN THE SPACE AT THE RIGHT.*

1. Some specialists are willing to give their services to the Government entirely free of charge; some feel that a nominal salary, such as will cover traveling expenses, is sufficient for a position that is recognized as being somewhat honorary in nature; many other specialists value their time so highly that they will not devote any of it to public service that does not repay them at a rate commensurate with the fees that they can obtain from a good private clientele.
The paragraph BEST supports the statement that the use of specialists by the Government
    A. is rare because of the high cost of securing such persons
    B. may be influenced by the willingness of specialists to serve
    C. enables them to secure higher salaries in private fields
    D. has become increasingly common during the past few years
    E. always conflicts with private demands for their services

1._____

2. The fact must not be overlooked that only about one-half of the international trade of the world crosses the oceans. The other half is merely exchanges of merchandise between countries lying alongside each other or at least within the same continent.
The paragraph BEST supports the statement that
    A. the most important part of any country's trade is transoceanic
    B. domestic trade is insignificant when compared with foreign trade
    C. the exchange of goods between neighboring countries is not considered international trade
    D. foreign commerce is not necessarily carried on by water
    E. about one-half of the trade of the world is international

2._____

3. Individual differences in mental traits assume importance in fitting workers to jobs because such personal characteristics are persistent and are relatively little influenced by training and experience.
The paragraph BEST supports the statement that training and experience
    A. are limited in their effectiveness in fitting workers to jobs
    B. do not increase a worker's fitness for a job
    C. have no effect upon a person's mental traits
    D. have relatively little effect upon the individual's chances for success
    E. should be based on the mental traits of an individual

3._____

2 (#1)

4. The competition of buyers tends to keep prices up, the competition of sellers to send them down. Normally, the pressure of competition among sellers is stronger than that among buyers since the seller has his article to sell and must get rid of it, whereas the buyer is not committed to anything.
   The paragraph BEST supports the statement that low prices are caused by
   A. buyer competition
   B. competition of buyers with sellers
   C. fluctuations in demand
   D. greater competition among sellers than among buyers
   E. more sellers than buyers

4.____

5. In seventeen states, every lawyer is automatically a member of the American Bar Association. In some other states and localities, truly representative organizations of the Bar have not yet come into being, but are greatly needed.
   The paragraph IMPLIES that
   A. representative Bar Associations are necessary in states where they do not now exist
   B. every lawyer is required by law to become a member of the Bar
   C. the Bar Association is a democratic organization
   D. some states have more lawyers than others
   E. every member of the American Bar Association is automatically a lawyer in seventeen states

5.____

KEY (CORRECT ANSWERS)

1. B
2. D
3. A
4. D
5. A

TEST 2

DIRECTIONS: Each question has five suggested answers, lettered A to E. Decide which one is the BEST answer. *PRINT THE LETTER OF THE CORRECT ANSWER IN THE SPACE AT THE RIGHT.*

1. We hear a great deal about the new education, and see a great deal of it in action. But the school house, though prodigiously magnified in scale, is still very much the same old school house.
   The paragraph IMPLIES
   A. the old education was, after all, better than the new
   B. although the modern school buildings are larger than the old ones, they have not changed very much in other respects
   C. the old school houses do not fit in with modern educational theories
   D. a fine school building does not make up for poor teachers
   E. schools will be schools

   1.____

2. No two human beings are of the same pattern—not even twins and the method of bringing out the best in each one necessarily according to the nature of the child.
   The paragraph IMPLIES that
   A. individual differences should be considered in dealing with children
   B. twins should be treated impartially
   C. it is an easy matter to determine the special abilities of children
   D. a child's nature varies from year to year
   E. we must discover the general technique of dealing with children

   2.____

3. Man inhabits today a world very different from that which encompassed even his parents and grandparents. It is a world geared to modern machinery—automobiles, airplanes, power plants; it is linked together and served by electricity.
   The paragraph IMPLIES that
   A. the world has no changed much during the last few generations
   B. modern inventions and discoveries have brought about many changes in man's way of living
   C. the world is run more efficiently today than it was in our grandparents' time
   D. man is much happier today than he was a hundred years ago
   E. we must learn to see man as he truly is, underneath the veneers of man's contrivances

   3.____

4. Success in any study depends largely upon the interest taken in that particular subject by the student. This being the case, each teacher earnestly hopes that her students will realize at the vey onset that shorthand can be made an intensely fascinating study.
   The paragraph IMPLIES that
   A. Everyone is interested in shorthand
   B. success in a study is entirely impossible unless the student finds the study very interesting

   4.____

C. if a student is eager to study shorthand, he is likely to succeed in it
D. shorthand is necessary for success
E. anyone who is not interested in shorthand will not succeed in business

5. The primary purpose of all business English is to move the reader to agreeable and mutually profitable action. This action may be indirect or direct, but in either case a highly competitive appeal for business should be clothed with incisive diction tending to replace vagueness and doubt with clarity, confidence, and appropriate action.
The paragraph IMPLIES that the
   A. ideal business letter uses words to conform to the reader's language level
   B. business correspondent should strive for conciseness in letter writing
   C. keen competition of today has lessened the value of the letter as an appeal for business
   D. writer of a business letter should employ incisive diction to move the reader to compliant and gainful action
   E. the writer of a business letter should be himself clear, confident, and forceful

5._____

KEY (CORRECT ANSWERS)

1. B
2. A
3. B
4. C
5. D

TEST 3

DIRECTIONS: Each question has five suggested answers, lettered A to E. Decide which one is the BEST answer. *PRINT THE LETTER OF THE CORRECT ANSWER IN THE SPACE AT THE RIGHT.*

1. To serve the community best, a comprehensive city plan must coordinate all physical improvements, even at the possible expense of subordinating individual desires, to the end that a city may grow in a more orderly way and provide adequate facilities for its people
   The paragraph IMPLIES that
   A. city planning provides adequate facilities for recreation
   B. a comprehensive city plan provides the means for a city to grow in a more orderly fashion
   C. individual desires must always be subordinated to civic changes
   D. the only way to serve a community is to adopt a comprehensive city plan
   E. city planning is the most important function of city government

   1.____

2. Facility in writing letters, the knack of putting into these quickly written letters the same personal impression that would mark an interview, and the ability to boil down to a one-page letter the gist of what might be called a five- or ten-minute conversation —all these are essential to effective work under conditions of modern business organization.
   The paragraph IMPLIES that
   A. letters are of more importance in modern business activities than ever before
   B. letters should be used in place of interviews
   C. the ability to write good letters is essential to effective work in modern business organization
   D. business letters should never be more than one page in length
   E. the person who can write a letter with great skill will get ahead more readily than others

   2.____

3. The general rule is that it is the city council which determines the amount to be raised by taxation and which therefore determines, within the law, the tax rates. As has been pointed out, however, no city council or city authority has the power to determine what kind of taxes should be levied.
   The paragraph IMPLIES that
   A. the city council has more authority than any other municipal body
   B. while the city council has a great deal of authority in the levying of taxes, its power is not absolute
   C. the kinds of taxes levied in different cities vary greatly
   D. the city council appoints the tax collectors
   E. the mayor determines the kinds of taxes to be levied

   3.____

83

4. The growth of modern business has made necessary mass production, mass distribution, and mass selling. As a result, the problems of personnel and industrial relations have increased so rapidly that grave injustice in the handling of personal relationships have frequently occurred. Personnel administration is complex because, as in all human problems, many intangible elements are involved. Therefore a thorough, systematic, and continuous study of the psychology of human behavior is essential to the intelligent handling of personnel.
The paragraph IMPLIES that
- A. complex modern industry makes impossible the personal relationships which formerly existed between employer and employee
- B. mass decisions are successfully applied to personnel problems
- C. the human element in personnel administration makes continuous study necessary to is intelligent application
- D. personnel problems are less important than the problems of mass production and mass distribution
- E. since personnel administration is so complex and costly, it should be subordinated to the needs of good industrial relations

4.____

5. The Social Security Act is striving toward the attainment of economic security for the individual and for his family. It was stated, in outlining this program, that security for the individual and for the family concerns itself with three factors: (1) decent homes to live in; (2) development of the natural resources of the country so as to afford the fullest opportunity to engage in productive work; and (3) safeguards against the major misfortunes of life. The Social Security Act is concerned with the third of these factors —"safeguards against misfortunes which cannot be wholly eliminated in this man-made world of ours."
The paragraph IMPLIES that the
- A. Social Security Act is concerned primarily with supplying to families decent homes in which to live
- B. development of natural resources is the only means of offering employment to the masses of the unemployed
- C. Social Security Act has attained absolute economic security for the individual and his family
- D. Social Security Act deals with the first (1) factor as stated in the paragraph above
- E. Social Security Act deals with the third (3) factor as stated in the paragraph above

5.____

KEY (CORRECT ANSWERS)

1. B
2. C
3. B
4. C
5. E

TEST 4

DIRECTIONS: Each question has five suggested answers, lettered A to E. Decide which one is the BEST answer. *PRINT THE LETTER OF THE CORRECT ANSWER IN THE SPACE AT THE RIGHT.*

PASSAGE 1

Free unrhymed verse has been practiced for some thousands of years and reaches back to the incantation which linked verse with the ritual dance. It provided a communal emotion; the aim of the cadenced phrases was to create a state of mind. The general coloring of free rhythms in the poetry of today is that of speech rhythm, composed in the sequence of the musical phrase, not in the sequence of the metronome, the regular beat. In the twenties, conventional rhyme fell into almost complete disuse. This liberation from rhyme became as well a liberation of rhyme. Freed of its exacting task of supporting lame verse, it would be applied with greater effect where wanted for some special effect. Such break in the tradition of rhymed verse had the healthy effect of giving it a fresh start, released from the hampering convention of too familiar cadences. This refreshing and subtilizing of the use of rhythm can be seen everywhere in the poetry today.

1. The title below that BEST expresses the ideas of this paragraph is: 1.____
   A. Primitive Poetry
   B. The Origin of Poetry
   C. Rhyme and Rhythm in Modern Verse
   D. Classification of Poetry
   E. Purposes in All Poetry

2. Free verse had its origin in primitive   2.____
   A. fairytales   B. literature   C. warfare
   D. chants   E. courtship

3. The object of early free verse was to   3.____
   A. influence the mood of the people   B. convey ideas
   C. produce mental pictures   D. create pleasing sounds
   E. provide enjoyment

PASSAGE 2

Control of the Mississippi had always been goals of nations having ambitions in the New World. LaSalle claimed it for France in 1682. Iberville appropriated it to France when he colonized Louisiana in 1700. Bienville founded New Orleans, its principal port, as a French city in 1718. The fleur-de-lis were the blazon of the delta country until 1762. Then Spain claimed all of Louisiana. The Spanish were easy neighbors. American products from western Pennsylvania and the Northwest Territory were barged down the Ohio and Mississippi to New Orleans; here they were reloaded on ocean-going vessels that cleared for the great seaports of the world.

4. The title below that BEST expresses the ideas of this paragraph is:
   A. Importance of Seaports
   B. France and Spain in the New World
   C. Early Control of the Mississippi
   D. Claims of European Nations
   E. American Trade on the Mississippi

5. Until 1762, the lower Mississippi area was held by
   A. England   B. Spain   C. the United States
   D. France   E. Indians

6. In doing business with Americans, the Spaniards were
   A. easy to outsmart
   B. friendly to trade
   C. inclined to charge high prices for use of their ports
   D. shrewd
   E. suspicious

PASSAGE 3

Our humanity is by no means so materialistic as foolish talk is continually asserting it to be. Judging by what I have learned about men and women, I am convinced that there is far more in them of idealistic willpower than ever comes to the surface of the world. Just as the water of streams is small in amount compared to that which flows underground, so the idealism which becomes visible is small in amount compared with that which men and women bear locked in their hearts, unreleased or scarcely released. To unbind what is bound, to bring the underground waters to the surface—mankind is waiting and longing for men who can do that.

7. The title below that BEST expresses the ideas of the paragraph is:
   A. Releasing Underground Riches
   B. The Good and Bad in Man
   C. Materialism in Humanity
   D. The Surface and the Depths of Idealism
   E. Unreleased Energy

8. Human beings are more idealistic than
   A. the water in underground streams
   B. their waiting and longing proves
   C. outward evidence shows
   D. the world
   E. other living creatures

PASSAGE 4

The total impression made by any work of fiction cannot be rightly understood without a sympathetic perception of the artistic aims of the writer. Consciously or unconsciously, he has accepted certain facts, and rejected or suppressed other facts, in order to give unity to the particular aspect of human life which he is depicting. No novelist possesses the impartiality, the indifference, the infinite tolerance of nature. Nature displays to use, with complete unconcern, the beautiful and the ugly, the precious and the trivial, the pure and the impure. But a writer must select the aspects of nature and human nature which are demanded by the work in hand. He is forced to select, to combine, to create.

9. The title below that BEST expresses the ideas of this paragraph is:
   A. Impressionists in Literature
   B. Nature as an Artist
   C. The Novelist as an Imitator
   D. Creative Technic of the Novelist
   E. Aspects of Nature

10. A novelist rejects some facts because they
    A. are impure and ugly
    B. would show he is not impartial
    C. are unrelated to human nature
    D. would make a bad impression
    E. mar the unity of his story

11. It is important for a reader to know
    A. the purpose of the author
    B. what facts the author omits
    C. both the ugly and the beautiful
    D. something about nature
    E. what the author thinks of human nature

PASSAGE 5

If you watch a lamp which is turned very rapidly on and off, and you keep your eyes open, "persistence of vision" will bridge the gaps of darkness between the flashes of light, and the lamp will seem to be continuously lit. This "topical afterglow" explains the magic produced by the stroboscope, a new instrument which seems to freeze the swiftest motions while they are still going on, and to stop time itself dead in its tracks. The "magic" is all in the eye of the beholder.

12. The "magic" of the stroboscope is due to
    A. continuous lighting
    B. intense cold
    C. slow motion
    D. behavior of the human eye
    E. a lapse of time

13. "Persistence of vision" is explained by
    A. darkness
    B. winking
    C. rapid flashes
    D. gaps
    E. after impression

KEY (CORRECT ANSWERS)

1. C
2. D
3. A
4. C
5. D
6. B
7. D
8. C
9. D
10. E
11. A
12. D
13. E

TEST 5

DIRECTIONS: Each question has five suggested answers, lettered A to E. Decide which one is the BEST answer. *PRINT THE LETTER OF THE CORRECT ANSWER IN THE SPACE AT THE RIGHT.*

PASSAGE 1

During the past fourteen years, thousands of top-lofty United States elms have been marked for death by the activities of the tiny European elm bark beetle. The beetles, however, do not do fatal damage. Death is caused by another importation, Dutch elm disease, a fungus infection which the beetles carry from tree to tree. Up to 1941, quarantine and tree-sanitation measures kept the beetles and the disease pretty well confined within 510 miles around metropolitan New York. War curtailed these measures and made Dutch elm disease a wider menace. Every household and village that prizes an elm-shaded lawn or commons must now watch for it. Since there is as yet no cure for it, the infected trees must be pruned or felled, and the wood must be burned in order to protect other healthy trees.

1. The title below that BEST expresses the ideas of this paragraph is: 1.____
   A. A Menace to Our Elms
   B. Pests and Diseases of the Elm
   C. Our Vanishing Elms
   D. The Need to Protect Dutch Elms
   E. How Elms are Protected

2. The danger of spreading the Dutch elm disease was increased by 2.____
   A. destroying infected trees   B. the war
   C. the lack of a cure   D. a fungus infection
   E. quarantine measures

3. The European elm bark beetle is a serious threat to our elms because it 3.____
   A. chews the bark
   B. kills the trees
   C. is particularly active on the eastern seaboard
   D. carries infection
   E. cannot be controlled

PASSAGE 2

It is elemental that the greater the development of man, the greater the problems he has to concern him. When he lived in a cave with stone implements, his mind no less than his actions was grooved into simple channels. Every new invention, every new way of doing things posed fresh problems for him. And, as he moved along the road, he questioned each step, as indeed he should, for he trod upon the beliefs of his ancestors. It is equally elemental to say that each step upon this later road posed more questions than the earlier ones. It is only the educated man who realizes the results of his actions; it is only the thoughtful one who questions his own decisions.

4. The title below that BEST expresses the ideas of this paragraph is:
   A. Channels of Civilization
   B. The Mark of a Thoughtful Man
   C. The Cave Man in Contrast with Man Today
   D. The Price of Early Progress
   E. Man's Never-Ending Challenge

PASSAGE 3

Spring is one of those things that man has no hand in, any more than he has a part in sunrise or the phases of the moon. Spring came before man was here to enjoy it, and it will go right on coming even if man isn't here some time in the future. It is a matter of solar mechanics and celestial order. And for all our knowledge of astronomy and terrestrial mechanics, we haven't yet been able to do more than bounce a radar beam off the moon. We couldn't alter the arrival of the spring equinox by as much as one second, if we tried.

Spring is a matter of growth, of chlorophyll, of bud and blossom. We can alter growth and change the time of blossoming in individual plants; but the forests still grow in nature's way, and the grass of the plains hasn't altered its nature in a thousand years. Spring is a magnificent phase of the cycle of nature; but man really hasn't any guiding or controlling hand in it. He is here to enjoy it and benefit by it. And April is a good time to realize it; by May perhaps we will want to take full credit.

5. The title below that BEST expresses the ideas of this passage is:
   A. The Marvels of the Spring Equinox
   B. Nature's Dependence on Mankind
   C. The Weakness of Man Opposed to Nature
   D. The Glories of the World
   E. Eternal Growth

6. The author of the passage states that
   A. man has a part in the phases of the moon
   B. April is a time for taking full-credit
   C. April is a good time to enjoy nature
   D. man has a guiding hand in spring
   E. spring will cease to be if civilization ends

PASSAGE 4

The walled medieval town was as characteristic of its period as the cut of a robber baron's beard. It sprang out of the exigencies of war, and it was not without its architectural charm, whatever is hygienic deficiencies may have been. Behind its high, thick walls not only the normal inhabitants but the whole countryside fought and cowered in an hour of need. The capitals of Europe now forsake the city when the sirens scream and death from the sky seems imminent. Will the fear of bombs accelerate the slow decentralization which began with the automobile and the wide distribution of electrical energy and thus reverse the medieval flow to the city?

7. The title below that BEST expresses the ideas in this paragraph is:
   A. A Changing Function of the Town
   B. The Walled Medieval Town
   C. The Automobile's Influence on City Life
   D. Forsaking the City
   E. Bombs Today and Yesterday

   7.____

8. Conditions in the Middle Ages made the walled town
   A. a natural development
   B. the most dangerous of all places
   C. a victim of fires
   D. lacking in architectural charm
   E. healthful

   8.____

9. Modern conditions may
   A. make cities larger
   B. make cities more hygienic
   C. protect against floods
   D. cause people to move from population centers
   E. encourage good architecture

   9.____

PASSAGE 5

The literary history of this nation began when the first settler from abroad of sensitive mind paused in his adventure long enough to feel that he was under a different sky, breathing new air and that a New World was all before him with only his strength and Providence for guides. With him began a new emphasis upon an old theme in literature, the theme of cutting loose and faring forth, renewed, under the powerful influence of a fresh continent for civilized literature, whose other flow has come from a nostalgia for the rich culture of Europe, so much of which was perforce left behind.

10. The title below that BEST expresses the ideas of this paragraph is:
    A. America's Distinctive Literature   B. Pioneer Authors
    C. The Dead Hand of the Past   D. Europe's Literary Grandchild
    E. America Comes of Age

    10.____

11. American writers, according to the author, because of their colonial experiences
    A. were antagonistic to European writers
    B. cut loose from Old World influences
    C. wrote only on New World events and characters
    D. created new literary themes
    E. gave fresh interpretation to an old literary idea

    11.____

KEY (CORRECT ANSWERS)

1. A
2. B
3. D
4. E
5. C
6. C
7. A
8. A
9. D
10. A
11. E

TEST 6

DIRECTIONS: Each question has five suggested answers, lettered A to E. Decide which one is the BEST answer. *PRINT THE LETTER OF THE CORRECT ANSWER IN THE SPACE AT THE RIGHT.*

1. Any business not provided with capable substitutes to fill all important positions is a weak business. Therefore, a foreman should train each man not on to perform his own particular duties but also to do those of two or three positions. The paragraph BEST supports the statement that
    A. dependence on substitutes is a sign of weak organization
    B. training will improve the strongest organization
    C. the foreman should be the most expert at any particular job under him
    D. every employee can be trained to perform efficiency work other than his own
    E. vacancies in vital positions should be provided for in advance

    1.____

2. The coloration of textile fabrics composed of cotton and wool generally requires two processes, as the process used in dyeing wool is seldom capable of fixing the color upon cotton. The usual method is to immerse the fabric in the requisite baths to dye the wool and then to treat the partially dyed material in the manner found suitable for cotton.
    The paragraph BEST supports the statement that the dyeing of textile fabrics composed of cotton and wool is
    A. less complicated than the dyeing of wool alone
    B. more successful when the material contains more cotton than wool
    C. not satisfactory when solid colors are desired
    D. restricted to two colors for any one fabric
    E. usually based upon the methods required for dyeing the different materials

    2.____

3. The serious investigator must direct his whole effort toward success in his work. If he wishes to succeed in each investigation, his work will be by no means easy, smooth, or peaceful; on the contrary, he will have to devote himself completely and continuously to a task that requires all his ability.
    The paragraph BEST supports the statement that an investigator's success depends most upon
    A. ambition to advance rapidly in the service
    B. persistence in the face of difficulty
    C. training and experience
    D. willingness to obey orders without delay
    E. the number of investigations which he conducts

    3.____

4. Honest people in one nation find it difficult to understand the viewpoint of honest people in another. State departments and their ministers exist for the purpose of explaining the viewpoints of one nation in terms understood by another. Some of their most important work lies in this direction.

    4.____

The paragraph BEST supports the statement that
- A. people of different nations may not consider matters in the same light
- B. it is unusual for many people to share similar ideas
- C. suspicion prevents understanding between nations
- D. the chief work of state departments is to guide relations between nations united by a common cause
- E. the people of one nation must sympathize with the viewpoints of others

5. Economy once in a while is just not enough. I expect to find it at every level of responsibility, from cabinet member to the newest and youngest recruit. Controlling waste is something like bailing a boat; you have to keep at it. I have no intention of easing up on my insistence on getting a dollar of value for each dollar we spend.
The paragraph BEST supports the statement that
   - A. we need not be concerned about items which cost less than a dollar
   - B. it is advisable to buy the cheaper of two items
   - C. the responsibility of economy is greater at high levels than at low levels
   - D. economy becomes easy with practice
   - E. economy is a continuing responsibility

KEY (CORRECT ANSWERS)

1. E
2. E
3. B
4. A
5. E

TEST 7

DIRECTIONS: Each question has five suggested answers, lettered A to E. Decide which one is the BEST answer. *PRINT THE LETTER OF THE CORRECT ANSWER IN THE SPACE AT THE RIGHT.*

1. On all permit imprint mail the charge for postage has been printed by the mailer before he presents it for mailing and pays the postage. Such mail of any class is mailable only at the post office that issued a permit covering it. Since the postage receipts for such mail represent only the amount of permit imprint mail detected and verified, employees in receiving, handling, and outgoing sections must be alert constantly to route such mail to the weighing section before it is handled or dispatched.
   The paragraph BEST supports the statement that, at post offices where permit mail is received for dispatch,
   A. dispatching units make a final check on the amount of postage payable on permit imprint mail
   B. employees are to check the postage chargeable on mail received under permit
   C. neither more nor less postage is to be collected than the amount printed on permit imprint mail
   D. the weighing section is primarily responsible for failure to collect postage on such mail
   E. unusual measures are taken to prevent unstamped mail from being accepted

   1.____

2. Education should not stop when the individual has been prepared to make a livelihood and to live in modern society. Living would be mere existence were there were no appreciation and enjoyment of the riches of art, literature, and science.
   The paragraph BEST supports the statement that true education
   A. is focused on the routine problems of life
   B. prepares one for full enjoyment of life
   C. deals chiefly with art, literature, and science
   D. is not possible for one who does not enjoy scientific literature
   E. disregards practical ends

   2.____

3. Insured and c.o.d. air and surface mail is accepted with the understanding that the sender guarantees any necessary forwarding or return postage. When such mail is forwarded or returned, it shall be rated up for collection of postage; except that insured or c.o.d. air mail weighing 8 ounces or less and subject to the 40 cents an ounce rate shall be forwarded by air if delivery will be advanced, and returned by surface means without additional postage.
   The paragraph BEST supports the statement that the return postage for undeliverable insured mail is
   A. included in the original prepayment on air mail parcels
   B. computed but not collected before dispatching surface patrol post mail to sender

   3.____

C. not computed or charged for any air mail that is returned by surface transportation
D. included in the amount collected when the sender mails parcel post
E. collected before dispatching for return if any amount due has been guaranteed

4. All undeliverable first-class mail, except first-class parcels and parcel post paid with first-class postage, which cannot be returned to the sender, is sent to a dead-letter branch. Undeliverable matter of the third- and fourth-classes of obvious value for which the sender does not furnish return postage and undeliverable first-class parcels and parcel-post matter bearing postage of the first-class, which cannot be returned, is sent to a dead parcel-post branch.
The paragraph BEST supports the statement that matter that is sent to a dead parcel-post branch includes all undeliverable
   A. mail, except for first-class letter mail, that appears to be valuable
   B. mail, except that of the first-class, on which the sender failed to prepay the original mailing costs
   C. parcels on which the mailer prepaid the first-class rate of postage
   D. third- and fourth-class matter on which the required return postage has not been paid
   E. parcels on which first-class postage has been prepaid, when the sender's address is not known

4.____

5. Civilization started to move rapidly when man freed himself of the shackles that restricted his search for truth.
The passage BEST supports the statement that the progress of civilization
   A. came as a result of man's dislike for obstacles
   B. did not begin until restrictions on learning were removed
   C. has been aided by man's efforts to find the truth
   D. is based on continually increasing efforts
   E. continues at a constantly increasing rate

5.____

KEY (CORRECT ANSWERS)

1. B
2. B
3. B
4. E

TEST 8

DIRECTIONS: Each question has five suggested answers, lettered A to E. Decide which one is the BEST answer. *PRINT THE LETTER OF THE CORRECT ANSWER IN THE SPACE AT THE RIGHT.*

1. E-mails should be clear, concise, and brief. Omit all unnecessary words. The parts of speech most often used in e-mails are nouns, verbs, adjectives, and adverbs. If possible, do without pronouns, prepositions, articles, and copulative verbs. Use simple sentences, rather than complex and compound.
The paragraph BEST supports the statement that in writing e-mails one should always use
   A. common and simple words
   B. only nouns, verbs, adjectives, and adverbs
   C. incomplete sentences
   D. only words essential to the meaning
   E. the present tense of verbs

   1.____

2. The function of business is to increase the wealth of the country and the value and happiness of life. It does this by supplying the material needs of men and women. When the nation's business is successfully carried on, it renders public service of the highest value.
The paragraph BEST supports the statement that
   A. all businesses which render public service are successful
   B. human happiness is enhanced only by the increase of material wants
   C. the value of life is increased only by the increase of wealth
   D. the material needs of men and women are supplied by well-conducted business
   E. business is the only field of activity which increases happiness

   2.____

3. In almost every community, fortunately, there are certain men and women known to be public-spirited. Others, however, may be selfish and act only as their private interests seem to require.
The paragraph BEST supports the statement that those citizens who disregard others are
   A. fortunate   B. needed
   C. found only in small communities   D. not known
   E. not public spirited

   3.____

KEY (CORRECT ANSWERS)

1. D
2. D
3. E

READING COMPREHENSION
UNDERSTANDING AND INTERPRETING WRITTEN MATERIAL
EXAMINATION SECTION
TEST 1

DIRECTIONS: Each question or incomplete statement is followed by several suggested answers or completions. Select the one that BEST answers the question or completes the statement. *PRINT THE LETTER OF THE CORRECT ANSWER IN THE SPACE AT THE RIGHT.*

Questions 1-3.

DIRECTIONS: Questions 1 through 3 are to be answered SOLELY on the basis of the following passage.

Accident proneness is a subject which deserves much more objective and competent study than it has received to date. In discussing accident proneness, it is important to differentiate between the employee who is a *repeater* and one who is truly accident-prone. It is obvious that any person put on work of which he knows little without thorough training in safe practice for the work in question will be liable to injury until he does learn the *how* of it. Few workmen left to their own devices will develop adequate safe practices. Therefore, they must be trained. Only those who fail to respond to proper training should be regarded as accident-prone. The repeater whose accident record ca be explained by a correctible physical defect, by correctible plant or machine hazards, by assignment to work for which he is not suited because of physical deficiencies or special abilities, cannot be fairly called accident prone.

1. According to the above passage, a person is considered accident prone if
   A. he has accidents regardless of the fact that he has been properly trained
   B. he has many accidents
   C. it is possible for him to have accidents
   D. he works at a job where accidents are possible

1.____

2. According to the above passage,
   A. workers will learn the safe way of doing things if left to their own intelligence
   B. most workers must be trained to be safe
   C. a worker who has had more than one accident has not been properly trained
   D. intelligent workers are always safe

2.____

3. According to the above passage, a person would not be called accident prone if the cause of his accident was
   A. a lack of interest in the job   B. recklessness
   C. a low level of intelligence   D. eyeglasses that don't fit properly

3.____

Questions 4-9.

DIRECTIONS: Each question consists of a statement. You are to indicate whether the statement is TRUE (T) or FALSE (F). Questions 4 through 9 are to be answered SOLELY on the basis of the following passage.

    Every accident should be reported even though the accident seems very unimportant. The man involved may be unharmed, yet it is necessary in the case of all accidents to forward a written report containing all the facts that show how the accident occurred, including the time and place. The reason for this action is that a situation which does not cause injury at one time may cause serious injury at another time. A written report informs the safety director of a dangerous condition and helps his investigation by supplying important facts. He can, therefore, take steps to eliminate the hazard.

4. Only serious accidents should be reported.   4.____

5. If the man involved in an accident is unharmed, it is not necessary to send through a report.   5.____

6. An accident report should show how the accident happened and include the time and place of the accident.   6.____

7. A situation which does not cause an injury at one time cannot cause serious injury at another time.   7.____

8. When a written report of an accident is made, it means that the safety director is informed of a dangerous condition.   8.____

9. The acts in an accident report do not help the safety director in his investigation of the accident.   9.____

Questions 10-17.

DIRECTIONS: Each question consists of a statement. You are to indicate whether the statement is TRUE (T) or FALSE (F). Questions 10 through 17 are to be answered SOLELY on the basis of the following passage.

    The Mayor is in charge of the city government. He has his office in City Hall in downtown. There are city rules, or laws, that all citizens must obey. For example, there is a law that no one can throw things on the sidewalks or into the streets. We want our city to be clean and beautiful. There are also traffic laws for the automobiles that use our city streets. For instance, the cars cannot go at more than a certain speed. The drivers must stop when the traffic lights turn red.
    If people do not obey these rules or city laws, a policeman may arrest them. These laws were made to protect other people who want to use the streets too.

10. The head of the city government is the Mayor.   10.____

11.	The Mayor's office is in the Municipal Building.	11.____
12.	The Mayor does not have to obey the city laws or rules.	12.____
13.	Anyone who throws things on the sidewalks is breaking the law.	13.____
14.	There is a traffic law that does not allow a car to go faster than a certain speed.	14.____
15.	A driver does not have to stop when the traffic lights turn red.	15.____
16.	A policeman may arrest a driver who does not obey the traffic laws.	16.____
17.	People who use the streets are not protected by the traffic laws.	17.____

Questions 18-25.

DIRECTIONS: Each question consists of a statement. You are to indicate whether the statement is TRUE (T) or FALSE (F). Questions 4 through 25 are to be 18answered SOLELY on the basis of the following passage.

NEW YORK CITY

The name of New York City, as it appears on all official documents, is *The City of New York*. This name applies to all five boroughs which consolidated in 1898 to form what is known as Greater New York. The five boroughs are Manhattan, The Bronx, Brooklyn, Queens, and Richmond. The term Greater New York is seldom used at the present time, and often the city is called New York City to distinguish it from New York State. The two Boroughs of Brooklyn and Queens are located on Long Island and the Borough of Richmond is located on Staten Island. The Borough of Manhattan is located on Manhattan Island, while The Bronx is located on the mainland of New York State. Because the city is large, covers much territory, and has so many people, the United States Post Office has divided the city for its own convenience; therefore, the post office address of people living in Manhattan is New York, New York. For those living in the Borough of Brooklyn, the post office address is Brooklyn, New York; and likewise, each borough has its own special post office address.

18.	New York City is referred to on all official documents as *Greater New York City*.	18.____
19.	The boroughs of New York City were joined together in 1898 to make up Greater New York.	19.____
20.	Greater New York is made up of five boroughs.	20.____
21.	The boroughs which make up New York City are: The Bronx, Richmond, Brooklyn, Queens, and Nassau.	21.____
22.	The borough of Queens is located on the mainland of New York State.	22.____

23. The Bronx and Brooklyn are part of Long Island.   23._____

24. A letter for Manhattan should be addressed to New York, New York.   24._____

25. Because New York City is so big, the Post Office has divided it into five different post office addresses.   25._____

KEY (CORRECT ANSWERS)

1.	A		11.	F
2.	B		12.	F
3.	D		13.	T
4.	F		14.	T
5.	F		15.	F
6.	T		16.	T
7.	F		17.	F
8.	T		18.	F
9.	F		19.	T
10.	T		20.	T

21.	F
22.	F
23.	F
24.	T
25.	T

TEST 2

DIRECTIONS: All questions are to be answered SOLELY on the basis of the information contained in the passage. Each question or incomplete statement is followed by several suggested answers or completions. Select the one that BEST answers the question or completes the statement. *PRINT THE LETTER OF THE CORRECT ANSWER IN THE SPACE AT THE RIGHT.*

Questions 1-4.

In the long run, a government will always encroach upon freedom to the extent which it has the power to do so; this is almost a natural law of politics since, whatever the intentions of the men who exercise political power, the sheer momentum of government leads to a constant pressure upon the liberties of the citizen. But in many countries, society has responded by throwing up its own defenses in the shape of social classes or organized corporations which, enjoying economic power and popular support, have been able to set limits to the scope of action of the executive. Such, for example, in England was the origin of all our liberties won from government by the stand first of the feudal nobility, then of churches and political parties, and latterly of trade unions, commercial organizations, and the societies for promoting various causes. Even European lands which were arbitrarily ruled by the powers of the monarchy, though absolute in theory, were in their exercise checked in a similar fashion. Indeed, the fascist of dictatorships of today are the first truly tyrannical governments which western Europe has known for centuries, and they have been rendered possible only because on coming to power they destroyed all forms of social organization which were in any way rivals to the state.

1. The MAIN idea of the above passage is BEST expressed as 1.____
 A. limited powers of monarchies   B. the ideal of liberal government
 C. functions of trade unions   D. ruthless ways of dictators

2. The writer maintains that there is a natural tendency for governments to 2.____
 A. become more democratic   B. become fascist
 C. increase individual liberties   D. assume more power

3. Monarchy was FIRST checked in England by the 3.____
 A. trade unions   B. church   C. people   D. nobles

4. Fascist dictatorships differ from monarchies of recent times in 4.____
 A. getting things done by sheer momentum
 B. promoting various causes
 C. exerting constant pressure on liberties
 D. destroying people's organizations

Questions 5-8.

Very early on a summer's morning, the nicest thing to look at is a beach, before the swimmers arrive. Usually all the litter has been picked up from the sand by the Park Department clean-up crew. Everything is quiet. All you can hear are the waves breaking and the sea gulls calling to each other. The beach opens to the public at 10 A.M. Long before that time, however, long lines of eager men, women, and children have driven up to the entrance. They form long lines that wind around the beach waiting for the signal to move.

103

5. According to the above passage, before 10 A.M., long lines are formed that are made up of
   A. cars
   B. clean-up crews
   C. men, women, and children
   D. Park Department trucks

   5.____

6. The season referred to in the above passage is
   A. fall   B. summer   C. winter   D. spring

   6.____

7. The place the above passage is describing is a
   A. beach   B. park   C. golf course   D. tennis court

   7.____

8. According to the above passage, one of the things you notice early in the morning is that
   A. radios are playing
   B. swimmers are there
   C. the sand is dirty
   D. the litter is gone

   8.____

Questions 9-10.

There have been almost as many definitions of *opinion* as there have been students of the problem, and the definitions have ranged from such a statement as *inconsistent views capable of being accepted by rational minds as true to the overt manifestation of an attitude*. There are, however, a number of clearly outstanding factors among the various definitions which form the sum total of the concept. Opinion is the stronghold of the individual. No *group* ever had an opinion, and there is no mechanism except that of the individual mind capable of forming an opinion. It is true, of course, that opinions can be altered or even created by the stimuli of environment. In the midst of individual diversity and confusion, every question as it rises into importance is subjected to a process of consolidation and clarification until there emerge certain views, each held and advocated in common by bodies of citizens. When a group of people accepts the same opinion, that opinion is public with respect to the group accepting it. When there is not unanimous opinion, there is not one public but two or more.

9. On the basis of the above passage, it may be INFERRED that
   A. all individual opinions are subjected to consolidation by the influence of environmental stimuli
   B. governments are influenced by opinions held in common by large groups of citizens
   C. some of the elements of the extremely varied definitions of *opinion* are compatible
   D. when there is no unanimity, there is no public opinion

   9.____

10. On the basis of the above passage, the MOST accurate of the following statement is:
    A. One definition of *opinion* implies that most individuals can accept inconsistent views on the same question
    B. One other definition of *opinion* implies that the individual's attitude concerning a question must be openly expressed before it can be considered as an opinion

    10.____

C. The individual opinion plays no part in the stand taken on a given question by a group after the individual has identified himself with the group
D. There are no group opinions formed on relatively unimportant issues because of individual confusion

Questions 11-13.

The word *propaganda* has fallen on evil days. As far as popular usage is concerned, its reputation by now is probably lost irretrievably, for its connotation is almost invariably sinister or evil. This is a pity for, in the struggle for men's minds, it is a weapon of great potential value. Indeed, in the race against time that we are running, its constructive use is indispensable. The student of propaganda must know that it is a term honorable in origin.

Propaganda is *good* or *bad* according to the virtue of the end to which it seeks to persuade us, and the methods it employs. Bad propaganda is distinguished by a disregard for the welfare of those at whom it is directed. Such disregard either derives from, or eventually results in, a lack of proper reverence for individuality, for the private person and our relation to him. For *man* is substituted mass, and the *mass* is manipulated for selfish purposes. The authoritarian reformist who believes he is acting *in the interest of the masses* is also involved in this same disregard for personal integrity. Its final outcome is always the same—a disregard for the individual. Good propaganda involves the deliberate avoidance of all casuistry. In so far as good propaganda operates upon us at a level of our weakness or disability, its intent must be to contribute a cure, not a sedative; inspiration, not an opiate; enlightenment, not accentuation of our ignorance.

11. Of the following, the MOST suitable title for the above passage is
    A. Propaganda and Society
    B. Propaganda For the Masses
    C. The Proper Meaning of Propaganda
    D. Uses and Misuses of Propaganda

12. On the basis of the above passage, it may be INFERRED that
    A. some propaganda may employ unscrupulous methods to persuade us to ends that are justified
    B. the definition of the word *propaganda* has been changed
    C. the method of frequent repetition is an example of bad propaganda
    D. the opportunity for the individual to challenge propaganda has decreased

13. On the basis of the above passage, it may be INFERRED that
    A. a reformer who believes in his cause should not employ propaganda to advance it
    B. good propaganda should be limited to operating against the levels of weakness of the individual
    C. propaganda may lose sight of the welfare of the individual in its appeal to the masses
    D. those who have privileged access to the media of mass communication must always accept high standards in their use of propaganda

Questions 14-15.

A steadfast concert for peace can never be maintained except by a partnership of democratic nations. No autocratic government could be trusted to keep faith within it or observe its covenants. It must be a league of honor, a partnership of opinion. Intrigue would eat its vitals away; the plotting of inner circles who could plan what they would, and render account to no one, would be a corruption seated at is very heart. Only free people can hold their purpose and their honor steady to a common end, and prefer the interests of mankind to any narrow interest of their own.

14. According to the above passage, only democratic nations can   14.____
    A. be free of plotting, intrigue, and corruption
    B. be trusted to do what is right and honorable
    C. plan programs which promote the interests of their country
    D. subordinate their own interests to those which benefit the entire world

15. It may be implied from the above passage that an autocratic government could   15.____
    NOT be trusted to respect its international agreements because it
    A. exemplifies the proverb that there is no honor among thieves
    B. is full of corruption, plots, and intrigue
    C. is principally concerned with the welfare of its own people
    D. would plot with other governments to advance their own mutual interests

Questions 16-17.

A gentleman is mainly occupied in removing the obstacles which hinder the free and unembarrassed action of those about him; and he concurs with their movements rather than takes the initiative himself. The true gentleman carefully avoids whatever may cause a jar or jolt in the minds of those with whom he is cast. His great concern is to put everyone at his ease and to make all feel at home. He is tender towards the bashful, gentle towards the distant, and merciful towards the absurd; he can recollect to whom he is speaking; he guards against unseasonable allusions, or topics which may irritate; he is seldom prominent in conversation, and never wearisome.

16. According to the above passage, a gentleman make it his business to   16.____
    A. discuss current issues of interest although controversial
    B. get the bashful to participate in the conversation
    C. introduce to one another guests who have not previously met
    D. remember the person with whom he is speaking

17. According to the above passage, one of the CHIEF characteristics of a   17.____
    gentleman is that he
    A. conducts himself in such a way as to avoid hurting the feelings if others
    B. keeps the conversation going, particularly when interest lags
    C. puts an unruly guest in his place politely but firmly
    D. shows his guests the ways in which they can best enjoy

18. Too often we retire people who are willing and able to continue working, according to Federal Security Agency Administrator Oscar R. Ewing in addressing the first National Conference on Aging; to point up the fact that chronological age is no longer an effective criterion in determining whether or not an individual is capable of working. The Second World War proved this point when it became necessary to hire older, experienced people to handle positions in business and industry vacated by personnel called to serve their country. As shown by production records set during the war period, the employment of older people helped us continue, and even better, our high level of production. It was also pointed out at the conference that our life expectancy is increasing and that the over-65 group will jump from 11,500,000 now to twenty million in 2015. A good many of these people are capable of producing and have a desire to work, but they are kept from gainful employment by a shortsightedness on the part of many employers which leads them to believe that young people can give them adequate service. It is true that the young person has greater agility and speed to offer, but on the other hand there is much to be gained from the experience, steadfastness, and maturity of judgment of the elderly worker.
The title that BEST expresses the ideas of the above passage is
   A. Increased Efficiency of Elderly Workers
   B. Misjudging Elderly Workers
   C. Lengthening the Span of Life
   D. New Jobs For the Aged

18.____

19. The question is whether night baseball will prove a boon or a disaster to the game. The big crowds now attending the night games, the brilliance of the spectacle, the miracle of the spinning turnstiles; all these seem sufficient evidence that what is needed is not less night ball, but more. The fact remains, however, that despite all apparent success, some of the shrewdest, most experienced men in baseball remain unconvinced of the miracle. They are steady in their preference for daytime baseball, and they view with increasing distrust the race towards more lights. It could be that these men are simply being obstinate. Yet, on the other hand, it could be that in reviewing the caliber of baseball as it is played at night, in speculating upon the future effect of night ball, they are not entirely unprophetic. It could even be, indeed, that they are dead right.
In his attitude toward the future of night baseball, the author expresses
   A. uncertainty   B. confidence   C. optimism   D. sharp criticism

19.____

20. We all know people who would welcome a new American car to their stables, but one cannot expect to find a sportscar man among them. He cannot be enticed into such a circus float without feeling soiled. He resents the wanton use of chromium as much as he shudders at the tail fins, the grotesquely convoluted bumpers, and other *dishonest* lines. He blanches at the enormous bustle that adds weight and useless space, drags on ramps and curbstones, and complicates the process of parking even in the car's own garage. The attitude of the owner of a Detroit product is reflected in the efforts of manufacturers to *take the drive out of driving*. The sportscar addict regards

20.____

this stand as outrageous. His interest in a car, he is forever telling himself and other captive listeners, lies in the fun of driving it, in *sensing its alertness on the road*, and in *pampering it as a thoroughbred*.

The above passage implies that sportscars are very
- A. colorful
- B. showy
- C. maneuverable
- D. roomy

Questions 21-25.

Fuel is conserved when a boiler is operating its most efficient load. The efficiency of a boiler will change as the output varies. Large amounts of air must be used at low ratings and so the heat exchanger is inefficient. As the output increases, the efficiency decreases due to an increase in flue gas temperature. Every boiler has an output rate for which its efficiency is highest. For example, in a water-tube boiler, the highest efficiency might occur at 120 percent of rated capacity while in a vertical fire-tube boiler highest efficiency might be at 70% of rated capacity. The type of fuel burned and cleanliness affects the maximum efficiency of the boiler. When a power plant contains a battery of boilers, a sufficient number should be kept in operation so as to maintain the output of individual units near their points of maximum efficiency. One of the boilers in the battery can be used as a regulator to meet the change in demand for steam while the other boilers could still operate at their most efficient rating. Boiler performance is expressed as the number of pounds of steam generated per pound of fuel.

21. According to the above passage, the number of pounds of steam generated per pound of fuel is a measure of boiler
    - A. size
    - B. performance
    - C. regulator input
    - D. bypass

22. According to the above passage, the HIGHEST efficiency of a vertical fire tube boiler might occur at _____ capacity.
    - A. 70% of rate
    - B. 80% of water tube
    - C. 95% of water tube
    - D. 120% of rated

23. According to the above passage, the MAXIMUM efficiency of a boiler is affected by
    - A. atmospheric temperature
    - B. atmospheric pressure
    - C. cleanliness
    - D. fire brick material

24. According to the above passage, a heat exchanger uses large amounts of air at low
    - A. fuel rates
    - B. ratings
    - C. temperatures
    - D. pressures

25. According to the above passage, one boiler in a battery of boilers should be used as a
    - A. demand
    - B. stand-by
    - C. regulator
    - D. safety

KEY (CORRECT ANSWERS)

1. D
2. D
3. D
4. D
5. C

6. B
7. A
8. D
9. C
10. B

11. D
12. A
13. C
14. D
15. D

16. D
17. A
18. B
19. A
20. C

21. B
22. A
23. C
24. B
25. C

TEST 3

DIRECTIONS: All questions are to be answered SOLELY on the basis of the information contained in the passage. Each question or incomplete statement is followed by several suggested answers or completions. Select the one that BEST answers the question or completes the statement. *PRINT THE LETTER OF THE CORRECT ANSWER IN THE SPACE AT THE RIGHT.*

Questions 1-7.

FIRST AID INSTRUCTIONS

The main purpose of first aid is to put the injured person in the best possible position until medical help arrives. This includes the performance of emergency treatment designed to save a life if a doctor is not immediately available. When an accident happens, a crowd usually collects around the victim. If nobody uses his head, the injured person fails to receive the care he needs. You must keep calm and cool at all times and, most important, it is your duty to take charge at an accident. The first thing for you to do is to see, insofar as possible, what is wrong with the injured person. Leave him where he is until the nature and extent of his injury are determined. If he is unconscious, he should not be moved except to lay him flat on his back if he is in some other position. Loosen the clothing of any seriously hurt person, and make him as comfortable as possible. Medical help should be called as soon as possible. You should remain with the injured person and send someone else to call the doctor. You should try to make sure that the one who calls for a doctor is able to give correct information as to the location of the injured person. In order to help the physician to know what equipment may be needed in each particular case, the person making the call should give the doctor as much information about the injury as possible.

1. If nobody uses his head at the scene of an accident, there is danger that
   A. a large crowd will gather
   B. emergency treatment will be needed
   C. names of witnesses will be missed
   D. the victim will not get the care he needs

2. The FIRST thing you should do at the scene of an accident is to
   A. call a doctor
   B. lay the injured person on his back
   C. find out what is wrong with the injured person
   D. loosen the clothing of the injured person

3. Until the nature and extent of the injuries are determined, you should
   A. move the injured person indoors
   B. let the injured person lie where he is
   C. carefully roll the injured person on his back
   D. give the injured person artificial respiration

4. If the injured person is unconscious, you should
   A. give him artificial respiration
   B. get some hot liquid like coffee into him
   C. lay him flat on his back
   D. move him to a comfortable location

   4.____

5. If a doctor is to be called, you should
   A. go make this call yourself since you have all the information
   B. go make this call yourself since you are in charge
   C. send someone who knows what happened
   D. send someone who is fast

   5.____

6. The person calling the doctor should give as much information as he has regarding the injury so that the doctor
   A. can bring the necessary equipment
   B. can decide whether he should come
   C. will know whom to notify
   D. can advise what should be done

   6.____

7. The MAIN purpose of first aid is to
   A. stop bleeding
   B. prevent further complications of the injury
   C. keep the patient comfortable
   D. determine what the injuries are

   7.____

Questions 8-13.

SELECTION OF TOURS OF DUTY

A selection of tours of duty for the winter season for Railroad Porters will begin on Monday, December 27, and conclude on Thursday, December 30.
The selection will take place in Room 828, 4th Floor, 370 Jay Street, Telephone 215, Extension 3870.
Railroad Porters whose names appear on the attached schedule will make selections at the time and date indicated.

8. The selection of tours of duty began on
   A. Monday   B. Tuesday   C. Wednesday   D. Thursday

   8.____

9. No selections of tours of duty were scheduled for December
   A. 28   B. 29   C. 30   D. 31

   9.____

10. The choice of tours of duty was PROBABLY based on
    A. age   B. seniority
    C. borough of residence   D. alphabetical listing of names

    10.____

11. The season for which the selection of tours of duty was made was the
    A. spring   B. summer   C. autumn   D. winter

    11.____

12. A porter making a selection had to do so 12.____
   A. before work B. after work
   C. on his day off D. at the time indicated

13. The selection was to be done by 13.____
   A. all station employees
   B. all porters
   C. only the porters whose names were on the schedule
   D. employees not satisfied with present schedules

Questions 14-16.

CAR INSPECTION AND CLEANING

RIGID INSPECTION: Subway cars are hauled into a repair yard and given a rigid inspection about three times a month.
SWEEING AND WASHING: Each car is swept every twenty-four hours. Its windows are washed every time it comes into a repair yard.
OVERHAUL: At the completion of 90,000 miles, the car is almost completely taken apart, cleaned, and painted.

14. Car windows are USUALLY washed at least once in 14.____
   A. one day B. three days
   C. ten days D. three months

15. If the average car traveled about 75,000 miles per year, it would NORMALLY be almost completely taken apart, cleaned, and painted about every 15.____
   A. 9 months B. year C. 15 months D. 2 years

16. If a car has been overhauled at the end of 90,000 miles, it would be brought back to the repair yard 16.____
   A. within one week for sweeping
   B. within two weeks for another overhaul
   C. after 90,000 miles for inspection if necessary
   D. within two weeks for a rigid inspection

Questions 17-19.

Into the nine square miles that make up Manhattan's business districts, about two million people travel each weekday to go to work—the equivalent of the combined populations of Boston, Baltimore, and Cincinnati. Some 140,000 drive there in cars, 200,000 take buses, and 100,000 ride the commuter railroads. The great majority, however, go by subway approximately 1.4 million people.

It is some ride. The last major improvement in the subway system was completed in 1935. The subways are dirty and noisy. Many local lines operate well beneath capacity, but many express lines are strained way beyond capacity—in particular, the lines to Manhattan, now overloaded by 39,000 passengers during peak hours.

But for all its discomforts, the subway system is inherently a far more efficient way of moving people than automobiles and highways. Making this system faster, more convenient, and more comfortable for people must be the core of the City's transportation effort.

17. The CENTRAL point of the above passage is that
    A. the equivalent of the combined populations of Boston, Baltimore, and Cincinnati commute into Manhattan's business district each weekday
    B. the improvement of the subway system is the key to the solution of moving people efficiently in and out of Manhattan's business district
    C. the subways are dirty and noisy, resulting in a terrible ride
    D. we should increase the ability of people to get in and out of Manhattan by cars, subways, and commuter railroads in order to ease the load from the subways

17.____

18. In accordance with the above passage, 1.4 million people commute by subway and _____ by other mass transportation means.
    A. 200,000   B. 100,000   C. 440,000   D. 300,000

18.____

19. From the information given in the above passage, one could logically conclude that, next to the subways, the transportation system that carries the LARGEST number of passengers is
    A. railroads   B. cars   C. buses   D. local lines

19.____

Questions 20-25.

DIRECTIONS: Questions 20 through 25 are to be answered SOLELY on the basis of the following passage. Each question consists of a statement. You are to indicate whether the statement is TRUE (T) or FALSE (F).

THE CITY

The City, which at one time in 1789-90 was the capital of the nation and which was also the capital of the State until 1796, has continued as the financial and economic capital of the United States and has grown to be the greatest city in the country.

The City is great because it has such a large population—a total of eight million persons in 2008. This population is larger than the total inhabitants of 41 of 75 of the largest countries in the world. The City requires many homes and buildings to accommodate its residents. The City consists of more than 725,000 buildings, more than half of which are one- and two-family houses owned by the occupants. More than five hundred hotels, with 128,000 rooms, are needed to take care of visitors to the City; it is estimated that between one and two hundred thousand people visit the City daily.

The harbor is so large that any six of the other leading seaports of the world could be placed in it. Its piers, to accommodate freight and passengers, number 417, and its waterfront covers 770 miles.

20. The City has been the capital of the United States and also the capital of the Senate.

20.____

5 (#3)

21. In 1988, the population of the City was greater than the total population of forty-one of seventy-five of the largest countries in the world. 21._____

22. Over half of all the buildings in the City are one- and two-family homes which are owned by the people who live in them. 22._____

23. A little under 200,000 people visit the City each year. 23._____

24. The harbor is larger than any other leading seaport. 24._____

25. The harbor is 471 miles long and has 770 piers to take care of passengers and cargo. 25._____

KEY (CORRECT ANSWERS)

1.	D		11.	D
2.	C		12.	D
3.	B		13.	C
4.	C		14.	C
5.	C		15.	C
6.	A		16.	D
7.	B		17.	B
8.	A		18.	D
9.	D		19.	C
10.	B		20.	T

21. T
22. T
23. F
24. T
25. F

READING COMPREHENSION
UNDERSTANDING AND INTERPRETING WRITTEN MATERIAL
EXAMINATION SECTION
TEST 1

DIRECTIONS: Each question or incomplete statement is followed by several suggested answers or completions. Select the one that BEST answers the question or completes the statement. *PRINT THE LETTER OF THE CORRECT ANSWER IN THE SPACE AT THE RIGHT.*

Questions 1-5.

DIRECTIONS: Questions 1 through 5 are to be answered SOLELY on the basis of the following passage.

The most effective control mechanism to prevent gross incompetence on the part of public employees is a good personnel program. The personnel officer in the line departments and the central personnel agency should exert positive leadership to raise levels of performance. Although the key factor is the quality of the personnel recruited, staff members other than personnel officers can make important contributions to efficiency. Administrative analysts, now employed in many agencies, make detailed studies of organization and procedures, with the purpose of eliminating delays, waste, and other inefficiencies. Efficiency is, however, more than a question of good organization and procedures; it is also the product of the attitudes and value of the public employees. Personal motivation can provide the will to be efficient. The best management studies will not result in substantial improvement of the performance of those employees who feel no great urge to wok up to their abilities.

1. The above passage indicates that the KEY factor in preventing gross incompetence of public employees is the
   A. hiring of administrative analysts to assist personnel people
   B. utilization of effective management studies
   C. overlapping of responsibility
   D. quality of the employees hired

2. According to the above passage, the central personnel agency staff SHOULD
   A. work more closely with administrative analysts in the line departments than with personnel officers
   B. make a serious effort to avoid jurisdictional conflicts with personnel officers in line departments
   C. contribute to improving the quality of work of public employees
   D. engage in a comprehensive program to change the public's negative image of public employees

3. The above passage indicates that efficiency in an organization can BEST be brought about by 3.____
   A. eliminating ineffective control mechanisms
   B. instituting sound organizational procedures
   C. promoting competent personnel
   D. recruiting people with desire to do good work

4. According to the above passage, the purpose of administrative analysts in a public agency is to 4.____
   A. prevent injustice to the public employee
   B. promote the efficiency of the agency
   C. protect the interests of the public
   D. ensure the observance of procedural due process

5. The above passage implies that a considerable rise in the quality of work of public employees can be brought about by 5.____
   A. encouraging positive employee attitudes toward work
   B. controlling personnel officers who exceed their powers
   C. creating warm personal associations among public employees in an agency
   D. closing loopholes in personnel organization and procedures

Questions 6-8.

DIRECTIONS: Questions 6 through 8 are to be answered SOLELY on the basis of the following passage.

EMPLOYEE NEEDS

The greatest waste in industry and in government may be that of human resources. This waste usually derives not from employees' unwillingness or inability, but from management's ineptness to meet the maintenance and motivational needs of employees. Maintenance needs refer to such needs as providing employees with safe places to work, written work rules, job security, adequate salary, employer-sponsored social activities, and with knowledge of their role in the overall framework of the organization. However, of greatest significance to employees are the motivational needs of job growth, achievement, responsibility, and recognition.

Although employee dissatisfaction may stem from either poor maintenance or poor motivation factors, the outward manifestation of the dissatisfaction may be very much like, i.e., negativism, complaints, deterioration of performance, and so forth. The improvement in the lighting of an employee's work area or raising his level of ay won't do much good if the source of the dissatisfaction is the absence of a meaningful assignment. By the same token, if an employee is dissatisfied with what he considers inequitable pay, the introduction of additional challenge in his work may simply make matters worse.

It is relatively easy for an employee to express frustration by complaining about pay, washroom conditions, fringe benefits, and so forth; but most people cannot easily express resentment in terms of the more abstract concepts concerning job growth, responsibility, and achievement.

It would be wrong to assume that there is no interaction between maintenance and motivational needs of employee. For example, conditions of high motivation often overshadow poor maintenance conditions. If an organization is in a period of strong growth and expansion, opportunities for job growth, responsibility, recognition, and achievement are usually abundant, but the rapid growth may have outrun the upkeep of maintenance factors. In this situation, motivation may be high, but only if employees recognize the poor maintenance conditions as unavoidable and temporary. The subordination of maintenance factors cannot go on indefinitely, even with the highest motivation.

Both maintenance and motivation factors influence the behavior of all employees, but employees are not identical and, furthermore, the needs of any individual do not remain orientation toward maintenance factors and those with greater sensitivity toward motivation factors.

A highly maintenance-oriented individual, preoccupied with the factors peripheral to his job rather than the job itself, is more concerned with comfort than challenge. He does not get deeply involved with his work but does with the condition of his work area, toilet facilities, and his time for going to lunch. By contrast, a strongly motivation-oriented employee is usually relatively indifferent to his surroundings and is caught up in the pursuit of work goals.

Fortunately, there are few people who are either exclusively maintenance-oriented or purely motivation-oriented. The former would be deadwood in an organization, while the latter might trample on those around him in his pursuit to achieve his goals.

6. With respect to employee motivational and maintenance needs, the management policies of an organization which is growing rapidly will probably result
    A. more in meeting motivational needs rather than maintenance needs
    B. more in meeting maintenance needs rather than motivational needs
    C. in meeting both of these needs equally
    D. in increased effort to define the motivational and maintenance needs of its employees

7. In accordance with the above passage, which of the following CANNOT be considered as an example of an employee maintenance need for railroad clerks?
    A. Providing more relief periods
    B. Providing fair salary increases at periodic intervals
    C. Increasing job responsibilities
    D. Increasing health insurance benefits

8. Most employees in an organization may be categorized as being interested in
    A. maintenance needs only
    B. motivational needs only
    C. both motivational and maintenance needs
    D. money only, to the exclusion of all other needs

Questions 9-11.

DIRECTIONS: Questions 9 through 11 are to be answered SOLELY on the basis of the following passage.

GOOD EMPLOYEE PRACTICES

As a city employee, you will be expected to take an interest in you work and perform the duties of your job to the best of your ability and in a spirit of cooperation. Nothing shows an interest in your work more than coming to work on time, not only at the start of the day but also when returning from lunch. If it is necessary for you to keep a personal appointment at lunch hour which might cause a delay in getting back to work on time, you should explain the situation to your supervisor and get his approval to come back a little late before you leave for lunch.

You should do everything that is asked of you willingly and consider important even the small jobs that your supervisor gives you. Although these jobs may seem unimportant, if you forget to do them or if you don't do them right, trouble may develop later.

Getting along well with your fellow workers will add much to the enjoyment of your work. You should respect your fellow workers and try to see their side when a disagreement arises. The better you get along with your fellow workers and your supervisor, the better you will like your job and the better you will be able to do it.

9. According to the above passage, in your job as a city employee, you are expected to
   A. show a willingness to cooperate on the job
   B. get your supervisor's approval before keeping any personal appointments at lunch hour
   C. avoid doing small jobs that seem unimportant
   D. do the easier jobs at the start of the day and the more difficult ones later on

10. According to the above passage, getting to work on time shows that you
    A. need the job
    B. have an interest in your work
    C. get along well with your fellow workers
    D. like your supervisor

11. According to the above passage, the one of the following statements that is NOT true is:
    A. If you do a small job wrong, trouble may develop
    B. You should respect your fellow workers
    C. If you disagree with a fellow worker, you should try to see his side of the story
    D. The less you get along with your supervisor, the better you will be able to do your job

Questions 12-15.

DIRECTIONS: Questions 12 through 15 are to be answered SOLELY on the basis of the following passage.

EMPLOYEE SUGGESTIONS

To increase the effectiveness of the city government, the city asks its employees to offer suggestions when they feel an improvement could be made in some government operation. The Employees' Suggestions Program was started to encourage city employees to do this. Through this Program, which is only for city employees, cash awards may be given to those whose suggestions are submitted and approved. Suggestions are looked for not only from supervisors but from all city employees as any city employee may get an idea which might be approved and contribute greatly to the solution of some problem of city government.

Therefore, all suggestions for improvement are welcome, whether they be suggestions on how to improve working conditions, or on how to increase the speed with which work is done, or on how to reduce or eliminate such things as waste, time losses, accidents or fire hazards. There are, however, a few types of suggestions for which cash awards cannot be given. An example of this type would be a suggestion to increase salaries or a suggestion to change the regulations about annual leave or about sick leave. The number of suggestions sent in has increased sharply during the past few years. It is hoped that it will keep increasing in the future in order to meet the city's needs for more ideas for improved ways of doing things.

12. According to the above passage, the MAIN reason why the city asks its employees for suggestions about government operations is to
    A. increase the effectiveness of the city government
    B. show that the Employees' Suggestion Program is working well
    C. show that everybody helps run the city government
    D. have the employee win a prize

13. According to the above passage, the Employees' Suggestion Program can approve awards ONLY for those suggestions that come from
    A. city employees
    B. city employees who are supervisors
    C. city employees who are not supervisors
    D. experienced employee of the city

14. According to the above passage, a cash award cannot be given through the Employees' Suggestion Program for a suggestion about
    A. getting work done faster
    B. helping prevent accidents on the job
    C. increasing the amount of annual leave for city employees
    D. reducing the chance of fire where city employees work

15. According to the above passage, the suggestions sent in during the past few years have
    A. all been approved
    B. generally been well written
    C. been mostly about reducing or eliminating waste
    D. been greater in number than before

Questions 16-18.

DIRECTIONS: Questions 16 through 18 are to be answered SOLELY on the basis of the following passage.

The supervisor will gain the respect of the members of his staff and increase his influence over them by controlling his temper and avoiding criticizing anyone publicly. When a mistake is made, the good supervisor will take it over with the employee quietly and privately. The supervisor will listen to the employee's story, suggest the better way of doing the job, and offer help so the mistake won't happen again. Before closing the discussion, the supervisor should try to find something good to say about other parts of the employee's work. Some praise and appreciation, along with instruction, is more likely to encourage an employee to improve in those areas where he is weakest.

16. A good title that would show the meaning of the above passage would be
    A. How to Correct Employee Errors
    B. How to Praise Employees
    C. Mistakes are Preventable
    D. The Weak Employee

17. According to the above passage, the work of an employee who has made a mistake is more likely to improve if the supervisor
    A. avoids criticizing him
    B. gives him a chance to suggest a better way of doing the work
    C. listens to the employee's excuses to see if he is right
    D. praises good work at the same time he corrects the mistake

18. According to the above passage, when a supervisor needs to correct an employee's mistake, it is important that he
    A. allow some time to go by after the mistake is made
    B. do so when other employee are not present
    C. show his influence with his tone of voice
    D. tell other employee to avoid the same mistake

Questions 19-23.

DIRECTIONS: Questions 19 through 23 are to be answered SOLELY on the basis of the following passage.

In studying the relationships of people to the organizational structure, it is absolutely necessary to identify and recognize the informal organizational structure. These relationships are necessary when coordination of a plan is attempted. They may be with *the boss*, line supervisors, staff personnel, or other representatives of the formal organization's hierarchy, and they may include the *liaison men* who serve as the leaders of the informal organization. An acquaintanceship with the people serving in these roles in the organization, and its formal counterpart, permits a supervisor to recognize sensitive areas in which it is simple to get conflict reaction. Avoidance of such areas, plus conscious efforts to inform other people of his own objectives for various plans, will usually enlist their aid and support. Planning *without* people can lead to disaster because the individuals who must act together to make any plan a success are more important than the plans themselves.

19. Of the following titles, the one that MOST clearly describes the above passage is
    A. Coordination of a Function
    B. Avoidance of Conflict
    C. Planning With People
    D. Planning Objectives

20. According to the above passage, attempts at coordinating plans may fail unless
    A. the plan's objectives are clearly set forth
    B. conflict between groups is resolved
    C. the plans themselves are worthwhile
    D. informal relationships are recognized

21. According to the above passage, conflict
    A. may, in some cases, be desirable to secure results
    B. produces more heat than light
    C. should be avoided at all costs
    D. possibilities can be predicted by a sensitive supervisor

22. The above passage implies that
    A. informal relationships are more important than formal structure
    B. the weakness of a formal structure depends upon informal relationships
    C. liaison men are the key people to consult when taking formal and informal structures into account
    D. individuals in a group are at least as important as the plans for the group

23. The above passage suggests that
    A. some planning can be disastrous
    B. certain people in sensitive areas should be avoided
    C. the supervisor should discourage acquaintanceships in the organization
    D. organizational relationships should be consciously limited

Questions 24-25.

DIRECTIONS: Questions 24 and 25 are to be answered SOLELY on the basis of the following passage.

Good personnel relations of an organization depend upon mutual confidence, trust, and good will. The basis of confidence is understanding. Most troubles start with people who do not understand each other. When the organization's intentions or motives are misunderstood, or when reasons for actions, practices, or policies are misconstrued, complete cooperation from individuals is not forthcoming. If management expects full cooperation from employees, it has a responsibility of sharing with them the information which is the foundation of proper understanding, confidence, and trust. Personnel management has long since outgrown the days when it was the vogue to *treat them rough and tell them nothing.* Up-to-date personnel management provides all possible information about the activities, aims, and purposes of the organization. It seems altogether creditable that a desire should exist among employees for such information which the best-intentioned executive might think would not interest them and which the worst-intentioned would think was none of their business.

24. The above passage implies that one of the causes of the difficulty which an organization might have with its personnel relations is that its employees
    A. have not expressed interest in the activities, aims, and purposes of the organization
    B. do not believe in the good faith of the organization
    C. have not been able to give full cooperation to the organization
    D. do not recommend improvements in the practices and policies of the organization

25. According to the above passage, in order for an organization to have good personnel relations, it is NOT essential that
    A. employees have confidence in the organization
    B. the purposes of the organization be understood by the employees
    C. employees have a desire for information about the organization
    D. information about the organization be communicated to employees

KEY (CORRECT ANSWERS)

1.	D		11.	D
2.	C		12.	A
3.	D		13.	A
4.	B		14.	C
5.	A		15.	D
6.	A		16.	A
7.	C		17.	D
8.	C		18.	B
9.	A		19.	C
10.	B		20.	D

21.	D
22.	D
23.	A
24.	B
25.	C

TEST 2

DIRECTIONS: Each question or incomplete statement is followed by several suggested answers or completions. Select the one that BEST answers the question or completes the statement. *PRINT THE LETTER OF THE CORRECT ANSWER IN THE SPACE AT THE RIGHT.*

Questions 1-8.

DIRECTIONS: Questions 1 through 8 are to be answered SOLELY on the basis of the following passage.

Important figures in education and in public affairs have recommended development of a private organization sponsored in part by various private foundations which would offer installment payment plans to full-time matriculated students in accredited colleges and universities in the United States and Canada. Contracts would be drawn to cover either tuition and fees, or tuition, fees, room and board in college facilities, from one year up to and including six years. A special charge, which would vary with the length of the contract, would be added to the gross repayable amount. This would be in addition to interest at a rate which would vary with the income of the parents. There would be a 3% annual interest charge for families with total income, before income taxes, of $50,000 or less. The rate would increase by 1/10 of 1% for every $1,000 of additional net income in excess of $50,000 up to a maximum of 10% interest. Contracts would carry an insurance provision on the life of the parent or guardian who signs the contract; all contracts must have the signature of a parent or guardian. Payment would be scheduled in equal monthly installments.

1. Which of the following students would be eligible for the payment plan described in the above passage? A
   A. matriculated student taking six semester hours toward a graduate degree
   B. matriculated student taking seventeen semester hours toward an undergraduate degree
   C. graduate matriculated at the University of Mexico taking eighteen semester hours toward a graduate degree
   D. student taking eighteen semester hours in a special pre-matriculation program

1.____

2. According to the above passage, the organization described would be sponsored in part by
   A. private foundations   B. colleges and universities
   C. persons in the field of education   D. persons in public life

2.____

3. Which of the following expenses could NOT be covered by a contract with the organization described in the above passage?
   A. Tuition amounting to $20,000 per year
   B. Registration and laboratory fees
   C. Meals at restaurants near the college
   D. Rent for an apartment in a college dormitory

3.____

123

4. The total amount to be paid would include ONLY the
    A. principal
    B. principal and interest
    C. principal, interest, and special charge
    D. principal, interest, special charge, and fee

5. The contract would carry insurance on the
    A. life of the student
    B. life of the student's parents
    C. income of the parents of the student
    D. life of the parent who signed the contract

6. The interest rate for an annual loan of $25,000 from the organization described in the above passage for a student whose family's net income was $55,000 should be
    A. 3%   B. 3.5%   C. 4%   D. 4.5%

7. The interest rate for an annual loan of $35,000 from the organization described in the above passage for a student whose family's net income was $100,000 should be
    A. 5%   B. 8%   C. 9%   D. 10%

8. John Lee has submitted an application for the installment payment plan described in the above passage. John's mother and father have a store which grossed $500,000 last year, but the income which the family received from the store was $90,000 before taxes. They also had $5,000 income from stock dividends. They paid $10,000 in income taxes.
    The amount of income upon which the interest should be based is
    A. $85,000   B. $90,000   C. $95,000   D. $105,000

Questions 9-13.

DIRECTIONS: Questions 9 through 13 are to be answered SOLELY on the basis of the following passage.

Since the organization chart is pictorial in nature, there is a tendency for it to be drawn in an artistically balanced and appealing fashion, regardless of the realities of actual organizational structure. In addition to being subject to this distortion, there is the difficulty of communicating in any organization chart the relative importance or the relative size of various component parts of an organizational structure. Furthermore, because of the need for simplicity of design, an organization chart can never indicate the full extent of the interrelationships among the component parts of an organization.

These interrelationships are often just as vital as the specifications which an organization chart endeavors to indicate. Yet, if an organization chart were to be drawn with all the wide variety of criss-crossing communication and cooperation networks existent within a typical organization, the chart would probably be much more confusing than informative. It is also obvious that no organization chart as such can prove or disprove that the organizational structure it represents is effective in realizing the objectives of the organization. At best, an organization chart can only illustrate some of the various factors to be taken into consideration in understanding, devising, or altering organizational arrangements.

9. According to the above passage, an organization chart can be expected to portray the
    A. structure of the organization along somewhat ideal lines
    B. relative size of the organizational units quite accurately
    C. channels of information distribution within the organization graphically
    D. extent of the obligation of each unit to meet the organizational objectives

9.____

10. According to the above passage, those aspects of internal functioning which are NOT shown on an organization chart
    A. can be considered to have little practical application in the operations of the organization
    B. might well be considered to be as important as the structural relationships which a chart does present
    C. could be the cause of considerable confusion in the operations of an organization which is quite large
    D. would be most likely to provide the information needed to determine the overall effectiveness of an organization

10.____

11. In the above passage, the one of the following conditions which is NOT implied as being a defect of an organization chart is that an organization chart may
    A. present a picture of the organizational structure which is different from the structure that actually exists
    B. fail to indicate the comparative size of various organizational units
    C. be limited in its ability to convey some of the meaningful aspects of organizational relationships
    D. become less useful over a period of time during which the organizational facts which it illustrated have changed

11.____

12. The one of the following which is the MOST suitable title for the above passage is
    A. The Design and Construction of an Organization Chart
    B. The Informal Aspects of an Organization Chart
    C. The Inherent Deficiencies of an Organization Chart
    D. The Utilization of a Typical Organization Chart

12.____

13. It can be inferred from the above passage that the function of an organization chart is to
    A. contribute to the comprehension of the organization form and arrangements
    B. establish the capabilities of the organization to operate effectively
    C. provide a balanced picture of the operations of the organization
    D. eliminate the need for complexity in the organization's structure

13.____

Questions 14-16.

DIRECTIONS: Questions 14 through 16 are to be answered SOLELY on the basis of the following passage.

In dealing with visitors to the school office, the school secretary must use initiative, tact, and good judgment. All visitors should be greeted promptly and courteously. The nature of their business should be determined quickly and handled expeditiously. Frequently, the secretary should be able to handle requests, deliveries, or passes herself. Her judgment should determine when a visitor should see members of the staff or the principal. Serious problems or doubtful cases should be referred to a supervisor.

14. In general, visitors should be handled by the 14.____
    A. school secretary B. principal
    C. appropriate supervisor D. person who is free

15. It is wise to obtain the following information from visitors: 15.____
    A. Name B. Nature of business
    C. Address D. Problems they have

16. All visitors who wish to see members of the staff should 16.____
    A. be permitted to do so B. produce identification
    C. do so for valid reasons only D. be processed by a supervisor

Questions 17-19.

DIRECTIONS: Questions 17 through 19 are to be answered SOLELY on the basis of the following passage.

Information regarding payroll status, salary differentials, promotional salary increments, deductions, and pension payments should be given to all members of the staff who have questions regarding these items. On occasion, if the secretary is uncertain regarding the information, the staff member should be referred to the principal or the appropriate agency. No question by a staff member regarding payroll status should be brushed aside as immaterial or irrelevant. The school secretary must always try to handle the question or pass it on to the person who can handle it.

17. If a teacher is dissatisfied with information regarding her salary status, as given 17.____
by the school secretary, the matter should be
    A. dropped
    B. passed on to the principal
    C. passed on by the secretary to proper agency or the principal
    D. made a basis for grievance procedures

18. The following is an adequate summary of the above passage: 18.____
    A. The secretary must handle all payroll matters
    B. The secretary must handle all payroll matter or know who can handle them
    C. The secretary or the principal must handle all payroll matters
    D. Payroll matter too difficult to handle must be followed up until they are solved

19. The above passage implies that
    A. many teachers ask immaterial questions regarding payroll status
    B. few teachers ask irrelevant pension questions
    C. no teachers ask immaterial salary questions
    D. no question regarding salary should be considered irrelevant

19.____

Questions 20-22.

DIRECTIONS: Questions 20 through 22 are to be answered SOLELY on the basis of the following passage.

The necessity for good speech on the part of the school secretary cannot be overstated. The school secretary must deal with the general public, the pupils, the members of the staff, and the school supervisors. In every situation which involves the general public, the secretary serves as a representative of the school. In dealing with pupils, the secretary's speech must serve as a model from which students may guide themselves. Slang, colloquialisms, malapropisms, and local dialects must be avoided.

20. The above passage implies that the speech pattern of the secretary must be
    A. perfect
    B. very good
    C. average
    D. on a level with that of the pupils

20.____

21. The last sentence indicates that slang
    A. is acceptable
    B. occurs in all speech
    C. might be used occasionally
    D. should be shunned

21.____

22. The above passage implies that the speech of pupils
    A. may be influenced
    B. does not change readily
    C. is generally good
    D. is generally poor

22.____

Questions 23-25.

DIRECTIONS: Questions 23 through 25 are to be answered SOLELY on the basis of the following passage.

The school secretary who is engaged in the task of filing records and correspondence should follow a general set of rules. Items which are filed should be available to other secretaries or to supervisors quickly and easily by means of the application of a modicum of common sense and good judgment. Items which, by their nature, may be difficult to find should be cross-indexed. Folders and drawers should be neatly and accurately labeled. There should never be a large accumulation of papers which have not been filed.

23. A good general rule to follow in filing is that materials should be
    A. placed in folders quickly
    B. neatly stored
    C. readily available
    D. cross-indexed

23.____

24. Items that are filed should be available to
    A. the secretary charged with the task of filing
    B. secretaries and supervisors
    C. school personnel
    D. the principal

25. A modicum of common sense means _____ common sense.
    A. an average amount of   B. a great deal of
    C. a little   D. no

KEY (CORRECT ANSWERS)

1.	B	11.	D
2.	A	12.	C
3.	C	13.	A
4.	C	14.	A
5.	D	15.	B
6.	B	16.	C
7.	B	17.	C
8.	C	18.	B
9.	A	19.	D
10.	B	20.	B

21. D
22. A
23. C
24. B
25. C

TEST 3

DIRECTIONS: Each question or incomplete statement is followed by several suggested answers or completions. Select the one that BEST answers the question or completes the statement. *PRINT THE LETTER OF THE CORRECT ANSWER IN THE SPACE AT THE RIGHT.*

Questions 1-4.

DIRECTIONS: Questions 1 through 4 are to be answered SOLELY on the basis of the following passage.

The proposition that administrative activity is essentially the same in all organizations appears to underlie some of the practices in the administration of private higher education. Although the practice is unusual in public education, there are numerous instances of industrial, governmental, or military administrators being assigned to private institutions of higher education and, to a lesser extent, of college and university presidents assuming administrative positions in other types of organizations. To test this theory that administrators are interchangeable, there is a need for systematic observation and classification. The myth that an educational administrator must first have experience in the teaching profession is firmly rooted in a long tradition that has historical prestige. The myth is bound up in the expectations of the public and personnel surrounding the administrator. Since administrative success depends significantly on how well an administrator meets the expectations others have of him, the myth may be more powerful than the special experience in helping the administrator attain organizational and educational objectives. Educational administrators who have risen through the teaching profession have often expressed nostalgia for the life of a teacher or scholar, but there is no evidence that this nostalgia contributes to administrative success.

1. Which of the following statements as completed is MOST consistent with the above passage?
   The greatest number of administrators has moved from
   A. industry and the military to government and universities
   B. government and universities to industry and the military
   C. government, the armed forces, and industry to colleges and universities
   D. colleges and universities to government, the armed forces, and industry

2. Of the following, the MOST reasonable inference from the above passage is that a specific area requiring further research is the
   A. place of myth in the tradition and history of the educational profession
   B. relative effectiveness of educational administrators from inside and outside the teaching profession
   C. performance of administrators in the administration of public colleges
   D. degree of reality behind the nostalgia for scholarly pursuits often expressed by educational administrators

1.____

2.____

129

3. According to the above passage, the value to an educational administrator of experience in the teaching profession
   A. lies in the first-hand knowledge he has acquired of immediate educational problems
   B. may lie in the belief of his colleagues, subordinates, and the public that such experience is necessary
   C. has been supported by evidence that the experience contributes to administrative success in educational fields
   D. would be greater if the administrator were able to free himself from nostalgia for his former duties

4. Of the following, the MOST suitable title for the above passage is
   A. Educational Administration, Its Problems
   B. The Experience Needed For Educational Administration
   C. Administration in Higher Education
   D. Evaluating Administrative Experience

Questions 5-6.

DIRECTIONS: Questions 5 and 6 are to be answered SOLELY on the basis of the following passage.

Management by objectives (MBO) may be defined as the process by which the superior and the subordinate managers of an organization jointly define its common goals, define each individual's major areas of responsibility in terms of the results expected of him and use these measure as guides for operating the unit and assessing the contribution of each of its members.

The MBO approach requires that after organizational goals are established and communicated, targets must be set for each individual position which are congruent with organizational goals. Periodic performance reviews and a final review using the objectives set as criteria are also basic to this approach.

Recent studies have shown that MBO programs are influenced by attitudes and perceptions of the boss, the company, the reward-punishment system, and the program itself. In addition, the manner in which the MBO program is carried out can influence the success of the program. A study done in the late sixties indicates that the best results are obtained when the manager sets goals which deal with significant problem areas in the organizational unit, or with the subordinate's personal deficiencies. These goals must be clear with regard to what is expected of the subordinate. The frequency of feedback is also important in the success of a management-by-objectives program. Generally, the greater the amount of feedback, the more successful the MBO program.

5. According to the above passage, the expected output for individual employees should be determined
   A. after a number of reviews of work performance
   B. after common organizational goals are defined
   C. before common organizational goals are defined
   D. on the basis of an employee's personal qualities

6. According to the above passage, the management-by-objectives approach requires
   A. less feedback than other types of management programs
   B. little review of on-the-job performance after the initial setting of goals
   C. general conformance between individual goals and organizational goals
   D. the setting of goals which deal with minor problem areas in the organization

Questions 7-10.

DIRECTIONS: Questions 7 through 10 are to be answered SOLELY on the basis of the following passage.

Management, which is the function of executive leadership, has as its principal phases the planning, organizing, and controlling of the activities of subordinate groups in the accomplishment of organizational objectives. Planning specifies the kind and extent of the factors, forces, and effects, and the relationships among them, that will be required for satisfactory accomplishment. The nature of the objectives and their requirements must be known before determinations can be made as to what must be done, how it must be done and why, where actions should take place, who should be responsible, and similar programs pertaining to the formulation of a plan. Organizing, which creates the conditions that must be present before the execution of the plan can be undertaken successfully, cannot be done intelligently without knowledge of the organizational objectives. Control, which has to do with the constraint and regulation of activities entering into the execution of the plan, must be exercised in accordance with the characteristics and requirements of the activities demanded by the plan.

7. The one of the following which is the MOST suitable title for the above passage is
   A. The Nature of Successful Organization
   B. The Planning of Management Functions
   C. The Importance of Organizational Functions
   D. The Principle Aspects of Management

8. It can be inferred from the above passage that the one of the following functions whose existence is essential to the existence of the other three is the
   A. regulation of the work needed to carry out a plan
   B. understanding of what the organization intends to accomplish
   C. securing of information of the factors necessary for accomplishment of objectives
   D. establishment of the conditions required for successful action

9. The one of the following which would NOT be included within any of the principal phases of the function of executive leadership as defined in the above passage is
   A. determination of manpower requirements
   B. procurement of required material
   C. establishment of organizational objectives
   D. scheduling of production

10. The conclusion which can MOST reasonably be drawn from the above passage is that the control phase of managing is most directly concerned with the 10.____
    A. influencing of policy determinations
    B. administering of suggestion systems
    C. acquisition of staff for the organization
    D. implementation of performance standards

Questions 11-12.

DIRECTIONS: Questions 11 and 12 are to be answered SOLELY on the basis of the following passage.

Under an open-and-above-board policy, it is to be expected that some supervisors will gloss over known shortcomings of subordinates rather than face the task of discussing team face-to-face. It is also to be expected that at least some employees whose job performance is below par will reject the supervisor's appraisal as biased and unfair. Be that as it may, these are inescapable aspects of any performance appraisal system in which human beings are involved. The supervisor who shies away from calling a spade a spade, as well as the employee with a chip on his shoulder, will each in his own way eventually be revealed in his true light—to the benefit of the organization as a whole.

11. The BEST of the following interpretations of the above passage is that 11.____
    A. the method of rating employee performance requires immediate revision to improve employee acceptance
    B. substandard performance ratings should be discussed with employees even if satisfactory ratings are not
    C. supervisors run the risk of being called unfair by the subordinates even though their appraisals are accurate
    D. any system of employee performance rating is satisfactory if used properly

12. The BEST of the following interpretations of the above passage is that 12.____
    A. supervisors generally are not open-and-above-board with their subordinates
    B. it is necessary for supervisors to tell employees objectively how they are performing
    C. employees complain when their supervisor does not keep them informed
    D. supervisors are afraid to tell subordinates their weaknesses

Questions 13-15.

DIRECTIONS: Questions 13 through 15 are to be answered SOLELY on the basis of the following passage.

During the last decade, a great deal of interest has been generated around the phenomenon of *organizational development,* or the process of developing human resources through conscious organization effort. Organizational development (OD) stresses improving interpersonal relationships and organizational skills, such as communication, to a much greater degree than individual training ever did. The kind of training that an organization should emphasize depends upon the present and future structure of the organization. If future organizations are to be unstable, shifting coalitions, then individual skills and abilities, particularly those emphasizing innovativeness, creativity, flexibility, and the latest technological knowledge, are crucial and individual training is most appropriate.

But if there is to be little change in organizational structure, then the main thrust of training should be group-oriented or organizational development. This approach seems better designed for overcoming hierarchical barriers, for developing a degree of interpersonal relationships which make communication along the chain of command possible, and for retaining a modicum of innovation and/or flexibility.

13. According to the above passage, group-oriented training is MOST useful in in
    A. developing a communications system that will facilitate understanding through the chain of command
    B. highly flexible and mobile organizations
    C. preventing the crossing of hierarchical barriers within an organization
    D. saving energy otherwise wasted on developing methods of dealing with rigid hierarchies

13._____

14. The one of the following conclusions which can be drawn MOST appropriately from the above passage is that
    A. behavioral research supports the use of organizational development training methods rather than individualized training
    B. it is easier to provide individualized training in specific skills than to set up sensitivity training programs
    C. organizational development eliminates innovative or flexible activity
    D. the nature of an organization greatly influences which training methods will be most effective

14._____

15. According to the above passage, the one of the following which is LEAST important for large-scale organizations geared to rapid and abrupt change is
    A. current technological information
    B. development of a high degree of interpersonal relationships
    C. development of individual skills and abilities
    D. emphasis on creativity

15._____

Questions 16-18.

DIRECTIONS: Questions 16 through 18 are to be answered SOLELY on the basis of the following passage.

The increase in the extent to which each individual is personally responsible to others is most noticeable in a large bureaucracy. No one person *decides* anything; each decision of any importance, is the product of an intricate process of brokerage involving individuals inside and outside the organization who feel some reason to be affected by the decision, or two have special knowledge to contribute to it. The more varied the organization's constituency, the more inside *veto-groups* will need to be taken into account. But even if no outside consultations were involved, sheer size would produce a complex process of decision. For a large organization is a deliberately created system of tensions into which each individual is expected to bring work-ways, viewpoints, and outside relationships markedly different from those of his colleagues. It is the administrator's task to draw from these disparate forces the elements of wise action from day to day, consistent with the purposes of the organization as a whole.

16. The above passage is essentially a description of decision-making as 16.____
    A. an organization process
    B. the key responsibility of the administrator
    C. the one best position among many
    D. a complex of individual decisions

17. Which one of the following statements BEST describes the responsibilities of an administrator? 17.____
    A. He modifies decisions and goals in accordance with pressures from within and outside the organization.
    B. He creates problem-solving mechanisms that rely on the varied interests of his staff and *veto-groups*.
    C. He makes determinations that will lead to attainment of his agency's objectives.
    D. He obtains agreement among varying viewpoints and interests

18. In the context of the operations of a central public personnel agency, a *veto-group* would LEAST likely consist of 18.____
    A. employee organizations
    B. professional personnel societies
    C. using agencies
    D. civil service newspapers

Questions 19-25.

DIRECTIONS: Questions 19 through 25 are to be answered SOLELY on the basis of the following passage, which is an extract from a report prepared for Department X, which outlines the procedure to be followed in the case of transfers of employees.

Every transfer, regardless of the reason therefore, requires completion of the record of transfer, Form DT411. To denote consent to the transfer, DT411 should contain the signatures of the transferee and the personnel officer(s) concerned, except that, in the case of an involuntary transfer, the signatures of the transferee's present and prospective supervisors shall be entered in Boxes 8A and 8B, respectively, since the transferee does not consent. Only a permanent employee may request a transfer; in such cases, the employee's attendance record shall be duly considered with regard to absences, latenesses, and accrued overtime balances. In the case of an inter-district transfer, the employee's attendance record must be included in Section 8A of the transfer request, Form DT410, by the personnel officer of the district from which the transfer is requested. The personnel officer of the district to which the employee requested transfer may refuse to accept accrued overtime balances in excess of ten days.

An employee on probation shall be eligible for transfer. If such employee is involuntarily transferred, he shall be credited for the period of time already served on probation. However, if such transfer is voluntary, the employee shall be required to serve the entire period of his probation in the new position. An employee who has occurred a disability which prevents him from performing his normal duties may be transferred during the period of such disability to other appropriate duties. A disability transfer requires the completion of either DT414 if the disability is job-connected, or Form DT415 if it is not a job-connected disability. In either case, the personnel officer of the district from which the transfer is made signs in Box 6A of the first two copies and the personnel officer of the district to which the transfer is made signs in Box 6B of the last two copies, or, in the case of an intra-district disability transfer, the personnel officer must sign in Box 6A of the first two copies and Box 6B of the last two copies.

19. When a personnel officer consents to an employee's request for transfer from his district, this procedure requires that the personnel officer sign Forms
    A. DT411
    B. DT410 and DT411
    C. DT411 and either Form DT414 or DT415
    D. DT410 and DT411, and either Form DT414 or DT415

20. With respect to the time record of an employee transferred against his wishes during his probationary period, this procedure requires that
    A. he serve the entire period of his probation in his present office
    B. he lose his accrued overtime balance
    C. his attendance record be considered with regard to absences and latenesses
    D. he be given credit for the period of time he has already served on probation

21. Assume you are a supervisor and an employee must be transferred into your office against his wishes.
    According to this procedure, the box you must sign on the record of transfer is
    A. 6A   B. 8A   C. 6B   D. 8B

22. Under this procedure, in the case of a disability transfer, when must Box 6A on Forms DT414 and DT415 be signed by the personnel officer of the district to which the transfer is being made?
    A. In all cases when either Form DT414 or Form DT415 is used
    B. In all cases when Form DT414 is used and only under certain circumstances when Form DT415 is used
    C. In all cases when Form DT415 is used and only under certain circumstances when Form DT414 is used
    D. Only under certain circumstances when either Form DT414 or Form DT415 is used

23. From the above passage, it may be inferred MOST correctly that the number of copies of Form DT414 is
    A. no more than 2
    B. at least 3
    C. at least 5
    D. more than the number of copies of Form DT415

24. A change in punctuation and capitalization only which would change one sentence into two and possibly contribute to somewhat greater ease of reading this report extract would be MOST appropriate in the
    A. 2nd sentence, 1st paragraph
    B. 3rd sentence, 1st paragraph
    C. next to the last sentence, 2nd paragraph
    D. 2nd sentence, 2nd paragraph

25. In the second paragraph, a word that is INCORRECTLY used is
    A. *shall* in the 1st sentence
    B. *voluntary* in the 3rd sentence
    C. *occurred* in the 4th sentence
    D. *intra-district* in the last sentence

KEY (CORRECT ANSWERS)

1.	C		11.	C
2.	B		12.	B
3.	B		13.	A
4.	B		14.	D
5.	B		15.	B
6.	C		16.	A
7.	D		17.	C
8.	B		18.	B
9.	C		19.	A
10.	D		20.	D

21.	D
22.	D
23.	B
24.	B
25.	C

CLERICAL ABILITIES TEST
EXAMINATION SECTION
TEST 1

DIRECTIONS: Each question or incomplete statement is followed by several suggested answers or completions. Select the one that BEST answers the question or completes the statement. *PRINT THE LETTER OF THE CORRECT ANSWER IN THE SPACE AT THE RIGHT.*

Questions 1-10.

DIRECTIONS: Questions 1 through 10 consist of lines of names, dates, and numbers. For each question, you are to choose the option (A, B, C, or D) in Column II which EXACTLY matches the information in Column I. *PRINT THE LETTER OF THE CORRECT ANSWER IN THE SPACE AT THE RIGHT.*

SAMPLE QUESTION

Column I
Schneider 11/16/75 581932

Column II
A. Schneider 11/16/75 518932
B. Schneider 11/16/75 581932
C. Schnieder 11/16/75 581932
D. Shnieder 11/16/75 518932

The correct answer is B. Only Option B shows the name, date, and number exactly as they are in Column I. Option A has a mistake in the number. Option C has a mistake in the name. Option D has a mistake in the name and in the number. Now answer Questions 1 through 10 in the same manner.

	Column I	Column II	
1.	Johnston 12/26/74 659251	A. Johnson 12/23/74 659251 B. Johston 12/26/74 659251 C. Johnston 12/26/74 695251 D. Johnston 12/26/74 659251	1.____
2.	Allison 1/26/75 9939256	A. Allison 1/26/75 9939256 B. Alisson 1/26/75 9939256 C. Allison 1/26/76 9399256 D. Allison 1/26/75 9993356	2.____
3.	Farrell 2/12/75 361251	A. Farell 2/21/75 361251 B. Farrell 2/12/75 361251 C. Farrell 2/21/75 361251 D. Farrell 2/12/75 361151	3.____

4. Guerrero 4/28/72 105689
   A. Guererro 4/28/72 105689
   B. Guerrero 4/28/72 105986
   C. Guerrero 4/28/72 105869
   D. Guerrero 4/28/72 105689

4.____

5. McDonnell 6/05/73 478215
   A. McDonnell 6/15/73 478215
   B. McDonnell 6/05/73 478215
   C. McDonnell 6/05/73 472815
   D. MacDonell 6/05/73 478215

5.____

6. Shepard 3/31/71 075421
   A. Sheperd 3/31/71 075421
   B. Shepard 3/13/71 075421
   C. Shepard 3/31/71 075421
   D. Shepard 3/13/71 075241

6.____

7. Russell 4/01/69 031429
   A. Russell 4/01/69 031429
   B. Russell 4/10/69 034129
   C. Russell 4/10/69 031429
   D. Russell 4/01/69 034129

7.____

8. Phillips 10/16/68 961042
   A. Philipps 10/16/68 961042
   B. Phillips 10/16/68 960142
   C. Phillips 10/16/68 961042
   D. Philipps 10/16/68 916042

8.____

9. Campbell 11/21/72 624856
   A. Campbell 11/21/72 624856
   B. Campbell 11/21/72 624586
   C. Campbell 11/21/72 624686
   D. Campbel 11/21/72 624856

9.____

10. Patterson 9/18/71 76199176
    A. Patterson 9/18/72 76191976
    B. Patterson 9/18/71 76199176
    C. Patterson 9/18/72 76199176
    D. Patterson 9/18/71 76919176

10.____

Questions 11-15.

DIRECTIONS: Questions 11 through 15 consist of groups of numbers and letters which you are to compare. For each question, you are to choose the option (A, B, C, or D) in Column I which EXACTLY matches the group of numbers and letters given in Column I.

SAMPLE QUESTION

Column I
B92466

Column II
A. B92644
B. B94266
C. A92466
D. B92466

The correct answer is D. Only Option D in Column II shows the group of numbers and letters EXACTLY as it appears in Column I. Now answer Questions 11 through 15 in the same manner.

Column I
11. 925AC5

Column II
A. 952CA5
B. 925AC5
C. 952AC5
D. 925CA6

11._____

12. Y006925

A. Y060925
B. Y006295
C. Y006529
D. Y006925

12._____

13. J236956

A. J236956
B. J326965
C. J239656
D. J932656

13._____

14. AB6952

A. AB6952
B. AB9625
C. AB9652
D. AB6925

14._____

15. X259361

A. X529361
B. X259631
C. X523961
D. X259361

15._____

Questions 16-25.

DIRECTIONS: Each of questions 16 through 25 consists of three lines of code letters and three lines of numbers. The numbers on each line should correspond with the code letters on the same line in accordance with the table below.

Code Letter	S	V	W	A	Q	M	X	E	G	K
Corresponding Number	0	1	2	3	4	5	5	7	8	9

On some of the lines, an error exists in the coding. Compare the letters and numbers in each question carefully. If you find an error or errors on:
    only one of the lines in the question, mark your answer A;
    any two lines in the question, mark your answer B;
    all three lines in the question, mark your answer C;
    none of the lines in the question, mark your answer D.

4 (#1)

SAMPLE QUESTION

WQGKSXG   2489068
XEKVQMA   6591453
KMAESXV   9527061

In the above sample, the first line is correct since each code letter listed has the correct corresponding number. On the second line, an error exists because code letter E should have the number 7 instead of the number 5. On the third line, an error exists because the code letter A should have the number 3 instead of the number 2. Since there are errors in two of the three lines, the correct answer is B. Now answer Questions 16 through 25 in the same manner.

16. SWQEKGA   0247983   16._____
     KEAVSXM   9731065
     SSAXGKQ   0036894

17. QAMKMVS   4259510   17._____
     MGGEASX   5897306
     KSWMKWS   9125920

18. WKXQWVE   2964217   18._____
     QKXXQVA   4966413
     AWMXGVS   3253810

19. GMMKASE   8559307   19._____
     AWVSKSW   3210902
     QAVSVGK   4310189

20. XGKQSMK   6894049   20._____
     QSVKEAS   4019730
     GSMXKMV   8057951

21. AEKMWSG   3195208   21._____
     MKQSVQK   5940149
     XGQAEVW   6843712

22. XGMKAVS   6858310   22._____
     SKMAWEQ   0953174
     GVMEQSA   8167403

23. VQSKAVE   1489317   23._____
     WQGKAEM   2489375
     MEGKAWQ   5689324

24. XMQVSKG   6541098   24._____
     QMEKEWS   4579720
     KMEVGKG   9571983

25. GKVAMEW   88912572   25.____
    AXMVKAE   3651937
    KWAGMAV   9238531

Questions 26-35.

DIRECTIONS: Each of Questions 26 through 35 consists of a column of figures. For each
             question, add the column of figures and choose the correct answer from the
             four choices given.

26. 5,665.43   26.____
     2,356.69
     6,447.24
     7,239.65

     A. 20,698.01   B. 21,709.01
     C. 21,718.01   D. 22,609.01

27. 817,209.55   27.____
     264,354.29
      82,368.76
     849,964.89

     A. 1,893.977.49   B. 1,989,988.39
     C. 2,009,077.39   D. 2,013,897.49

28. 156,366.89   28.____
     249,973.23
     823,229.49
      56,869.45

     A. 1,286,439.06   B. 1,287,521.06
     C. 1,297,539.06   D. 1,296,421.06

29.   23,422.15   29.____
     149,696.24
     238,377.53
      86,289.79
     505,533.63

     A. 989,229.34   B. 999,879.34
     C. 1,003,330.34   D. 1,023,329.34

6 (#1)

30. 2,468,926.70
     656,842.28
     49,723.15
     832,369.59

   A. 3,218,062.72
   C. 4,007,861.72
   B. 3,808,092.72
   D. 4,818,192.72

30.____

31. 524,201.52
     7,775,678.51
     8,345,299.63
     40,628,898.08
     31,374,670.07

   A. 88,646,647.81
   C. 88,648,647.91
   B. 88,646,747.91
   D. 88,648,747.81

31.____

32. 6,824,829.40
     682,482.94
     5,542,015.27
     775,678.51
     7,732,507.25

   A. 21,557,513.37
   C. 22,567,503.37
   B. 21,567,513.37
   D. 22,567,513.37

32.____

33. 22,109,405.58
     6,097,093.43
     5,050,073.99
     8,118,050.05
     4,313,980.82

   A. 45,688,593.87
   C. 45,689,593.87
   B. 45,688,603.87
   D. 45,689,603.87

33.____

34. 79,324,114.19
     99,848,129.74
     43,331,653.31
     41,610,207.14

   A. 264,114,104.38
   C. 265,114,114.38
   B. 264,114,114.38
   D. 265,214,104.38

34.____

35. 33,729,653.94
    5,959,342.58
    26,052,715.47
    4,452,669.52
    7,079,953.59

35.____

A. 76,374,334.10
C. 77,274,335.10

B. 76,375,334.10
D. 77,275,335.10

Questions 36-40.

DIRECTIONS: Each of Questions 36 through 40 consists of a single number in Column I and four options in Column II. For each question, you are to choose the option (A, B, C, or D) in Column II which EXACTLY matches the number in Column I.

SAMPLE QUESTION

Column I
5965121

Column II
A. 5956121
B. 5965121
C. 5966121
D. 5965211

The correct answer is B. Only Option B shows the number EXACTLY as it appears in Column I. Now answer Questions 36 through 40 in the same manner.

Column I
36. 9643242

Column II
A. 9643242
B. 9462342
C. 9642442
D. 9463242

36.____

37. 3572477

A. 3752477
B. 3725477
C. 3572477
D. 3574277

37.____

38. 5276101

A. 5267101
B. 5726011
C. 5271601
D. 5276101

38.____

39. 4469329

A. 4496329
B. 4469329
C. 4496239
D. 4469239

39.____

40. 2326308   A. 2236308
                B. 2233608
                C. 2326308
                D. 2323608

40._____

KEY (CORRECT ANSWERS)

1.	D	11.	B	21.	A	31.	D
2.	A	12.	D	22.	C	32.	A
3.	B	13.	A	23.	B	33.	B
4.	D	14.	A	24.	D	34.	A
5.	B	15.	D	25.	A	35.	C
6.	C	16.	D	26.	B	36.	A
7.	A	17.	C	27.	D	37.	C
8.	C	18.	A	28.	A	38.	D
9.	A	19.	D	29.	C	39.	B
10.	B	20.	B	30.	C	40.	C

TEST 2

DIRECTIONS: Each question or incomplete statement is followed by several suggested answers or completions. Select the one that BEST answers the question or completes the statement. *PRINT THE LETTER OF THE CORRECT ANSWER IN THE SPACE AT THE RIGHT.*

Questions 1-5.

DIRECTIONS: Each of Questions 1 through 5 consists of a name and a dollar amount. In each question, the name and dollar amount in Column II should be an EXACT copy of the name and dollar amount in Column I. If there is:
    a mistake only in the name, mark your answer A;
    a mistake only in the dollar amount, mark your answer B;
    a mistake in both the name and the dollar amount, mark your answer C;
    no mistake in either the name or the dollar amount, mark your answer D.

SAMPLE QUESTION

Column I	Column II
George Peterson	George Petersson
$125.50	$125.50

Compare the name and dollar amount in Column II with the name and dollar amount in Column I. The name *Petersson* in Column II is spelled *Peterson* in Column I. The amount is the same in both columns. Since there is a mistake only in the name, the answer to the sample question is A. Now answer Questions 1 through 5 in the same manner.

	Column I	Column II	
1.	Susanne Shultz $3440	Susanne Schultz $3440	1.____
2.	Anibal P. Contrucci $2121.61	Anibel P. Contrucci $2112.61	2.____
3.	Eugenio Mendoza $12.45	Eugenio Mendozza $12.45	3.____
4.	Maurice Gluckstadt $4297	Maurice Gluckstadt $4297	4.____
5.	John Pampellonne $4656.94	John Pammpellonne $4566.94	5.____

Questions 6-11.

DIRECTIONS: Each of Questions 6 through 11 consist of a set of names and addresses, which you are to compare. In each question, the name and addresses in Column II should be an EXACT copy of the name and address in Column I. If there is:
- a mistake only in the name, mark your answer A;
- a mistake only in the address, mark your answer B;
- a mistake in both the name and address, mark your answer C;
- no mistake in either the name or address, mark your answer D.

SAMPLE QUESTION

Column I
Michael Filbert
456 Reade Street
New York, N.Y. 10013

Column II
Michael Filbert
645 Reade Street
New York, N.Y. 10013

Since there is a mistake only in the address (the street number should be 456 instead of 645), the answer to the sample question is B. Now answer Questions 6 through 11 in the same manner.

	Column I	Column II	
6.	Hilda Goettelmann 55 Lenox Rd. Brooklyn, N.Y. 11226	Hilda Goettelman 55 Lenox Ave. Brooklyn, N.Y. 11226	6.____
7.	Arthur Sherman 2522 Batchelder St. Brooklyn, N.Y. 11235	Arthur Sharman 2522 Batcheder St. Brooklyn, N.Y. 11253	7.____
8.	Ralph Barnett 300 West 28 Street New York, New York 10001	Ralph Barnett 300 West 28 Street New York, New York 10001	8.____
9.	George Goodwin 135 Palmer Avenue Staten Island, New York 10302	George Godwin 135 Palmer Avenue Staten Island, New York 10302	9.____
10.	Alonso Ramirez 232 West 79 Street New York, N.Y. 10024	Alonso Ramirez 223 West 79 Street New York, N.Y. 10024	10.____
11.	Cynthia Graham 149-34 83 Street Howard Beach, N.Y. 11414	Cynthia Graham 149-35 83 Street Howard Beach, N.Y. 11414	11.____

Questions 12-20.

DIRECTIONS: Questions 12 through 20 are problems in subtraction. For each question do the subtraction and select your answer from the four choices given.

12. 232,921.85
    -179,587.68

    A. 52,433.17 B. 52,434.17
    C. 53,334.17 D. 53,343,17

    12.____

13. 5,531,876.29
    -3,897,158.36

    A. 1,634,717.93 B. 1,644,718.93
    C. 1,734,717.93 D. 1,7234,718.93

    13.____

14. 1,482,658.22
    -937,925.76

    A. 544,633.46 B. 544,732.46
    C. 545,632.46 D. 545,732.46

    14.____

15. 937,828.17
    -259,673.88

    A. 678,154.29 B. 679,154.29
    C. 688,155.39 D. 699,155.39

    15.____

16. 760,412.38
    -263,465.95

    A. 496,046.43 B. 496,946.43
    C. 496,956.43 D. 497,046.43

    16.____

17. 3,203,902.26
    -2,933,087.96

    A. 260,814.30 B. 269,824.30
    C. 270,814.30 D. 270,824.30

    17.____

18. 1,023,468.71
    -934,678.88

    A. 88,780.83 B. 88,789.83
    C. 88,880.83 D. 88,889.83

    18.____

19. 831,549.47
     -772,814.78

    A. 58,734.69   B. 58,834.69
    C. 59,735.69   D. 59,834.69

20. 6,306,181.74
     -3,617,376.99

    A. 2,687,904.99   B. 2,688,904.99
    C. 2,689,804.99   D. 2,799,905.99

Questions 21-30.

DIRECTIONS: Each of Questions 21 through 30 consists of three lines of code letters and three lines of numbers. The numbers on each line should correspond with the code letters on the same line in accordance with the table below.

Code Letter	J	U	B	T	Y	D	K	R	L	P
Corresponding Number	0	1	2	3	4	5	5	7	8	9

On some of the lines, an error exists in the coding. Compare the letters and numbers in each question carefully. If you find an error or errors on:
  only *one* of the lines in the question, mark your answer A;
  any *two* lines in the question, mark your answer B;
  all *three* lines in the question, mark your answer C;
  none of the lines in the question, mark your answer D.

SAMPLE QUESTION

    BJRPYUR   2079417
    DTBPYKJ   5328460
    YKLDBLT   4685283

In the above sample, the first line is correct since each code letter listed has the correct corresponding number. On the second line, an error exists because code letter P should have the number 9 instead of the number 8. The third line is correct since each code letter listed has the correct corresponding number. Since there is an error in *one* of the three lines, the correct answer is A. Now answer Questions 21 through 30 in the same manner.

21. BYPDTJL   2495308
     PLRDTJU   9815301
     DTJRYLK   5207486

22. RPBYRJK   7934706
     PKTYLBU   9624821
     KDLPJYR   6489047

5 (#2)

23.	TPYBUJR	3942107	23.____
	BYRKPTU	2476931	
	DUKPYDL	5169458	
24.	KBYDLPL	6345898	24.____
	BLRKBRU	2876261	
	JTULDYB	0318542	
25.	LDPYDKR	8594567	25.____
	BDKDRJL	2565708	
	BDRPLUJ	2679810	
26.	PLRLBPU	9858291	26.____
	LPYKRDJ	88936750	
	TDKPDTR	3569527	
27.	RKURPBY	7617924	27.____
	RYUKPTJ	7426930	
	RTKPTJD	7369305	
28.	DYKPBJT	5469203	28.____
	KLPJBTL	6890238	
	TKPLBJP	3698209	
29.	BTPRJYL	2397148	29.____
	LDKUTYR	8561347	
	YDBLRPJ	4528190	
30.	ULPBKYT	1892643	30.____
	KPDTRBJ	6953720	
	YLKJPTB	4860932	

KEY (CORRECT ANSWERS)

1.	A	11.	D	21.	B
2.	C	12.	C	22.	C
3.	A	13.	A	23.	D
4.	D	14.	B	24.	B
5.	C	15.	A	25.	A
6.	C	16.	B	26.	C
7.	C	17.	C	27.	A
8.	D	18.	B	28.	D
9.	A	19.	A	29.	B
10.	B	20.	B	30.	D

EXAMINATION SECTION
TEST 1

DIRECTIONS: Each question or incomplete statement is followed by several suggested answers or completions. Select the one that BEST answers the question or completes the statement. *PRINT THE LETTER OF THE CORRECT ANSWER IN THE SPACE AT THE RIGHT.*

Questions 1-5.

DIRECTIONS: Questions 1 through 5 consist of a sentence with an underlined word. For each question, select the choice that is CLOSEST in meaning to the underlined word.

EXAMPLE
This division reviews the fiscal reports of the agency.
In this sentence, the word *fiscal* means MOST NEARLY
    A. financial   B. critical   C. basic   D. personnel
The correct answer is A. "financial" because "financial" is closest to *fiscal*.
Therefore, the answer is A.

1. Every good office worker needs basic skills.
   The word *basic* in this sentence means
     A. fundamental   B. advanced   C. unusual   D. outstanding

2. He turned out to be a good instructor.
   The word *instructor* in this sentence means
     A. student   B. worker   C. typist   D. teacher

3. The quantity of work in the office was under study.
   In this sentence, the word *quantity* means
     A. amount   B. flow   C. supervision   D. type

4. The morning was spent examining the time records.
   In this sentence, the word *examining* means
     A. distributing   B. collecting   C. checking   D. filing

5. The candidate filled in the proper spaces on the form.
   In this sentence, the word *proper* means
     A. blank   B. appropriate   C. many   D. remaining

Questions 6-8.

DIRECTIONS: Questions 6 through 8 are to be answered SOLELY on the basis of the information contained in the following paragraph.

The increase in the number of public documents in the last two centuries closely matches the increase in population in the United States. The great number of public documents has become a serious threat to their usefulness. It is necessary to have programs which will reduce the number of public documents that are kept and which will, at the same time, assure keeping those that have value. Such programs need a great deal of thought to have any success.

6. According to the above paragraph, public documents may be less useful if 6.____
   A. the files are open to the public
   B. the record room is too small
   C. the copying machine is operated only during normal working hours
   D. too many records are being kept

7. According to the above paragraph, the growth of the population in the United 7.____
   States has matched the growth in the quantity of public documents for a period of MOST NEARLY _____ years.
   A. 50   B. 100   C. 200   D. 300

8. According to the above paragraph, the increased number of public documents 8.____
   has made it necessary to
   A. find out which public documents are worth keeping
   B. reduce the great number of public documents by decreasing government services
   C. eliminate the copying of all original public documents
   D. avoid all new copying devices

Questions 9-10.

DIRECTIONS: Questions 9 and 10 are to be answered SOLELY on the basis of the information contained in the following paragraph.

The work goals of an agency can best be reached if the employees understand and agree with these goals. One way to gain such understanding and agreement is for management to encourage and seriously consider suggestions from employees in the setting of agency goals.

9. On the basis of the above paragraph, the BEST way to achieve the work goals 9.____
   of an agency is to
   A. make certain that employees work as hard as possible
   B. study the organizational structure of the agency
   C. encourage employees to think seriously about the agency's problems
   D. stimulate employee understanding of the work goals

10. On the basis of the above paragraph, understanding and agreement with agency goals can be gained by 10._____
    A. allowing the employees to set agency goals
    B. reaching agency goals quickly
    C. legislative review of agency operations
    D. employee participation in setting agency goals

Questions 11-15.

DIRECTIONS: Each of Questions 11 through 15 consists of a group of four words. One word in each group is incorrectly spelled. For each question, print the letter of the correct answer in the space at the right that is the same as the letter next to the word which is INCORRECTLY spelled.

EXAMPLE

A. housing   B. certain   C. budgit   D. money

The word "budgit" is incorrectly spelled, because the correct spelling should be "budget." Therefore, the correct answer is C.

11. A. sentince   B. bulletin   C. notice   D. definition   11._____
12. A. appointment   B. exactly   C. typest   D. light   12._____
13. A. penalty   B. suparvise   C. consider   D. division   13._____
14. A. schedule   B. accurate   C. corect   D. simple   14._____
15. A. suggestion   B. installed   C. proper   D. agincy   15._____

Questions 16-20.

DIRECTIONS: Each Question 16 through 20 consists of a sentence which may be
    A. incorrect because of bad word usage, or
    B. incorrect because of bad punctuation, or
    C. incorrect because of bad spelling, or
    D. correct
    Read each sentence carefully. Then print in the space at the right A, B, C, or D, according to the answer you choose from the four choices listed above. There is only one type of error in each incorrect sentence. If there is no error, the sentence is correct.

EXAMPLE

George Washington was the father of his contry.
This sentence is incorrect because of bad spelling ("contry" instead of "country").
Therefore, the answer is C.

16. The assignment was completed in record time but the payroll for it has not yet been preparid. 16.____

17. The operator, on the other hand, is willing to learn me how to use the mimeograph. 17.____

18. She is the prettiest of the three sisters. 18.____

19. She doesn't know; if the mail has arrived. 19.____

20. The doorknob of the office door is broke. 20.____

21. A clerk can process a form in 15 minutes.
    How many forms can that clerk process in six hours?
       A. 10   B. 21   C. 24   D. 90 21.____

22. An office staff consists of 120 people. Sixty of them have been assigned to a special project. Of the remaining staff, 20 answer the mail, 10 handle phone calls, and the rest operate the office machines.
    The number of people operating the office machines is
       A. 20   B. 30   C. 40   D. 45 22.____

23. An office worker received 65 applications but on the first day had to return 26 of them for being incomplete and on the second day 25 had to be returned for being incomplete.
    How many applications did NOT have to be returned?
       A. 10   B. 12   C. 14   D. 16 23.____

24. An office worker answered 63 phone calls in one day and 91 phone calls the next day.
    For these 2 days, what was the average number of phone calls he answered per day?
       A. 77   B. 28   C. 82   D. 93 24.____

25. An office worker processed 12 vouchers of $8.50 each, 3 vouchers of $3.68 each, and 2 vouchers of $1.29 each.
    The TOTAL dollar amount of these vouchers is
       A. $116.04   B. $117.52   C. $118.62   D. $119.04 25.____

KEY (CORRECT ANSWERS)

1.	A	11.	A
2.	D	12.	C
3.	A	13.	B
4.	C	14.	C
5.	B	15.	D
6.	D	16.	C
7.	C	17.	A
8.	A	18.	D
9.	D	19.	B
10.	D	20.	A

21.	C
22.	B
23.	C
24.	A
25.	C

TEST 2

DIRECTIONS: Each question or incomplete statement is followed by several suggested answers or completions. Select the one that BEST answers the question or completes the statement. *PRINT THE LETTER OF THE CORRECT ANSWER IN THE SPACE AT THE RIGHT.*

Questions 1-5.

DIRECTIONS: Each Question from 1 through 5 lists four names. The names may not be exactly the same. Compare the names in each question and mark your answer
- A if all the names are different
- B if only two names are exactly the same
- C if only three names are exactly the same
- D if all four names are exactly the same

EXAMPLE
Jensen, Alfred E.
Jensen, Alfred E.
Jensan, Alfred E.
Jensen, Fred E.

Since the name Jensen, Alfred E. appears twice and is exactly the same in both places, the correct answer is B.

1. A. Riviera, Pedro S. B. Rivers, Pedro S. 1.____
   C. Riviera, Pedro N. D. Riviera, Juan S.

2. A. Guider, Albert B. Guidar, Albert 2.____
   C. Giuder, Alfred D. Guider, Albert

3. A. Blum, Rona B. Blum, Rona 3.____
   C. Blum, Rona D. Blum, Rona

4. A. Raugh, John B. Raugh, James 4.____
   C. Raughe, John D. Raugh, John

5. A. Katz, Stanley B. Katz, Stanley 5.____
   C. Katze, Stanley D. Katz, Stanley

Questions 6-10.

DIRECTIONS: Each Question 6 through 10 consists of numbers or letters in Columns I and II. For each question, compare each line of Column I with its corresponding line in Column II and decide how many lines in Column I are EXACTLY the same as their corresponding lines in Column II. In your answer space, mark your answer
- A if only ONE line in Column I is exactly the same as its corresponding line in Column II
- B if only TWO lines in Column I are exactly the same as their corresponding lines in Column II

2 (#2)

    C if only THREE lines in Column I are exactly the same as their corresponding lines in Column II
    D if all FOUR lines in Column I are exactly the same as their corresponding lines in Column II

EXAMPLE

Column I	Column II
1776	1776
1865	1865
1945	1945
1976	1978

Only three lines in Column I are exactly the same as their corresponding lines in Column II. Therefore, the correct answer is C.

	Column I	Column II	
6.	5653 8727 ZPSS 4952	5653 8728 ZPSS 9453	6.____
7.	PNJP NJPJ JNPN PNJP	PNPJ NJPJ JNPN PNPJ	7.____
8.	effe uWvw KpGj vmnv	eFfe uWvw KpGg vmnv	8.____
9.	5232 PfrC zssz rwwr	5232 PfrN zzss rwww	9.____
10.	czws cecc thrm lwtz	czws cece thrm lwtz	10.____

Questions 11-15.

DIRECTIONS: Questions 11 through 15 have lines of letters and numbers. Each letter should be matched with its number in accordance with the following table.

Letter	F	R	C	A	W	I	F	N	B	T
Matching Number	0	1	2	3	4	5	6	7	8	9

From the table you can determine that the letter F has the matching number 0 below it, the letter R has the matching number 1 below, etc.

For each question, compare each line of letters and numbers carefully to see if each letter has its correct matching number. If all the letters and numbers are matched correctly in

- *none* of the lines of the question, mark your answer A
- only *one* of the lines of the question, mark your answer B
- only *two* of the lines of the question, mark your answer C
- *all three* lines of the question, mark your answer D

EXAMPLE

WBCR	4826
TLBF	9580
ATNE	3986

There is a mistake in the first line because the letter R should have its matching number 1 instead of the number 6.

The second line is correct because each letter shown has the correct matching number.

There is a mistake in the third line because the letter N should have the matching number 7 instead of the number 8.

Since all the letters and numbers are correct matched in only one of the lines in the sample, the correct answer is B.

11. EBCT   6829   11._____
     ATWR   3961
     NLBW   7584

12. RNCT   1729   12._____
     LNCR   5728
     WAEB   5368

13. NTWB   7948   13._____
     RABL   1385
     TAEF   9360

14. LWRB   5417   14._____
     RLWN   1647
     CBWA   2843

15. ABTC   3792   15._____
     WCER   5261
     AWCN   3417

16. Your job often brings you into contact with the public.   16._____
    Of the following, it would be MOST desirable to explain the reasons for official actions to people coming into your office for assistance because such explanations
    A. help build greater understanding between the public and your agency
    B. help build greater self-confidence in city employees
    C. convince the public that nothing they do can upset a city employee
    D. show the public that city employees are intelligent

17. Assume that you strongly dislike one of your co-workers.
    You should FIRST
    A. discuss your feeling with the co-worker
    B. demand a transfer to another office
    C. suggest to your supervisor that the co-worker should be observed carefully
    D. try to figure out the reason for this dislike before you say or do anything

17.____

18. An office worker who has problems accepting authority is MOST likely to find it difficult to
    A. obey rules
    B. understand people
    C. assist other employees
    D. follow complex instructions

18.____

19. The employees in your office have taken a dislike to one person and frequently annoy her.
    Your supervisor should
    A. transfer this person to another unit at the first opportunity
    B. try to find out the reason for the staff's attitude before doing anything about it
    C. threaten to transfer the first person observed bothering this person
    D. ignore the situation

19.____

20. Assume that your supervisor has asked a worker in your office to get a copy of a report out of the files. You notice the worker as accidentally pulled out the wrong report.
    Of the following, the BEST way for you to handle this situation is to tell
    A. the worker about all the difficulties that will result from this error
    B. the worker about her mistake in a nice way
    C. the worker to ignore this error
    D. your supervisor that this worker needs more training in how to use the files

20.____

21. Filing systems differ in their efficiency.
    Which of the following is the BEST way to evaluate the efficiency of a filing system? A
    A. number of times used per day
    B. amount of material that is received each day for filing
    C. amount of time it takes to locate material
    D. type of locking system used

21.____

22. In planning ahead so that a sufficient amount of general office supplies is always available, it would be LEAST important to find out the
    A. current office supply needs of the staff
    B. amount of office supplies used last year
    C. days and times that office supplies can be ordered
    D. agency goals and objectives

22.____

23. The MAIN reason for establishing routine office work procedures is that once a routine is established
    A. work need not be checked for accuracy
    B. all steps in the routine will take an equal amount of time to perform
    C. each time the job is repeated, it will take less time to perform
    D. each step in the routine will not have to be planned all over again each time

24. When an office machine centrally located in an agency must be shut down for repairs, the bureaus and divisions using this machine should be informed of the
    A. expected length of time before the machine will be in operation again
    B. estimated cost of repairs
    C. efforts being made to avoid future repairs
    D. type of new equipment which the agency may buy in the future to replace the machine being repaired

25. If the day's work is properly scheduled, the MOST important result would be that the
    A. supervisor will not have to do much supervision
    B. employee will know what to do next
    C. employee will show greater initiative
    D. job will become routine

KEY (CORRECT ANSWERS)

1.	A	11.	C
2.	B	12.	B
3.	D	13.	D
4.	B	14.	B
5.	C	15.	A
6.	B	16.	A
7.	B	17.	D
8.	B	18.	A
9.	A	19.	B
10.	C	20.	B

21. C
22. D
23. D
24. A
25. B

EXAMINATION SECTION
TEST 1

DIRECTIONS: Each question or incomplete statement is followed by several suggested answers or completions. Select the one that BEST answers the question or completes the statement. *PRINT THE LETTER OF THE CORRECT ANSWER IN THE SPACE AT THE RIGHT.*

1. Assume that a few co-workers meet near your desk and talk about personal matters during working hours. Lately, this practice has interfered with your work. In order to stop this practice, the BEST action for you to take FIRST is to
   A. ask your supervisor to put a stop to the co-workers' meeting near your desk
   B. discontinue any friendship with this group
   C. ask your co-workers not to meet near your desk
   D. request that your desk be moved to another location

   1.____

2. In order to maintain office coverage during working hours, your supervisor has scheduled your lunch hour from 1 P.M. to 2 P.M. and your co-workers' lunch hour from 12 P.M. to 1 P.M. Lately, your co-worker has been returning late from lunch each day. As a result, you don't get a full hour since you must return to the office by 2 P.M.
   Of the following, the BEST action for you to take FIRST is to
   A. explain to your co-worker in a courteous manner that his lateness is interfering with your right to a full hour for lunch
   B. tell your co-worker that his lateness must stop or you will report him to your supervisor
   C. report your co-worker's lateness to your supervisor
   D. leave at 1 P.M. for lunch, whether your co-worker has returned or not

   2.____

3. Assume that, as an office worker, one of your jobs is to open mail sent to your unit, read the mail for content, and send the mail to the appropriate person to handle. You accidentally open and begin to read a letter marked *personal* to a co-worker.
   Of the following, the BEST action for you to take is to
   A. report to your supervisor that your co-worker is receiving personal mail at the office
   B. destroy the letter so that your co-worker does not know you saw it
   C. reseal the letter and place it on the co-worker's desk without saying anything
   D. bring the letter to your co-worker and explain that you opened it by accident

   3.____

4. Suppose that in evaluating your work, your supervisor gives you an overall rating, but states that you sometimes turn in work with careless errors.
The BEST action for you to take would be to
   A. ask a co-worker who is good at details to proofread your work
   B. take time to do a careful job, paying more attention to detail
   C. continue working as usual since occasional errors are to be expected
   D. ask your supervisor if she would mind correcting your errors

5. Assume that you are taking a telephone message for a co-worker who is not in the office at the time.
Of the following, the LEAST important item to write on the message is the
   A. length of the call   B. name of the caller
   C. time of the call   D. telephone number of the caller

Questions 6-13.

DIRECTIONS: Questions 6 through 13 each consist of a sentence which may or may not be an example of good English. The underlined parts of each sentence may be correct or incorrect. Examine each sentence, considering grammar, punctuation, spelling, and capitalization. If the English usage in the underlined parts of the sentence given is better than any of the changes in the underlined words suggested in Options B, C, or D, choose Option A. If the changes in the underlined words suggested in Options B, C, or D would make the sentence correct, choose the correct option. Do not choose an option that will change the meaning of the sentence.

6. This Fall, the office will be closed on Columbus Day, October 9th.
   A. Correct as is   B. fall...Columbus Day, October
   C. Fall...Columbus day, October   D. fall...Columbus Day, october

7. This manual discribes the duties performed by an Office Aide.
   A. Correct as is   B. describe the duties performed
   C. discribe the duties performed   D. describes the duties performed

8. There weren't no paper in the supply closet.
   A. Correct as is   B. weren't any
   C. wasn't any   D. wasn't no

9. The new employees left there office to attend a meeting.
   A. Correct as is   B. they're
   C. their   D. thier

10. The office worker started working at 8:30 a.m.
    A. Correct as is   B. 8:30 a.m.
    C. 8;30 a,m.   D. 8:30 am.

11. The alphabet, or A to Z sequence are the basis of most filing systems.
    A. Correct as is   B. alphabet, or A to Z sequence, is
    C. alphabet, or A to Z sequence are   D. alphabet, or A too Z sequence, is

12. Those file cabinets are five feet tall.　　　　　　　　　　　　　　　　　　　　　　　　12.____
    A. Correct as is　　　　　　　　　B. Them...feet
    C. Those...foot　　　　　　　　　 D. Them...foot

13. The Office Aide checked the register and finding the date of the meeting.　　13.____
    A. Correct as is　　　　　　　　　B. regaster and finding
    C. register and found　　　　　　 D. regaster and found

Questions 14-21.

DIRECTIONS: Each of Questions 14 through 21 has two lists of numbers. Each list contains three sets of numbers. Check each of the three sets in the list on the right to see if they are the same as the corresponding set in the list on the left. Mark your answers
　　A. if none of the sets in the right list are the same as those in the left list
　　B. if only one of the sets in the right list are the same as those in the left list
　　C. if only two of the sets in the right list are the same as those in the left list
　　D. if all three sets in the right list are the same as those in the left list

14.　7354183476　　　　7354983476　　　　　　　　　　　　　　　　　　　　　　　　14.____
　　 4474747744　　　　4474747774
　　 57914302311　　　 57914302311

15.　7143592185　　　　7143892185　　　　　　　　　　　　　　　　　　　　　　　　15.____
　　 8344517699　　　　8344518699
　　 9178531263　　　　9178531263

16.　2572114731　　　　257214731　　　　　　　　　　　　　　　　　　　　　　　　16.____
　　 8806835476　　　　8806835476
　　 8255831246　　　　8255831246

17.　331476853821　　　331476858621　　　　　　　　　　　　　　　　　　　　　　17.____
　　 6976658532996　　 6976655832996
　　 3766042113715　　 3766042113745

18.　8806663315　　　　8806663315　　　　　　　　　　　　　　　　　　　　　　　 18.____
　　 74477138449　　　 74477138449
　　 211756663666　　　211756663666

19.　990006966996　　　99000696996　　　　　　　　　　　　　　　　　　　　　　　19.____
　　 53022219743　　　 53022219843
　　 4171171117717　　 4171171177717

20.　24400222433004　　24400222433004　　　　　　　　　　　　　　　　　　　　　20.____
　　 5300030055000355　 5300030055500355
　　 20000075532002022　20000075532002022

4 (#1)

21. 6111666406600011116   61116664066001116   21.____
     7111300117001100733   7111300117001100733
     26666446664476518   26666446664476518

Questions 22-25.

DIRECTIONS: Each of Questions 22 through 25 has two lists of names and addresses. Each list contains three sets of names and addresses. Check each of the three sets in the list on the right to see if they are the same as the corresponding set in the list on the left. Mark your answers
  A. if none of the sets in the right list are the same as those in the left list
  B. if only one of the sets in the right list are the same as those in the left list
  C. if only two of the sets in the right list are the same as those in the left list
  D. if all three sets in the right list are the same as those in the left list

22. Mary T. Berlinger   Mary T. Berlinger   22.____
     2351 Hampton St.   2351 Hampton St.
     Monsey, N.Y. 20117   Monsey, N.Y. 20117

     Eduardo Benes   Eduardo Benes
     473 Kingston Avenue   473 Kingston Avenue
     Central Islip, N.Y. 11734   Central Islip, N.Y. 11734

     Alan Carrington Fuchs   Alan Carrington Fuchs
     17 Gnarled Hollow Road   17 Gnarled Hollow Road
     Los Angeles, CA 91635   Los Angeles, CA 91685

23. David John Jacobson   David John Jacobson   23.____
     178 35 St. Apt. 4C   178 53 St. Apt. 4C
     New York, N.Y. 00927   New York, N.Y. 00927

     Ann-Marie Calonella   Ann-Marie Calonella
     7243 South Ridge Blvd.   7243 South Ridge Blvd.
     Bakersfield, CA 96714   Bakersfield, CA 96714

     Pauline M. Thompson   Pauline M. Thomson
     872 Linden Ave.   872 Linden Ave.
     Houston, Texas 70321   Houston, Texas 70321

24. Chester LeRoy Masterton   Chester LeRoy Masterson   24.____
     152 Lacy Rd.   152 Lacy Rd.
     Kankakee, Ill. 54532   Kankakee, Ill. 54532

     William Maloney   William Maloney
     S. LaCrosse Pla.   S. LaCross Pla.
     Wausau, Wisconsin 52146   Wausau, Wisconsin 52146

5 (#1)

    Cynthia V. Barnes　　　　　　　　　　Cynthia V. Barnes
    16 Pines Rd.　　　　　　　　　　　　16 Pines Rd.
    Greenpoint, Miss. 20376　　　　　　Greenpoint, Miss. 20376

25. Marcel Jean Frontenac　　　　　　　Marcel Jean Frontenac　　　　　　　25._____
    6 Burton On The Water　　　　　　　6 Burton On The Water
    Calender, Me. 01471　　　　　　　　Calender, Me. 01471

    J. Scott Marsden　　　　　　　　　　J. Scott Marsden
    174 S. Tipton St.　　　　　　　　　　174 Tipton St.
    Cleveland, Ohio　　　　　　　　　　　Cleveland, Ohio

    Lawrence T. Haney　　　　　　　　　Lawrence T. Haney
    171 McDonough St.　　　　　　　　　171 McDonough St.
    Decatur, Ga. 31304　　　　　　　　　Decatur, Ga. 31304

KEY (CORRECT ANSWERS)

1.	C		11.	B
2.	A		12.	A
3.	D		13.	C
4.	B		14.	B
5.	A		15.	B
6.	B		16.	C
7.	D		17.	A
8.	C		18.	D
9.	C		19.	A
10.	B		20.	C

    21. C
    22. C
    23. B
    24. B
    25. C

TEST 2

DIRECTIONS: Each question or incomplete statement is followed by several suggested answers or completions. Select the one that BEST answers the question or completes the statement. *PRINT THE LETTER OF THE CORRECT ANSWER IN THE SPACE AT THE RIGHT.*

Questions 1-6.

DIRECTIONS: Questions 1 through 6 are to be answered SOLELY on the basis of the information contained in the following passage.

Duplicating is the process of making a number of identical copies of letters, document, etc. from an original. Some duplicating processes make copies directly from the original document. Other duplicating processes require the preparation of a special master, and copies are then made from the master. Four of the most common duplicating processes are stencil, fluid, offset, and xerox.

In the stencil process, the typewriter is used to cut the words into a master called a stencil. Drawings, charts, or graphs can be cut into the stencil using a stylus. As many as 3,500 good-quality copies can be reproduced from one stencil. Various grades of finished paper from inexpensive mimeograph to expensive bond can be used.

The fluid process is a good method of copying from 50 to 125 good-quality copies from a master, which is prepared with a special dye. The master is placed on the duplicator, and special paper with a hard finish is moistened and then passed through the duplicator. Some of the dye on the master is dissolved, creating an impression on the paper. The impression becomes lighter as more copies are made; and once the dye on the master is used up, a new master must be made.

The offset process is the most adaptable office duplicating process because this process can be used for making a few copies or many copies. Masters can be made on paper or plastic for a few hundred copies, or on metal plates for as many as 75,000 copies. By using a special technique called photo-offset, charts, photographs, illustrations, or graphs can be reproduced on the master plate. The offset process is capable of producing large quantities of fine, top-quality copies on all types of finished paper.

The xerox process reproduces an exact duplicate from an original. It is the fastest duplicating method because the original material is placed directly on the duplicator, eliminating the need to make a special master. Any kind of paper can be used. The xerox process is the most expensive duplicating process; however, it is the best method of reproducing small quantities of good-quality copies of reports, letters, official documents, memos, or contracts.

1. Of the following, the MOST efficient method of reproducing 5,000 copies of a graph is
   A. stencil
   B. fluid
   C. offset
   D. xerox

1.____

2. The offset process is the MOST adaptable office duplicating process because
   A. it is the quickest duplicating method
   B. it is the least expensive duplicating method
   C. it can produce a small number or large number of copies
   D. a softer master can be used over and over again

3. Which one of the following duplicating processes uses moistened paper?
   A. Stencil   B. Fluid   C. Offset   D. Xerox

4. The fluid process would be the BEST process to use for reproducing
   A. five copies of a school transcript
   B. fifty copies of a memo
   C. five hundred copies of a form letter
   D. five thousand copies of a chart

5. Which one of the following duplicating processes does NOT require a special master?
   A. Fluid   B. Xerox   C. Offset   D. Stencil

6. Xerox is NOT used for all duplicating jobs because
   A. it produces poor-quality copies
   B. the process is too expensive
   C. preparing the master is too time-consuming
   D. it cannot produce written reports

7. Assume a city agency has 775 office workers.
   If 2 out of 25 office workers were absent on a particular day, how many office workers reported to work on that day?
   A. 713   B. 744   C. 750   D. 773

Questions 8-11,

DIRECTIONS: In Questions 8 through 11, select the choice that is CLOSEST in meaning to the underlined word.

SAMPLE: This division reviews the fiscal reports of the agency.
In this sentence, the word *fiscal* means MOST NEARLY
A. financial   B. critical   C. basic   D. personnel

The correct answer is A, financial, because financial is closest to *fiscal*.

8. A central file eliminates the need to retain duplicate material.
   The word *retain* means MOST NEARLY
   A. keep   B. change   C. locate   D. process

9. Filing is a routine office task.
   Routine means MOST NEARLY
   A. proper   B. regular   C. simple   D. difficult

10. Sometimes a word, phrase, or sentence must be <u>deleted</u> to correct an error. 10.____
    Deleted means MOST NEARLY
    A. removed   B. added   C. expanded   D. improved

11. Your supervisor will <u>evaluate</u> your work. 11.____
    Evaluate means MOST NEARLY
    A. judge   B. list   C. assign   D. explain

Questions 12-19.

DIRECTIONS: The code table below shows 10 letters with matching numbers. For each Question 12 through 19, there are three sets of letters. Each set of letters is followed by a set of numbers which may or may not match their correct letter according to the code table. For each question, check all three sets of letters and numbers and mark your answer
   A. if no pairs are correctly matched
   B. if only one pair is correctly matched
   C. if only two pairs are correctly matched
   D. if all three pairs are correctly matched

CODE TABLE

T	M	V	D	S	P	R	G	B	H
1	2	3	4	5	6	7	8	9	0

SAMPLE QUESTION: TMVDSP   123456
                    RGBHTM   789011
                    DSPRGB   256789

In the sample question above, the first set of numbers correctly matches its set of letters. But the second and third pairs contain mistakes. In the second pair, M is incorrectly matched with number 1. According to the code table, letter M should be correctly matched with number 2. In the third pair, the letter D is incorrectly matched with number 2. According to the code table, letter D should be correctly matched with number 4. Since only one of the pairs is correctly matched, the answer to this sample question is B.

12. RSBMRM   759262   12.____
    GDSRVH   845730
    VDBRTM   349713

13. TGVSDR   183247   13.____
    SMHRDP   520647
    TRMHSR   172057

14. DSPRGM   456782   14.____
    MVDBHT   234902
    HPMDBT   062491

15. BVPTRD   936184   15._____
    GDPHMB   807029
    GMRHMV   827032

16. MGVRSH   283750   16._____
    TRDMBS   174295
    SPRMGV   567283

17. SGBSDM   489542   17._____
    MGHPTM   290612
    MPBMHT   269301

18. TDPBHM   146902   18._____
    VPBMRS   369275
    GDMBHM   842902

19. MVPTBV   236194   19._____
    PDRTMB   647128
    BGTMSM   981232

Questions 20-25.

DIRECTIONS: In each of Questions 20 through 25, the names of four people are given. For each question, choose as your answer the one of the four names given which should be filed FIRST according to the usual system of alphabetical filing of names, as described in the following paragraph.

In filing names, you must start with the last name. Names are filed in order of the first letter of the last name, then the second letter, etc. Therefore, BAILY would be filed before BROWN, which would be filed before COLT. A name with fewer letters of the same type comes first; i.e., Smith before Smithe. If the last names are the same, the names are filed alphabetically by the first name. If the first name is an initial, a name with an initial would come before a first name that starts with the same letter as the initial. Therefore, I. BROWN would come before IRA BROWN. Finally, if both last name and first name are the same, the name would be filed alphabetically by the middle name, one again an initial coming before a middle name which starts with the same letter as the initial. If there is no middle name at all, the name would come before those with middle initials or names.

SAMPLE QUESTION: A. Lester Daniels
                  B. William Dancer
                  C. Nathan Danzig
                  D. Dan Lester

The last names beginning with D are filed before the last name beginning with L. Since DANIELS, DANCER, and DANZIG all begin with the same three letters, you must look at the fourth letter of the last name to determine which name should be filed first. C comes before I or Z in the alphabet, so DANCER is filed before DANIELS or DANZIG. Therefore, the answer to the above sample question is B.

5 (#2)

20. A. Scott Biala B. Mary Byala 20.____
    C. Martin Baylor D. Francis Bauer

21. A. Howard J. Black B. Howard Black 21.____
    C. J. Howard Black D. John H. Black

22. A. Theodora Garth Kingston B. Theadore Barth Kingston 22.____
    C. Thomas Kingston D. Thomas T. Kingston

23. A. Paulette Mary Huerta B. Paul M. Huerta 23.____
    C. Paulette L. Huerta D. Peter A. Huerta

24. A. Martha Hunt Morgan B. Martin Hunt Morgan 24.____
    C. Mary H. Morgan D. Martine H. Morgan

25. A. James T. Meerschaum B. James M. Mershum 25.____
    C. James F. Mearshaum D. James N. Meshum

KEY (CORRECT ANSWERS)

1.	C		11.	A
2.	C		12.	B
3.	B		13.	B
4.	B		14.	C
5.	B		15.	A
6.	B		16.	D
7.	A		17.	A
8.	A		18.	D
9.	B		19.	A
10.	A		20.	D

21. B
22. B
23. B
24. A
25. C

TEST 3

DIRECTIONS: Each question or incomplete statement is followed by several suggested answers or completions. Select the one that BEST answers the question or completes the statement. *PRINT THE LETTER OF THE CORRECT ANSWER IN THE SPACE AT THE RIGHT.*

1. Which one of the following statements about proper telephone usage is NOT always correct?
   When answering the telephone, you should
   A. know whom you are speaking to
   B. give the caller your undivided attention
   C. identify yourself to the caller
   D. obtain the information the caller wishes before you do your other work

   1.____

2. Assume that, as a member of a worker's safety committee in your agency, you are responsible for encouraging other employees to follow correct safety practices. While you are working on your regular assignment, you observe an employee violating a safety rule.
   Of the following, the BEST action for you to take FIRST is to
   A. speak to the employee about safety practices and order him to stop violating the safety rule
   B. speak to the employee about safety practices and point out the safety rule he is violating
   C. bring the matter up in the next committee meeting
   D. report this violation of the safety rule to the employee's supervisor

   2.____

3. Assume that you have been temporarily assigned by your supervisor to do a job which you do not want to do.
   The BEST action for you to take is to
   A. discuss the job with your supervisor, explaining why you do not want to do it
   B. discuss the job with your supervisor and tell her that you will not do it
   C. ask a co-worker to take your place on this job
   D. do some other job that you like; your supervisor may give the job you do not like to someone else

   3.____

4. Assume that you keep the confidential personnel files of employees in your unit. A friend asks you to obtain some information from the file of one of your co-workers.
   The BEST action to take is to _____ to your friend.
   A. ask the co-worker if you can give the information
   B. ask your supervisor if you can give the information
   C. give the information
   D. refuse to give the information

   4.____

Questions 5-8.

DIRECTIONS: Questions 5 through 8 are to be answered SOLELY on the basis of the information contained in the following passage.

City government is committed to providing a safe and healthy work environment for all city employees. An effective agency safety program reduces accidents by educating employees about the types of careless acts which can cause accidents. Even in an office, accidents can happen. If each employee is aware of possible safety hazards, the number of accidents on the job can be reduced.

Careless use of office equipment can cause accidents and injuries. For example, file cabinet drawers which are filled with papers can be so heavy that the entire cabinet could tip over from the weight of one open drawer.

The bottom drawers of desks and file cabinets should never be left open since employees can easily trip over open drawers and injure themselves.

When reaching for objects on a high shelf, an employee should use a strong, sturdy object such as a stepstool to stand on. Makeshift platforms made out of books, papers, or boxes can easily collapse. Even chairs can slide out from under foot, causing serious injury.

Even at an employee's desk, safety hazards can occur. Frayed or cut wires should be repaired or replaced immediately. Computers which are not firmly anchored to the desk or table could fall, causing injury.

Smoking is one of the major causes of fires in the office. A lighted match or improperly extinguished cigarette thrown into a wastebasket filled with paper could cause a major fire with possible loss of life. Where smoking is permitted, ashtrays should be used. Smoking is particularly dangerous in offices were flammable chemicals are used.

5. The goal of an effective safety program is to
    A. reduce office accidents
    B. stop employees from smoking on the job
    C. encourage employees to continue their education
    D. eliminate high shelves in offices

6. Desks and file cabinets can become safety hazards when
    A. their drawers are left open
    B. they are used as wastebaskets
    C. they are makeshift
    D. they are not anchored securely to the floor

7. Smoking is especially hazardous when it occurs
    A. near exposed wires
    B. in a crowded office
    C. in an area where flammable chemicals are used
    D. where books and papers are stored

8. Accidents are likely to occur when
    A. employees' desks are cluttered with books and papers
    B. employees are not aware of safety hazards
    C. employees close desk drawers
    D. stepstools are used to reach high objects

9. Assume that part of your job as a worker in the accounting division of a city agency is to answer the telephone.
   When you first answer the telephone, it is LEAST important to tell the caller
   A. your title
   B. your name
   C. the name of your unit
   D. the name of your agency

10. Assume that you are assigned to work as a receptionist, and your duties are to answer phones, greet visitors, and do other general office work. You are busy with a routine job when several visitors approach your desk.
    The BEST action to take is to
    A. ask the visitors to have a seat and assist them after your work is completed
    B. tell the visitors that you are busy and they should return at a more convenient time
    C. stop working long enough to assist the visitors
    D. continue working and wait for the visitors to ask you for assistance

11. Assume that your supervisor has chosen you to take a special course during hours to learn a new payroll procedure. Although you know that you were chosen because of your good work record, a co-worker, who feels that he should have been chosen, has been telling everyone in your unit that the choice was unfair.
    Of the following, the BEST way to handle this situation FIRST is to
    A. suggest to the co-worker that everything in life is unfair
    B. contact your union representative in case your co-worker presents a formal grievance
    C. tell your supervisor about your co-worker's complaints and let her handle the situation
    D. tell the co-worker that you were chosen because of your superior work record

12. Assume that while you are working on an assignment which must be completed quickly, a supervisor from another unit asks you to obtain information for her.
    Of the following, the BEST way to respond to her request is to
    A. tell her to return in an hour since you are busy
    B. give her the names of some people in her own unit who could help her
    C. tell her you are busy and refer her to a co-worker
    D. tell her that you are busy and ask her if she could wait until you finish your assignment

13. A co-worker in your unit is often off from work because of illness. Your supervisor assigns the co-worker's work to you when she is not there. Lately, doing her work has interfered with your own job.
    The BEST action for you to take FIRST is to
    A. discuss the problem with your supervisor
    B. complete your own work before starting your co-worker's work
    C. ask other workers in your unit to assist you
    D. work late in order to get the jobs done

14. During the month of June, 40,587 people attended a city-owned swimming pool. 14.____
In July, 13,014 more people attended the swimming pool than the number that
had attended in June. In August, 39,655 people attended the swimming pool.
The TOTAL number of people who attended the swimming pool during the
months of June, July, and August was
   A. 80,242 B. 93,256 C. 133,843 D. 210,382

Questions 15-22.

DIRECTIONS: Questions 15 through 22 test how well you understand what you read. It will be necessary for you to read carefully because your answers to these questions must be based ONLY on the information in the following paragraphs.

The telephone directory is made up of two books. The first book consists of the introductory section and the alphabetical listing of names section. The second book is the classified directory (also known as the yellow pages). Many people who are familiar with one book do not realize how useful the other can be. The efficient office worker should become familiar with both books in order to make the best use of this important source of information.

The introductory section gives general instructions for finding numbers in the alphabetical listing and classified directory. This section also explains how to use the telephone company's many services, including the operator and information services, gives examples of charges for local and long-distance calls, and lists area codes for the entire country. In addition, this section provides a useful zip code map.

The alphabetical listing of names section lists the names, addresses, and telephone numbers of subscribers in an area. Guide names, or *telltales*, are on the top corner of each page. These guide names indicate the first and last name to be found on that page. *Telltales* help locate any particular name quickly. A cross-reference spelling is also given to help locate names which are spelled several different ways. City, state, and federal government agencies are listed under the major government heading. For example, an agency of the federal government would be listed under *United States Government*.

The classified directory, or yellow pages, is a separate book. In this section are advertising services, public transportation line maps, shopping guides, and listings of businesses arranged by the type of product or services they offer. This book is most useful when looking for the name or phone number of a business when all that is known is the type of product offered and the address, or when trying to locate a particular type of business in an area. Businesses listed in the classified directory can usually be found in the alphabetical listing of names section. When the name of the business is known, you will find the address or phone number more quickly in the alphabetical listing of names section.

15. The introductory section provides 15.____
   A. shopping guides   B. government listings
   C. business listings   D. information services

16. Advertising services would be found in the 16.____
   A. introductory section   B. alphabetical listing of names section\
   C. classified directory   D. information services

17. According to the information in the above passage for locating government agencies, the Information Office of the Department of Consumer Affairs of New York City government would be alphabetically listed FIRST under
    A. *I* for Information Offices
    B. *D* for Department of Consumer Affairs
    C. *N* for New York City
    D. *G* for government

18. When the name of a business is known, the QUICKEST way to find the phone number is to look in the
    A. classified directory
    B. introductory section
    C. alphabetical listing of name section
    D. advertising service section

19. The QUICKEST way to find the phone number of a business when the type of service a business offers and its address is known is to look in the
    A. classified directory
    B. alphabetical listing of names section
    C. introductory section
    D. information service

20. What is a *telltale*?
    A. An alphabetical listing
    B. A guide name
    C. A map
    D. A cross-reference listing

21. The BEST way to find a postal zip code is to look in the
    A. classified directory
    B. introductory section
    C. alphabetical listing of names section
    D. government heading

22. To help find names which have several different spellings, the telephone directory provides
    A. cross-reference spelling
    B. *telltales*
    C. spelling guides
    D. advertising services

23. Assume that your agency has been given $2,025 to purchase file cabinets. If each file cabinet costs $135, how many file cabinet can your agency purchase?
    A. 8   B. 10   C. 15   D. 16

24. Assume that your unit ordered 14 staplers at a total cost of $30.20 and each stapler cost the same.
    The cost of one stapler was MOST NEARLY
    A. $1.02   B. $1.61   C. $2.16   D. $2.26

25. Assume that you are responsible for counting and recording licensing fees collected by your department. On a particular day, your department collected in fees 40 checks in the amount of $6 each, 80 checks in the amount of $4 each, 45 twenty dollar bills, 30 ten dollar bills, 42 five dollar bills, and 186 one dollar bills.
The TOTAL amount in fees collected on that day was
   A. $1,406   B. $1,706   C. $2,156   D. $2,356

26. Assume that you are responsible for your agency's petty cash fund. During the month of February, you pay out 7 $2.00 subway fares and one taxi fare for $10.85. You pay out nothing else from the fund. At the end of February, you count the money left in the fund and find 3 one dollar bills, 4 quarters, 5 dimes, and 4 nickels.
The amount of money you had available in the petty cash fund at the BEGINNING of February was
   A. $4.70   B. $16.35   C. $24.85   D. $29.55

27. You overhear your supervisor criticize a co-worker for handling equipment in an unsafe way. You feel that the criticism may be unfair.
Of the following, it would be BEST for you to
   A. take your co-worker aside and tell her how you feel about your supervisor's comments
   B. interrupt the discussion and defend your co-worker to your supervisor
   C. continue working as if you had not overheard the discussion
   D. make a list of other workers who have violated safety rules and give it to your supervisor

28. Assume that you have been assigned to work on a long-term project with an employee who is known for being uncooperative.
In beginning to work with this employee, it would be LEAST desirable for you to
   A. understand why the person is uncooperative
   B. act in a calm manner rather than an emotional manner
   C. be appreciative of the co-worker's work
   D. report the co-worker's lack of cooperation to your supervisor

29. Assume that you are assigned to sell tickets at a city-owned ice skating rink. An adult ticket costs $4.50, and a children's ticket costs $2.25. At the end of a day, you find that you have sold 36 adult tickets and 80 children's tickets.
The TOTAL amount of money you collected for that day was
   A. $244.80   B. $318.00   C. $342.00   D. $348.00

30. If each office worker files 487 index cards in one hour, how many card can 26 office workers file in one hour?
   A. 10,662   B. 12,175   C. 12,662   D. 14,266

KEY (CORRECT ANSWERS)

1.	D	11.	C	21.	B
2.	B	12.	D	22.	A
3.	A	13.	A	23.	C
4.	D	14.	C	24.	C
5.	A	15.	D	25.	C
6.	A	16.	C	26.	D
7.	C	17.	C	27.	C
8.	B	18.	C	28.	D
9.	A	19.	A	29.	C
10.	C	20.	B	30.	C

PREPARING WRITTEN MATERIAL

PARAGRAPH REARRANGEMENT
COMMENTARY

The sentences that follow are in scrambled order. You are to rearrange them in proper order and indicate the letter choice containing the correct answer at the space at the right.

Each group of sentences in this section is actually a paragraph presented in scrambled order. Each sentence in the group has a place in that paragraph; no sentence is to be left out. You are to read each group of sentences and decide upon the best order in which to put the sentences so as to form a well-organized paragraph.

The questions in this section measure the ability to solve a problem when all the facts relevant to its solution are not given.

More specifically, certain positions of responsibility and authority require the employee to discover connection between events sometimes, apparently, unrelated. In order to do this, the employee will find it necessary to correctly infer that unspecified events have probably occurred or are likely to occur. This ability becomes especially important when action must be taken on incomplete information.

Accordingly, these questions require competitors to choose among several suggested alternatives, each of which presents a different sequential arrangement of the events. Competitors must choose the MOST logical of the suggested sequences.

In order to do so, they may be required to draw on general knowledge to infer missing concepts or events that are essential to sequencing the given events. Competitors should be careful to infer only what is essential to the sequence. The plausibility of the wrong alternatives will always require the inclusion of unlikely events or of additional chains of events which are NOT essential to sequencing the given events.

It's very important to remember that you are looking for the best of the four possible choices, and that the best choice of all may not even be one of the answers you're given to choose from.

There is no one right way to solve these problems. Many people have found it helpful to first write out the order of the sentences, as they would have arranged them, on their scrap paper before looking at the possible answers. If their optimum answer is there, this can save them some time. If it isn't, this method can still give insight into solving the problem. Others find it most helpful to just go through each of the possible choices, contrasting each as they go along. You should use whatever method feels comfortable and works for you.

While most of these types of questions are not that difficult, we've added a higher percentage of the difficult type, just to give you more practice. Usually there are only one or two questions on this section that contain such subtle distinctions that you're unable to answer confidently. And you then may find yourself stuck deciding between two possible choices, neither of which you're sure about.

EXAMINATION SECTION
TEST 1

DIRECTIONS: Each question or incomplete statement is followed by several suggested answers or completions. Select the one that BEST answers the question or completes the statement. *PRINT THE LETTER OF THE CORRECT ANSWER IN THE SPACE AT THE RIGHT.*

Questions 1-4.

DIRECTIONS: Questions 1 through 4 are to be answered on the basis of the following passage.

A State department which is interested in finding acceptable solutions to the operational problems of specific types of community self-help organizations recently sent two of its staff members to meet with one such organization. At that meeting, the leaders of the community organization voiced the need for increased activity planning input of a more detailed nature from the citizens regularly served by that organization. There followed a discussion of a number of information-gathering methods, including surveys by telephone, questionnaires mailed to the citizens' residences, in-person interviews with the citizens, and the placing of suggestion boxes in the organization's headquarters building. Concern was expressed by one of the leaders that the organization's funds be spent judiciously. The State department representatives present promised to investigate the possibility of a matching fund grant of money to the organization.

Later, the proposed survey was conducted using questionnaires completed by those citizens who visited the organization's headquarters. The results of the survey included the information that twice as many citizens wanted more educational activities scheduled than wanted more social activities scheduled, whereas one-half of those who wanted more educational activities scheduled were interested mainly in special job training.

1. A similar survey conducted by a State department employee involved special job training. That survey uncovered the information below. The following four sentences are to be rearranged to form the most effective and logical paragraph.
   Select the letter representing the BEST sequence for these sentences.
   I. The majority of those who are still in this group are ethnic minorities.
   II. The number of economically disadvantaged people who enjoyed their special job training is larger than the number of economically disadvantaged people who did not enjoy it.
   III. Thirty-five percent of all those who are economically disadvantaged are not ethnic minorities.
   IV. Eighty percent of those who have completed special job training in the past ten years are economically disadvantaged.
   The CORRECT answer is:
   A. IV, I, III, II   B. I, III, II, IV   C. IV, II, I, III   D. I, II, III, IV

   1.____

2. In the above reading passage, the word *judiciously* means MOST NEARLY
   A. legally   B. immediately   C. prudently   D. uniformly

   2.____

3. Based only on the information in the reading passage, which one of the following statements is MOST fully supported?
   A. The leaders of the community organization in question wanted to increase the quantity and quality of feedback about that organization's suggestion boxes.
   B. The number of citizens surveyed who wanted more educational activities scheduled and were mainly interested in special job training was the same as the number of citizens surveyed who wanted more social activities to be scheduled.
   C. At the meeting concerned, matching funds were promised to the community organization in question by the two State department representatives present.
   D. Telephone surveys generally yield more accurate information than do surveys conducted through the use of mailed questionnaires.

3.____

4. The following four sentences are to be rearranged to form the most effective and logical paragraph.
   Select the letter representing the BEST sequence for these sentences.
   I. Formal surveys of citizens within a community also convey to those citizens the interest of the community leadership in hearing the citizens' ideas about community improvement.
   II. Such surveys can provide needed input into the process of establishing specific community program goals.
   III. Formally conducted surveys of community residents often yield valuable information to the local area leaders responsible for community-based programs.
   IV. No community should formulate these goals without attempting to obtain the views of its citizenry.
   The CORRECT answer is:
   A. III, I, IV, II   B. I, III, II, IV   C. III, II, IV, I   D. IV, III, II, I

4.____

Questions 5-8.

DIRECTIONS: Questions 5 through 8 are to be answered on the basis of the following passage.

The Smith Paint Company, which currently employs 2,000 persons, has been in existence for 20 years. A new chemical plant, Futuron, was recently developed by an employee of that company. This paint was released for public use a month ago on a trial basis. The sales were phenomenal, and there is a great demand for more Futuron to be manufactured. The profits to be made by increased manufacturing and sale of Futuron could place the Smith Paint Company in a leading role in the paint industry.

The Smith Paint Company currently produces 2 million gallons of the more traditional paint per year. The Smith Paint Company's Board of Directors wishes to reduce its production of this traditional paint by 50%, and to produce 1 million gallons of Futuron per year.

The employees are quite concerned about this potential production change. A public nonprofit research group has been investigating the chemical make-up of Futuron. Initial research indicates that negative physical reactions may result from working closely with the chemicals necessary to manufacture Futuron. For this reason, most of the company employees do not want the proposed change in production to occur. The members of the Board of Directors, however, argue that the research results are too inconclusive to cause great concern. They say that the company would lose 25% to 50% of its potential profit if the large-scale manufacturing of Futuron is not initiated immediately.

5. Seventy-five percent of the Smith Paint Company's current employees were hired during its first 10 years of operation. Fifteen percent were hired in the past five years. During the five-year interval between the first ten years and the most recent five years, 40 persons were hired per year.
What percentage of its total employees were hired during the Smith Paint Company's first 13 years of operation?
   A. 75%   B. 81%   C. 85%   D. 90%

6. Assume that the total possible profit the Smith Paint Company could make during its first year of manufacturing the proposed amount of Futuron would be $1.00 per gallon. The purchase of new machinery would reduce this first-year profit by 50%. The anticipated delay, during the first production year, in establishing large-scale manufacturing facilities would reduce the total possible profit by an additional 25%.
Given this information, what would be the actual profit made from the first year of manufacturing Futuron?
   A. $250,000   B. $375,000   C. $500,000   D. $750,000

7. In the reading passage, the word *inconclusive* means MOST NEARLY
   A. ineluctable   B. incorrect
   C. unreasonable   D. indeterminate

8. Based on the information in the reading passage, which of the following statements represents the MOST accurate conclusion?
   A. The proposed reduction in the production of its traditional paint would not financially injure the Smith Paint Company.
   B. A greater proportion of the Smith Paint Company's employees are in favor of the proposed increase in Futuron production than are opposed to it.
   C. The increased Futuron production proposed by the Smith Paint Company's Board of Directors would cause that company's employees considerable health damage.
   D. Positive public response to the sale of Futuron suggests that considerable profit can be made by increasing the manufacturing and sale of Futuron.

KEY (CORRECT ANSWERS)

1. A 5. B
2. C 6. A
3. B 7. D
4. C 8. D

SOLUTIONS TO PROBLEMS

1. For the following reasons, Choice A is correct and the other three choices are incorrect.

   a. Both Choice B and Choice D begin with Sentence I, which states, *The majority of those who are still in this group are ethnic minorities.* The paragraph cannot logically begin with a statement such as Sentence I, because no one reading the paragraph would know what *this group* refers to. Therefore, Choice B and Choice D are not correct and may be eliminated from consideration.

   b. Both Choice A and Choice B begin with Sentence IV, which states, *Eighty percent of those who have completed special job training in the past ten years are economically disadvantaged.* The problem then becomes selecting the best sequence of the other three sentences so that they most logically follow the initial Sentence IV.

   c. If you select Choice C, then you are choosing Sentence II as the correct second sentence. Sentence II states, *The number of economically disadvantaged people who enjoyed their special job training is larger than the number of economically disadvantaged people who did not enjoy it.* Then Sentence I would be the third sentence. However, that would not be logical, because you could not tell whether *this group* in Sentence I refers to *economically disadvantaged people who enjoyed their special job training* or whether *this group* refers to *economically people who did not enjoy it*. Therefore, Choice C is not correct.

   d. By the process of elimination, only Choice A remains. Choice A specifies Sentence I as the second sentence, which is logically correct in that *this group* in Sentence I will then refer to those who are *economically disadvantaged* in Sentence IV. The two remaining sentences also refer back to *economically disadvantaged*, thus creating a paragraph that reads logically from start to finish. Therefore, Choice A is the correct answer.

2. Choices B and D should be eliminated from further consideration due to the context in which the word *judiciously* was used in the reading passage. Specifically, concern was expressed that funds be spent judiciously. Nothing in the paragraph suggests a need for concern if the funds were not spent immediately or uniformly. Choice A must be considered, because public funds should be spent legally. However, the word *judiciously* is related to the word *judgment* rather than to the word *judiciary*. It is the latter word that has to do with courts of law and is related to legality, so Choice A is incorrect. On the other hand, *judiciously* and *prudently* both mean *wisely* and *with direction*. Therefore, Choice C is correct.

3. Choice B is the correct choice. No matter what numbers you apply, Choice B still will be correct. This is because when you multiply any number by two and then divide the result in half, you end up with the same number that you begin with. For example, suppose that 20 citizens wanted more social activities. Twice that number (40 citizens) wanted more educational activities. But of those 40 citizens, one-half (20 citizens) wanted mainly special job training.

Choice A is incorrect because, first of all, the organization did not have any suggestion boxes; although suggestion boxes were discussed, questionnaires ultimately were used instead. In addition, Choice A is incorrect because it was input about the planning of activities that the leaders of the community organization wanted rather than feedback concerning suggestion boxes.

Choice C also is not correct. Instead of promising the matching funds, the State department representatives promised to investigate (or look into) the possibility of obtaining the matching funds.

Choice D is incorrect because the reading passage does not tell whether telephone surveys or mailed questionnaires provide more accurate information. Remember, the instructions for this question state that the question is to be answered ONLY on the information in the applicable reading passage.

4. The correct answer is Choice C. Choice A and Choice C both begin with Sentence III, which certainly could be the logical first sentence of a paragraph. However, the next sentence (Sentence I) in Choice A leaves the initial topic of obtaining information from citizens. The third sentence in Choice A would be Sentence IV, *No community should formulate these goals without attempting to obtain the views of its citizenry.* The words *these goals* do not logically refer to anything in the previous two sentences, so Choice A is incorrect.

Choice B also is incorrect because the word *also* in its first sentence (Sentence I) has nothing to logically refer to. *Also* would have to be used in a sentence that comes later in the paragraph.

Choice D has the same problem as Choice A. Choice D begins with Sentence IV, which starts off, *No community should formulate these goals....* Again, the words *these goals* need to refer to something in a previous sentence about goals in order to be logically correct.

5. Choice B is correct. Here are the mathematical computations you might use to arrive at the correct answer of 81%.

   a. The reading passage states that the Smith Paint Company currently employs 2,000 persons. The first part of this question states that 75% of those current employees were hired during the first ten years that the company was in operation. By multiplying 75% by 2,000, you would find that 1,500 of the current employees were hired during the company's first ten years.

   b. The question asks about the first 13 years of the company's operation rather than just the first ten years. Therefore, you need the arithmetical information for the three years that immediately followed the first ten years. You know from the reading passage that the company has been operating for 20 years. You have the information for the first ten years. Twenty minus ten leaves the most recent ten years.

c. You know from the question that 40 persons were hired each year during the five-year period of time between the first ten years and the most recent five years. However, you need the information about only the first three years. By multiplying 40 persons per year by three years, you would find that 120 people were hired during the first three years that came immediately after the first ten years of the company's operation.

d. Next, you would need to add 1,500 people (for the first ten years) and 120 people (for the next three years). That would give you a total of 1,620 people hired during the first 13 years.

e. The question asks for the percentage of the Smith Paint Company's total employees hired during its first 13 years. You know that the total number of employees is 2,000. The question then is: 1,620 people is what percentage of 2,000 people? By dividing 2,000 into 1,620, you would find that the correct answer is 81%.

Choice A is incorrect because it deals with only the first ten years that the company was in operation, rather than the first 13 years. If you took 1,500 people (from Step a in the explanatory material for the correct answer) and divided that number by 2,000 people, you would arrive at 75%, which is not correct.

Choice C is incorrect. If you correctly arrived at 1,500 people for the first ten years but then incorrectly dealt with the next five years instead of the next three years, you would end up with the wrong answer of 85%. First, you would multiply 40 people by five years and end up with 200 people. Next, you would add 200 to 1,500 and end up with 1,700 people. Finally, you would divide 1,700 by 2,000 and get 85%.

Choice D also is incorrect. If you correctly arrived at 1,500 people for the first ten years but then used the information for the most recent five years instead of the information for the five years that came just before the most recent five years, you would end up with the incorrect answer of 90%. First, you would find from the question that 15% of the total employees were hired in the past five years. Next, you would multiply 15% by 2,000 total employees and end up with 300. Next, you would add 1,500 employees and 300 employees, ending up with a total of 1,800 employees. By dividing 1,800 by 2,000, you would arrive at 90%.

6. Choice A is correct. Here are the mathematical computations you would need to make to arrive at the correct answer of $250,000.

   a. The reading passage states that the amount of Futuron proposed for manufacture each year is 1 million gallons. The question states that the possible profit per gallon would be $1.00. By multiplying $1.00 by 1,000,000, you would find that $1,000,000 would be the total possible profit to be made during the first year.

   b. The question states that the $1,000,000 possible profit would have to be reduced by 50% because of the purchase of new machinery, plus by an additional 25% due to the delay in establishing manufacturing facilities. The possible profit must, therefore, be reduced by 50% plus 25%, or by a total of 75%, leaving only 25% of the $1,000,000 as possible profit.

c. By multiplying 25% by $1,000,000, you would arrive at $250,000 as the actual profit which would be made.

Choice B is incorrect. If the two profit reductions were incorrectly multiplied by one another (50% times 25%) and the product (12½%) added to 50%, there would have been a net reduction of 62 ½%, yielding $375,000. However, the two profit reductions are independent of each other and should be added together.

Choice C also is incorrect. It would occur if you only took into account the 50% profit reduction. However, as the paragraph states, you must also deduct an additional 25% of the total profit.

Choice D ($75,000) would be made if you incorrectly multiplied the total profit reduction (75%) by $1,000,000. However, the question asks for the profit, not the profit reduction.

7. Both *indeterminate* and *inconclusive* mean *vague* and *indefinite*, so Choice D is correct. Choice A is incorrect, because the word *ineluctable* means *inescapable* or *inevitable*. The reading passage does not support the conclusion that the research results are incorrect or unreasonable, so Choice B and Choice C can be eliminated from consideration.

8. Choice D is correct. The reading passage states, *The sales were phenomenal, and there is a great demand for more Futuron to be manufactured. The profits to be made by increasing the manufacturing and sale of Futuron could place the Smith Paint Company in a leading role in the paint industry.* Since the sales of Futuron were phenomenal (remarkable; extraordinary) and there still is a great demand for it, the suggestion of considerable future profit is reasonable.

Choice A is not the most accurate conclusion based on the reading passage. The financial impact of decreasing the production of the traditional paint cannot be ascertained. Therefore, it is not certain that the proposed 50% reduction in the manufacturing of the Smith Paint Company's traditional paint would not financially injure that company. Certainly, Choice D is a more accurate conclusion.

Choice B is incorrect. A greater proportion of the employees being in favor of the proposed increase in Futuron production than not being in favor of it implies that over 50% of the employees are in favor of it. However, the reading passage states that most of the employees (which, logically, means over 50% of the employees) do not want the proposed change to occur.

Choice C also is not the most accurate conclusion. It states that the proposed increase in Futuron production would cause employees considerable health damage. The reading passage is not definite on this issue of health damage. It states, *Initial research indicates that negative physical reactions may result from working closely with the chemicals necessary….* How serious the health damage might be is not stated in the reading passage.

PREPARING WRITTEN MATERIAL
PARAGRAPH REARRANGEMENT
EXAMINATION SECTION
TEST 1

DIRECTIONS: The following groups of sentences need to be arranged in an order that makes sense. Select the letter preceding the sequence that represents the best sentence order. *PRINT THE LETTER OF THE CORRECT ANSWER IN THE SPACE AT THE RIGHT.*

1.
   I. The ostrich egg shell's legendary toughness makes it an excellent substitute for certain types of dishes or dinnerware, and in parts of Africa ostrich shells are cut and decorated for use as containers for water.
   II. Since prehistoric times, people have used the enormous egg of the ostrich as a part of their diet, a practice which has required much patience and hard work—to hard boil an ostrich egg takes about four hours.
   III. Opening the egg's shell, which is rock hard and nearly an inch thick, requires heavy tools, such as a saw or chisel; from inside, a baby ostrich must use a hornlike projection on its beak as a miniature pick-axe to escape from the egg.
   IV. The offspring of all higher-order animals originate from single egg cells that are carried by mothers, and most of these eggs are relatively small, often microscopic.
   V. The egg of the African ostrich, however, weighs a massive thirty pounds, making it the largest single cell on earth, and a common object of human curiosity and wonder.

   The BEST order is:
   A. V, IV, I, II, III   B. I, IV, V, III, II   C. IV, II, III, V, I   D. IV, V, II, III, I

   1.____

2.
   I. Typically only a few feet high on the open sea, individual tsunami have been known to circle the entire globe two or three times if their progress is not interrupted, but are not usually dangerous until they approach the shallow water that surrounds land masses.
   II. Some of the most terrifying and damaging hazards caused by earthquakes are tsunami, which were once called "tidal waves"—a poorly chosen name, since these waves have nothing to do with tides.
   III. Then a wave, slowed by the sudden drag on the lower part of its moving water column, will pile upon itself, sometimes reaching a height of over 100 feet.
   IV. Tsunami (Japanese for "great harbor wave") are seismic waves that are caused by earthquakes near oceanic trenches, and once triggered, can travel up to 600 miles an hour on the open ocean.
   V. A land-shoaling tsunami is capable of extraordinary destruction; some tsunami have deposited large boats miles inland, washed out two-foot-thick seawalls, and scattered locomotive trains over long distances.

   The BEST order is:
   A. IV, I, III, II, V   B. I, III, IV, II, V   C. V, I, III, II, IV   D. II, IV, I, III, V

   2.____

3. I. Soon, by the 1940s, jazz was the most popular type of music among American intellectuals and college students.
    II. In the early days of jazz, it was considered "lowdown" music, or music that was played only in rough, disreputable bars and taverns.
    III. However, jazz didn't take too long to develop from early ragtime melodies into more complex, sophisticated forms, such as Charlie Parker's "bebop" style of jazz.
    IV. After charismatic band leaders such as Duke Ellington and Count Basie brought jazz to a larger audience, and jazz continued to evolve into more complicated forms, white audiences began to accept and even to enjoy the new American art form.
    V. Many white Americans, who then dictated the tastes of society, were wary of music that was played almost exclusively in black clubs in the poorer sections of cities and towns.
    The BEST order is:
    A. V, IV, III, II, I   B. II, V, III, IV, I   C. IV, V, III, I, II   D. I, II, IV, III, V

4. I. Then, hanging in a windless place, the magnetized end of the needle would always point to the south.
    II. The needle could then be balanced on the rim of a cup, or the edge of a fingernail, but this balancing act was hard to maintain, and the needle often fell off.
    III. Other needles would point to the north, and it was important for any traveler finding his way with a compass to remember which kind of magnetized needle he was carrying.
    IV. To make some of the earliest compasses in recorded history, ancient Chinese "magicians" would rub a needle with a piece of magnetized iron called a lodestone.
    V. A more effective method of keeping the needle free to swing with its magnetic pull was to attach a strand of silk to the center of the needle with a tiny piece of wax.
    The BEST order is:
    A. IV, II, V, I, III   B. IV, III, V, II, I   C. IV, V, II, I, III   D. IV, I, III, V, II

5. I. The now-famous first mate of the *H.M.S. Bounty*, Fletcher Christian, founded one of the world's most peculiar civilizations in 1790.
    II. The men knew they had just committed a crime for which they could be hanged, so they set sail for Pitcairn, a remote, abandoned island in the far eastern region of the Polynesian archipelago, accompanied by twelve Polynesian women and six men.
    III. In a mutiny that has become legendary, Christian and the others forced Captain Bligh into a lifeboat and set him adrift off the coast of Tonga in April of 1789.
    IV. In early 1790, the *Bounty* landed at Pitcairn Island, where the men lived out the rest of their lives and founded an isolated community which to this day includes direct descendants of Christian and the other Crewmen.

V. The *Bounty*, commanded by Captain William Bligh, was in the middle of a global voyage, and Christian and his shipmates had come to the conclusion that Bligh was a reckless madman who would lead them to their deaths unless they took the ship from him.

The BEST order is:
  A. IV, V, III, II, I   B. I, III, V, II, IV   C. I, V, III, II, IV   D. III, I, V, IV, II

6.
  I. But once the vines had been led to make orchids, the flowers had to be carefully hand-pollinated, because unpollinated orchids usually lasted less than a day, wilting and dropping off the vine before it had even become dark.
  II. The Totonac farmers discovered that looping a vine back around once it reached a five-foot height on its host tree would cause the vine to flower.
  III. Though they knew how to process the fruit pods and extract vanilla's flavoring agent, the Totonacs also knew that a wild vanilla vine did not produce abundant flowers or fruit.
  IV. Wild vines climbed along the trunks and canopies of trees, and this constant upward growth diverted most of the vine's energy to making leaves instead of the orchid flowers that once pollinated, would produce the flavorful pods.
  V. Hundreds of years before vanilla became a prized food flavoring in Europe and the Western World, the Totonac Indians of the Mexican Gulf Coast were skilled cultivators of the vanilla vine, whose fruit they literally worshipped as a goddess.

The BEST order is:
  A. II, III, IV, I, V   B. II, IV, III, I, V   C. V, III, IV, II, I   D. III, IV, I, II, V

7.
  I. Once airborne, the spider is at the mercy of the air currents—usually the spider takes a brief journey, traveling close to the ground, but some have been found in air samples collected as high as 10,000 feet, or been reported landing on ships far out at sea.
  II. Once a young spider has hatched, it must leave the environment into which it was born as quickly as possible, in order to avoid competing with its hundreds of brothers and sisters for food.
  III. The silk rises into warm air currents, and as soon as the pull feels adequate the spider lets go and drifts up into the air, suspended from the silk strand in the same way that a person might parasail.
  IV. To help young spiders do this, many species have adapted a practice known as "aerial dispersal," or, in common speech, "ballooning."
  V. A spider that wants to leave its surroundings quickly will climb to the top of a grass system or twig, face into the wind, and aim its back end into the air, releasing a long stream of silk from the glands near the tip of its abdomen.

The BEST order is:
  A. V, IV, II, III, I   B. V, II, IV, I, III   C. II, V, IV, III, I   D. II, IV, V, III, I

8. I. For about a year, Tycho worked at a castle in Prague with a scientist named Johannes Kepler, but their association was cut short by another argument that drove Kepler out of the castle, to later develop, on his own, the theory of planetary orbits.
   II. Tycho found life without a nose embarrassing, so he made a new nose for himself out of silver, which reportedly remained glued to his face for the rest of his life.
   III. Tycho Brahe, the 17th-century Danish astronomer, is today more famous for his odd and arrogant personality than for any contribution he has made to our knowledge of the stars and planets.
   IV. Early in his career, as a student at Rostock University, Tycho got into an argument with another student about who was the better mathematician, and the two became so angry that the argument turned into a sword fight, during which Tycho's nose was sliced off.
   V. Later in his life, Tycho's arrogance may have kept him from playing a part in one of the greatest astronomical discoveries in history: the elliptical orbits of the solar system's planets.
   The BEST order is:
   A. I, IV, II, III, V   B. IV, II, III, V, I   C. IV, II, I, III, V   D. III, IV, II, V, I

9. I. The processionaries are so used to this routine that if a person picks up the end of a silk line and brings it back to the origin—creating a closed circle—the caterpillars may travel around and around for days, sometimes starving or freezing, without changing course.
   II. Rather than relying on sight or sound, the other caterpillars, who are lined up end-to-end behind the leader, travel to and from their nests by walking on this silk line, and each will reinforce it by laying down its own marking line as it passes over.
   III. In order to insure the safety of individuals, the processionary caterpillar nests in a tree with dozens of other caterpillars, and at night, when it is safest, they all leave together in search of food.
   IV. The processionary caterpillar of the European continent is a perfect illustration of how much some inspect species rely on instinct in their daily routines.
   V. As they leave their nests, the processionaries form a single-file line behind a leader who spins and lays out a silk line to mark the chosen path.
   The BEST order is:
   A. IV, III, V, II, I   B. III, V, IV, II, I   C. III, V, II, I, IV   D. IV, V, III, I, II

10. I. Often, the child is also given a handcrafted walker or push cart, to provide support for its first upright explorations.
    II. In traditional Indian families, a child's first steps are celebrated as a ceremonial event, rooted in ancient myth.
    III. These carts are often intricately designed to resemble the chariot of Krishna, an important figure in Indian mythology.
    IV. The sound of these anklet bells is intended to mimic the footsteps of the legendary child Rama, who is celebrated in devotional songs throughout India.

V. When the child's parents see that the child is ready to begin walking, they will fit it with specially designed ankle bracelets, adorned with gently ringing bells.

The BEST order is:
A. II, III, IV, I, V   B. II, V, III, I, IV   C. V, IV, I, III, II   D. V, III, II, I, IV

11. I. The settlers planted Osage oranges all across Middle America, and today long lines and rectangles of Osage orange trees can still be seen on the prairies, running along the former boundaries of farms that no longer exist.
II. After trying sod walls and water-filled ditches with no success, American farmers began to look for a plant that was adaptable to prairie weather, and that could be trimmed into a hedge that was "pig-tight, horse-high, and bull-strong."
III. The tree, so named because it bore a large (but inedible) fruit the size of an orange, was among the sturdiest and hardiest of American trees, and was prized among Native Americans for the strength and flexibility of bows which were made from its wood.
IV. The first people to practice agriculture on the American flatlands were faced with an important problem: what would they use to fence their land in a place that was almost entirely without trees or rocks?
V. Finally, an Illinois farmer brought the settlers a tree that was native to the land between the Red and Arkansas rivers, a tree called the Osage orange.

The BEST order is:
A. II, I, V, III, IV   B. I, II, III, IV, V   C. IV, II, V, III, I   D. IV, II, I, III, V

12. I. After about ten minutes of such spirited and complicated activity, the head dancer is free to make up his or her own movements while maintaining the interest of the New Year's crowd.
II. The dancer will then perform a series of leg kicks, while at the same time operating the lion's mouth with his own hand and moving the ears and eyes by means of a string which is attached to the dancer's own mouth.
III. The most difficult role of this dance belongs to the one who controls the lion's head; this person must lead all the other "parts" of the lion through the choreographed segments of the dance.
IV. The head dancer begins with a complex series of steps. alternately stepping forward with the head raised, and then retreating a few steps while lowering the head, a movement that is intended to create the impression that the lion is keeping a watchful eye for anything evil.
V. When performing a traditional Chinese New Year's lion dance, several performers must fit themselves inside a large lion costume and work together to enact different parts of the dance.

The BEST order is:
A. V, III, IV, II, I   B. III, IV, II, V, I   C. III, I, V, IV, II   D. IV, II, III, V, I

13. I. For many years the shell of the chambered nautilus was treasured in Europe for its beauty and intricacy, but collectors were unaware that they were in possession of the structure that marked a "missing link" in the evolution of marine mollusks.
II. The nautilus, however, evolved a series of enclosed chambers in its shell, and invented a new use for the structure: the shell began to serve as a buoyancy device.
III. Equipped with this new flotation device, the nautilus did not need the single, muscular foot of its predecessors, but instead developed flaps, tentacles, and a gentle form of jet propulsion that transformed it into the first mollusk able to take command of its own density and explore a three-dimensional world.
IV. By pumping and adjusting air pressure into the chambers, the nautilus could spend the day resting on the bottom, and then rise toward the surface at night in search of food.
V. The nautilus shell looks like a large snail shell, similar to those of its ancestors, who used their shells as protective coverings while they were anchored to the sea floor.
The BEST order is:
A. V, II, IV, I, III   B. V, I, II, III, IV   C. I, II, V, III, IV   D. I, V, II, IV, III

14. I. While France and England battled for control of the region, the Acadiens prospered on the fertile farmland, which was finally secured by England in 1713.
II. Early in the 17th century, settlers from Western France founded a colony called Acadie in what is now the Canadian province of Nova Scotia.
III. At this time, English officials feared the presence of spies among the Acadiens who might be loyal to their French homeland, and the Acadiens were deported to spots along the Atlantic and Caribbean shores of America.
IV. The French settlers remained on this land, under English rule, for around forty years, until the beginning of the French and Indian War, another conflict between France and England.
V. As the Acadien refugees drifted toward a final home in Southern Louisiana, neighbors shortened their name to "Cadien," and finally "Cajun," the name which the descendants of early Acadiens still call themselves.
The BEST order is:
A. I, IV, II, III, V   B. II, I, III, V, IV   C. II, I, IV, III, V   D. V, II, III, IV, I

15. I. Traditional households in the Eastern and Western regions of Africa serve two meals a day—one at around noon, and the other in the evening.
II. The starch is then used in the way that Americans might use a spoon, to scoop up a portion of the main dish on the person's plate.
III. The reason for the starch's inclusion in every meal has to do with taste as well as nutrition; African food can be very spicy, and the starch is known to cool the burning effect of the main dish.
IV. When serving these meals, the main dish is usually served on individual plates, and the starch is served on a communal plate, from which diners break off a piece of bread or scoop rice or fufu in their fingers.

V. The typical meals usually consist of a thick stew or soup as the main course, and an accompanying starch—either bread, rice, or *fufu*, a starchy grain paste similar in consistency to mashed potatoes.
The BEST order is:
  A. V, II, III, IV, I   B. V, I, IV, III, II   C. I, IV, V, III, II   D. I, V, IV, II, III

16.
  I. In the early days of the American Midwest, Indiana settlers sometimes came together to hold an event called an apple peeling, where neighboring settlers gathered at the homestead of a host family to help prepare the hosts' apple crop for cooking, canning, and making apple butter.
  II. At the beginning of the event, each peeler sat down in front of a ten- or twenty-gallon stone jar and was given a crock of apples and a paring knife.
  III. Once a peeler had finished with a crock, another was placed next to him; if the peeler was an unmarried man, he kept a strict count of the number of apples he had peeled, because the winner was allowed to kiss the girl of his choice.
  IV. The peeling usually ended by 9:30 in the evening, when the neighbors gathered in the host family's parlor for a dance social.
  V. The apples were peeled, cored, and quartered, and then placed into the jar.
The BEST order is:
  A. I, V, III, IV, II   B. II, V, III, IV, I   C. I, II, V, III, IV   D. II, I, V, IV, III

16._____

17.
  I. If your pet turtle is a land turtle and is native to temperate climates, it will stop eating some time in October, which should be your cue to prepare the turtle for hibernation.
  II. The box should then be covered with a wire screen, which will protect the turtle from any rodents or predators that might want to take advantage of a motionless and helpless animal.
  III. When your turtle hasn't eaten for a while and appears ready to hibernate, it should be moved to its winter quarters, most likely a cellar or garage, where the temperature should range between 40° and 45°F.
  IV. Instead of feeding the turtle, you should bathe it every day in warm water, to encourage the turtle to empty its intestines in preparation for its long winter sleep.
  V. Here the turtle should be placed in a well-ventilated box whose bottom is covered with a moisture-absorbing layer of clay beads, and then filled three-fourths full with almost dry peat moss or wood chips, into which the turtle will burrow and sleep for several months.
The BEST order is:
  A. I, IV, III, V, II   B. III, IV, II, V, I   C. III, II, IV, I, V   D. IV, V, II, III, I

17._____

18.
  I. Once he has reached the nest, the hunter uses two sturdy bamboo poles like huge chopsticks to pull the next away from the mountainside, into a large basket that will be lowered to people waiting below.
  II. The world's largest honeybees colonize the Nealese mountainsides, building honeycombs as large as a person on sheer rock faces that are often hundreds of feet high.

18._____

III. In the remote mountain country of Nepal, a small band of "honey hunters" carry out a tradition so ancient that 10,000 year-old drawings of the practice have been found in the caves of Nepal.
IV. To harvest the honey and beeswax from these combs, a honey hunter climbs above the nests, lowers a long bamboo-fiber ladder over the cliff, and then climbs down.
V. Throughout this dangerous practice, the hunter is stung repeatedly, and only the veterans, with skin that has been toughened over the years, are able to return from a hunt without the painful swelling caused by stings.
The BEST order is:
A. II, IV, III, V, I   B. II, IV, I, V, III   C. V, III, II, IV, I   D. III, II, IV, I, V

19. I. After the Romans left Britain, there were relentless attacks on the islands from the barbarian tribes of northern Germany—the Angles, Saxons, and Jutes.
II. As the empire weakened, Roman soldiers withdrew from Britain, leaving behind a country that continued to practice the Christian religion that had been introduced by the Romans.
III. Early Latin writings tell of a Christian warrior named Arturius (Arthur, in English) who led the British citizens to defeat these barbarian invades, and brought an extended period of peace to the lands of Britain.
IV. Long ago, the British Isles were part of the far-flung Roman Empire that extended across most of Europe and into Africa and Asia.
V. The romantic legend of King Arthur and his knights of the Round Table, one of the most popular and widespread stories of all time, appears to have some foundation in history.
The BEST order is:
A. V, IV, III, II, I   B. V, IV, II, I, III   C. IV, V, II, III, I   D. IV, III, II, I, V

19.____

20. I. The cylinder was allowed to cool until it could stand on its own, and then it was cut from the tube and split down the side with a single straight cut.
II. Nineteenth-century glassmakers, who had not yet discovered the glazier's modern techniques for making panes of glass, had to create a method for converting their blown gas into flat sheets.
III. The bubble was then pierced at the end to make a hole that opened up while the glassmaker gently spun it, creating a cylinder of glass.
IV. Turned on its side and laid on a conveyor belt, the cylinder was strengthened, or tempered, by being heated again and cooled very slowly, eventually flattening out into a single rectangular of glass.
V. To do this, the glassmaker dipped the end of a long tube into melted glass and blew into the other end of the tube, creating an expanding bubble of glass.
The BEST order is:
A. II, V, III, IV, I   B. II, IV, V, III, I   C. III, V, II, IV, I   D. III, I, IV, V, II

20.____

21. I. The splints are almost always hidden, but horses are occasionally born whose splinted toes project from the leg on either side, just above the hoof.
    II. The second and fourth toes remained, but shrank to thin splints of bone that fused invisibly to the horse's leg bone.
    III. Horses are unique among mammals, having evolved feet that each end in what is essentially a single toe, capped by a large, sturdy hoof.
    IV. Julius Caesar, an emperor of ancient Rome, was said to have owned one of these three-toed horses, and considered it so special that he would not permit anyone else to ride it.
    V. Though the horse's earlier ancestors possessed the traditional mammalian set of five toes on each foot, the horse has retained only its third toe; its first and fifth toes disappeared completely as the horse evolved.
    The BEST order is:
      A. III, V, II, I, IV   B. V, III, II, IV, I   C. III, II, V, I, IV   D. V, II, III, I, IV

22. I. The new building materials—some of which are twenty feet long, and weigh nearly six tons—were transported to Pohnpei on rafts, and were brought into their present position by using hibiscus fiber ropes and leverage to move the stone columns upward along the inclined trunks of coconut palm trees.
    II. The ancestors built great fires to heat the stone, and then poured cool seawater on the columns, which caused the stone to contract and split along natural fracture lines.
    III. The now-abandoned enclave of Nan Madol, a group of 92 man-made islands off the shore of the Micronesian island of Pohnpei, is estimated to have been built around the year 500 A.D.
    IV. The islanders say their ancestors quarried stone columns from a nearby island, where large basalt columns were formed by the cooling of molten lava.
    V. The structures of Nan Madol are remarkable for the sheer size of some of the stone "longs" or columns that were used to create the walls of the offshore community, and today anthropologists can only rely on the information of existing local people for clues about how Nan Madol was built.
    The BEST order is:
      A. V, IV, III, II, I   B. V, III, I, IV, II   C. III, V, IV, II, I   D. III, I, IV, II, V

23. I. One of the most easily manipulated substances on earth, glass can be made into ceramic tiles that are composed of over 90% air.
    II. NASA's space shuttles are the first spacecraft ever designed to leave and re-enter the earth's atmosphere while remaining intact.
    III. These ceramic tiles are such effective insulators that when a tile emerges from the oven in which it was fired, it can be held safely in a person's hand by the edges while its interior still glows at a temperature well over 2000°F.
    IV. Eventually, the engineers were led to a material that is as old as our most ancient civilization.
    V. Because the temperature during atmospheric re-entry is so incredibly hot, it took NASA's engineers some time to find a substance capable of protecting the shuttles.

The BEST order is:
A. V, II, I, II, IV B. II, V, IV, I, III C. II, III, I, IV, V D. V, IV, III, I, II

24. I. The secret to teaching any parakeet to talk is patience, and the understanding that when a bird talks," it is simply imitating what it hears, rather than putting ideas into words.
    II. You should stay just out of sight of the bird and repeat the phrase you want it to learn, for at least fifteen minutes every morning and evening.
    III. It is important to leave the bird without any words of encouragement or farewell; otherwise it might combine stray remarks or phrases, such as "Good night," with the phrase you are trying to teach it.
    IV. For this reason, to train your bird to imitate your words you should keep it free of any distractions, especially other noises, while you are giving it "lesson."
    V. After your repetition, you should quietly leave the bird alone for a while, to think over what it has just heard.
    The BEST order is:
    A. I, IV, II, V, III B. I, II, IV, III, V C. III, II, I, V, IV D. III, I, V, IV, II

24.____

25. I. As a school approaches, fishermen from neighboring communities join their fishing boats together as a fleet, and string their gill nets together to make a huge fence that is held up by cork floats.
    II. At a signal from the party leaders, or *nakura*, the family members pound the sides of the boats or beat the water with long poles, creating a sudden and deafening noise.
    III. The fishermen work together to drag the trap into a half-circle that may reach 300 yards in diameter, and then the families move their boats to form the other half of the circle around the school of fish.
    IV. The school of fish flee from the commotion into the awaiting trap, where a final wall of net is thrown over the open end of the half-circle, securing the day's haul.
    V. Indonesian people from the area around the Sulu islands live on the sea, in floating villages made of lashed-together or stilted homes, and make much of their living by fishing their home waters for migrating schools of snapper, scad, and other fish.
    The BEST order is:
    A. I, V, III, IV, II B. I, II, IV, III, V C. V, I, II, III, IV D. V, I, III, II, IV

25.____

KEY (CORRECT ANSWERS)

1. D
2. D
3. B
4. A
5. C

6. C
7. D
8. D
9. A
10. B

11. C
12. A
13. D
14. C
15. D

16. C
17. A
18. D
19. B
20. A

21. A
22. C
23. B
24. A
25. D

PREPARING WRITTEN MATERIAL
EXAMINATION SECTION
TEST 1

DIRECTIONS: Each of the sentences in this test may be classified under one of the following four categories:
A. *Incorrect* because of faulty grammar or sentence structure
B. *Incorrect* because of faulty punctuation
C. *Incorrect* because of faulty capitalization
D. *Correct*

Examine each sentence carefully to determine under which of the above four options it is best classified. Then, in the space at the right, print the capital letter preceding the option which is the BEST of the four suggested above.

(Each incorrect sentence contains but one type of error. Consider a sentence to be correct if it contains none of the types of errors mentioned, even though there may be other correct ways of expressing the same thought.)

1. This fact, together with those brought out at the previous meeting, prove that the schedule is satisfactory to the employees.   1.____

2. Like many employees in scientific fields, the work of bookkeepers and accountants requires accuracy and neatness.   2.____

3. "What can I do for you," the secretary asked as she motioned to the visitor to take a seat.   3.____

4. Our representative, Mr. Charles will call on you next week to determine whether or not your claim has merit.   4.____

5. We expect you to return in the spring; please do not disappoint us.   5.____

6. Any supervisor, who disregards the just complaints of his subordinates, is remiss in the performance of his duty.   6.____

7. Because she took less than an hour for lunch is no reason for permitting her to leave before five o'clock.   7.____

8. "Miss Smith," said the supervisor, "Please arrange a meeting of the staff for two o'clock on Monday."   8.____

9. A private company's vacation and sick leave allowance usually differs considerably from a public agency.   9.____

10. Therefore, in order to increase the efficiency of operations in the department, a report on the recommended changes in procedures was presented to the departmental committee in charge of the program.   10.____

11. We told him to assign the work to whoever was available. 11._____

12. Since John was the most efficient of any other employee in the bureau, he received the highest service rating. 12._____

13. Only those members of the national organization who resided in the middle West attended the conference in Chicago. 13._____

14. The question of whether the office manager has as yet attained, or indeed can ever hope to secure professional status is one which has been discussed for years. 14._____

15. No one knew who to blame for the error which, we later discovered, resulted in a considerable loss of time. 15._____

KEY (CORRECT ANSWERS)

1.	A	6.	B	11.	D
2.	A	7.	A	12.	A
3.	B	8.	C	13.	C
4.	B	9.	A	14.	B
5.	D	10.	D	15.	A

TEST 2

DIRECTIONS: Each of the sentences in this test may be classified under one of the following four categories:
- A. *Incorrect* because of faulty grammar or sentence structure
- B. *Incorrect* because of faulty punctuation
- C. *Incorrect* because of faulty capitalization
- D. *Correct*

1. The National alliance of Businessmen is trying to persuade private businesses to hire youth in the summertime.   1.____

2. The supervisor who is on vacation, is in charge of processing vouchers.   2.____

3. The activity of the committee at its conferences is always stimulating.   3.____

4. After checking the addresses again, the letters went to the mailroom.   4.____

5. The director, as well as the employees, are interested in sharing the dividends.   5.____

KEY (CORRECT ANSWERS)

1. C
2. B
3. D
4. A
5. A

TEST 3

DIRECTIONS: In each of the following groups of sentences, one of the four sentences is faulty in grammar, punctuation, or capitalization. Select the INCORRECT sentence in each case.

1. A. Sailing down the bay was a thrilling experience for me.
    B. He was not consulted about your joining the club.
    C. This story is different than the one I told you yesterday.
    D. There is no doubt about his being the best player.

    1.____

2. A. He maintains there is but one road to world peace.
    B. It is common knowledge that a child sees much he is not supposed to see.
    C. Much of the bitterness might have been avoided if arbitration had been resorted to earlier in the meeting.
    D. The man decided it would be advisable to marry a girl somewhat younger than him.

    2.____

3. A. In this book, the incident I liked least is where the hero tries to put out the forest fire.
    B. Learning a foreign language will undoubtedly give a person a better understanding of his mother tongue.
    C. His actions made us wonder what he planned to do next.
    D. Because of the war, we were unable to travel during the summer vacation.

    3.____

4. A. The class had no sooner become interested in the lesson than the dismissal bell rang.
    B. There is little agreement about the kind of world to be planned at the peace conference.
    C. "Today," said the teacher, "we shall read 'The Wind in the Willows,' I am sure you'll like it.
    D. The terms of the legal settlement of the family quarrel handicapped both sides for many years.

    4.____

5. A. I was so surprised that I was not able to say a word.
    B. She is taller than any other member of the class.
    C. It would be much more preferable if you were never seen in his company.
    D. We had no choice but to excuse her for being late.

    5.____

KEY (CORRECT ANSWERS)

1. C
2. D
3. A
4. C
5. C

TEST 4

DIRECTIONS: In each of the following groups of sentences, one of the four sentences is faulty in grammar, punctuation, or capitalization. Select the INCORRECT sentence in each case.

1. A. Please send me these data at the earliest opportunity.
   B. The loss of their material proved to be a severe handicap.
   C. My principal objection to this plan is that it is impracticable.
   D. The doll had laid in the rain for an hour and was ruined.

   1.____

2. A. The garden scissors, left out all night in the rain, were in a badly rusted condition.
   B. The girls felt bad about the misunderstanding which had arisen
   C. Sitting near the campfire, the old man told John and I about many exciting adventures he had had.
   D. Neither of us is in a position to undertake a task of that magnitude.

   2.____

3. A. The general concluded that one of the three roads would lead to the besieged city.
   B. The children didn't, as a rule, do hardly anything beyond what they were told to do.
   C. The reason the girl gave for her negligence was that she had acted on the spur of the moment.
   D. The daffodils and tulips look beautiful in that blue vase.

   3.____

4. A. If I was ten years older, I should be interested in this work.
   B. Give the prize to whoever has drawn the best picture.
   C. When you have finished reading the book, take it back to the library.
   D. My drawing is as good as or better than yours.

   4.____

5. A. He asked me whether the substance was animal or vegetable.
   B. An apple which is unripe should not be eaten by a child.
   C. That was an insult to me who am your friend.
   D. Some spy must of reported the matter to the enemy.

   5.____

6. A. Limited time makes quoting the entire message impossible.
   B. Who did she say was going?
   C. The girls in your class have dressed more dolls this year than we.
   D. There was such a large amount of books on the floor that I couldn't find a place for my rocking chair.

   6.____

7. A. What with his sleeplessness and his ill health, he was unable to assume any responsibility for the success of the meeting.
   B. If I had been born in February, I should be celebrating my birthday soon.
   C. In order to prevent breakage, she placed a sheet of paper between each of the plates when she packed them.
   D. After the spring shower, the violets smelled very sweet.

   7.____

8. A. He had laid the book down very reluctantly before the end of the lesson.
    B. The dog, I am sorry to say, had lain on the bed all night.
    C. The cloth was first lain on a flat surface; then it was pressed with a hot iron.
    D. While we were in Florida, we lay in the sun until we were noticeably tanned.

9. A. If John was in New York during the recent holiday season, I have no doubt he spent most of the time with his parents.
    B. How could he enjoy the television program; the dog was barking and the baby was crying.
    C. When the problem was explained to the class, he must have been asleep.
    D. She wished that her new dress were finished so that she could go to the party.

10. A. The engine not only furnishes power but light and heat as well.
    B. You're aware that we've forgotten whose guilt was established, aren't you?
    C. Everybody knows that the woman made many sacrifices for her children.
    D. A man with his dog and gun is a familiar sight in this neighborhood.

KEY (CORRECT ANSWERS)

1.	D	6.	D
2.	C	7.	B
3.	B	8.	C
4.	A	9.	B
5.	D	10.	A

TEST 5

DIRECTIONS: Each of Questions 1 through 5 consists of a sentence which may be classified appropriately under one of the following four categories:
- A. *Incorrect* because of faulty grammar
- B. *Incorrect* because of faulty punctuation
- C. *Incorrect* because of faulty spelling
- D. *Correct*

Examine each sentence carefully. Then, print in the space at the right the letter preceding the category which is the BEST of the four suggested above
(Note: Each incorrect sentence contains only one type of error. Consider a sentence correct if it contains no errors, although there may be other correct ways of writing the sentence.)

1. Of the two employees, the one in our office is the most efficient.   1.____

2. No one can apply or even understand, the new rules and regulations.   2.____

3. A large amount of supplies were stored in the empty office.   3.____

4. If an employee is occassionally asked to work overtime, he should do so willingly.   4.____

5. It is true that the new procedures are difficult to use but, we are certain that you will learn them quickly.   5.____

6. The office manager said that he did not know who would be given a large allotment under the new plan.   6.____

7. It was at the supervisor's request that the clerk agreed to postpone his vacation.   7.____

8. We do not believe that it is necessary for both he and the clerk to attend the conference.   8.____

9. All employees, who display perseverance, will be given adequate recognition.   9.____

10. He regrets that some of us employees are dissatisfied with our new assignments.   10.____

11. "Do you think that the raise was merited," asked the supervisor?   11.____

12. The new manual of procedure is a valuable supplament to our rules and regulations.   12.____

13. The typist admitted that she had attempted to pursuade the other employees to assist her in her work.   13.____

14. The supervisor asked that all amendments to the regulations be handled by you and I. 14.____

15. The custodian seen the boy who broke the window. 15.____

KEY (CORRECT ANSWERS)

1. A   6. D   11. B
2. B   7. D   12. C
3. A   8. A   13. C
4. C   9. B   14. A
5. B   10. D   15. A

PREPARING WRITTEN MATERIAL
EXAMINATION SECTION
TEST 1

DIRECTIONS: Each of the sentences in this test may be classified under one of the following four categories:
- A. Faulty because of incorrect grammar or word usage
- B. Faulty because of incorrect punctuation
- C. Faulty because of incorrect capitalization or incorrect spelling
- D. Correct

Examine each sentence carefully to determine under which of the above four options it is best classified. Then, in the space to the right, print the capital letter preceding the option which is the BEST of the four suggested above. (Note that each faulty sentence contains but one type of error. Consider a sentence to be correct if it contains none of the types of errors mentioned, even though there may be other correct ways of expressing the same thought.)

1. He sent the notice to the clerk who you hired yesterday. 1.____

2. It must be admitted, however that you were not informed of this change. 2.____

3. Only the employee who have served in this grade for at least two years are eligible for promotion. 3.____

4. The work was divided equally between she and Mary. 4.____

5. He thought that you were not available at that time. 5.____

6. When the messenger returns; please give him this package. 6.____

7. The new secretary prepared, typed, addressed, and delivered, the notices. 7.____

8. Walking into the room, his desk can be seen at the rear. 8.____

9. Although John has worked here longer than She, he produces a smaller amount of work. 9.____

10. She said she could of typed this report yesterday. 10.____

11. Neither one of these procedures are adequate for the efficient performance of this task. 11.____

12. The typewriter is the tool of the typist; the cash register, the tool of the cashier. 12.____

13. "The assignment must be completed as soon as possible" said the supervisor. 13.____

14. As you know, office handbooks are issued to all new Employees. 14.____

15. Writing a speech is sometimes easier than to deliver it before an audience. 15.____

16. Mr. Brown our accountant, will audit the accounts next week. 16.____

17. Give the assignment to whomever is able to do it most efficiently. 17.____

18. The supervisor expected either your or I to file these reports. 18.____

KEY (CORRECT ANSWERS)

1.	A	11.	A
2.	B	12.	C
3.	D	13.	B
4.	A	14.	C
5.	D	15.	A
6.	B	16.	B
7.	B	17.	A
8.	A	18.	A
9.	C		
10.	A		

TEST 2

DIRECTIONS: Each of the sentences in this test may be classified under one of the following four categories:
- A. Faulty because of incorrect grammar or word usage
- B. Faulty because of incorrect punctuation
- C. Faulty because of incorrect capitalization or incorrect spelling
- D. Correct

Examine each sentence carefully to determine under which of the above four options it is best classified. Then, in the space to the right, print the capital letter preceding the option which is the BEST of the four suggested above. (Note that each faulty sentence contains but one type of error. Consider a sentence to be correct if it contains none of the types of errors mentioned, even though there may be other correct ways of expressing the same thought.)

1. The fire apparently started in the storeroom, which is usually locked.
2. On approaching the victim, two bruises were noticed by this officer.
3. The officer, who was there examined the report with great care.
4. Each employee in the office had a seperate desk.
5. All employees including members of the clerical staff, were invited to the lecture.
6. The suggested Procedure is similar to the one now in use.
7. No one was more pleased with the new procedure than the chauffeur.
8. He tried to persaude her to change the procedure.
9. The total of the expenses charged to petty cash were high.
10. An understanding between him and I was finally reached.

KEY (CORRECT ANSWERS)

1. D
2. A
3. B
4. C
5. B
6. C
7. D
8. C
9. A
10. A

TEST 3

DIRECTIONS: Each of the sentences in this test may be classified under one of the following four categories:
- A. Faulty because of incorrect grammar or word usage
- B. Faulty because of incorrect punctuation
- C. Faulty because of incorrect capitalization or incorrect spelling
- D. Correct

Examine each sentence carefully to determine under which of the above four options it is best classified. Then, in the space to the right, print the capital letter preceding the option which is the BEST of the four suggested above. (Note that each faulty sentence contains but one type of error. Consider a sentence to be correct if it contains none of the types of errors mentioned, even though there may be other correct ways of expressing the same thought.)

1. They told both he and I that the prisoner had escaped.   1._____

2. Any superior officer, who, disregards the just complaint of his subordinates, is remiss in the performance of his duty.   2._____

3. Only those members of the national organization who resided in the Middle West attended the conference in Chicago.   3._____

4. We told him to give the national organization assignment to whoever was available.   4._____

5. Please do not disappoint and embarass us by not appearing in court.   5._____

6. Although the office's speech proved to be entertaining, the topic was not relevent to the main theme of the conference.   6._____

7. In February all new officers attended a training course in which they were learned in their principal duties and the fundamental operating procedure of the department.   7._____

8. I personally seen inmate Jones threaten inmates Smith and Green with bodily harm if they refused to participate in the plot.   8._____

9. To the layman, who on a chance visit to the prison observes everything functioning smoothly, the maintenance of prison discipline may seem to be a relatively easily realizable objective.   9._____

10. The prisoners in cell block fourty were forbidden to sit on the cell cots during the recreation hour.   10._____

KEY (CORRECT ANSWERS)

1.	A	6.	C
2.	B	7.	A
3.	C	8.	A
4.	D	9.	D
5.	C	10.	C

TEST 4

DIRECTIONS: Each of the sentences in this test may be classified under one of the following four categories:
  A. Faulty because of incorrect grammar or word usage
  B. Faulty because of incorrect punctuation
  C. Faulty because of incorrect capitalization or incorrect spelling
  D. Correct

Examine each sentence carefully to determine under which of the above four options it is best classified. Then, in the space to the right, print the capital letter preceding the option which is the BEST of the four suggested above. (Note that each faulty sentence contains but one type of error. Consider a sentence to be correct if it contains none of the types of errors mentioned, even though there may be other correct ways of expressing the same thought.)

1. I cannot encourage you any. 1._____
2. You always look well in those sort of clothes. 2._____
3. Shall we go to the park? 3._____
4. The man whome he introduced was Mr. Carey. 4._____
5. She saw the letter laying here this morning. 5._____
6. It should rain before the Afternoon is over. 6._____
7. They have already went home. 7._____
8. That Jackson will be elected is evident. 8._____
9. He does not hardly approve of us. 9._____
10. It was he, who won the prize. 10._____

KEY (CORRECT ANSWERS)

1. A   6. C
2. A   7. A
3. D   8. D
4. C   9. A
5. A   10. B

TEST 5

DIRECTIONS: Each of the sentences in this test may be classified under one of the following four categories:
- A. Faulty because of incorrect grammar or word usage
- B. Faulty because of incorrect punctuation
- C. Faulty because of incorrect capitalization or incorrect spelling
- D. Correct

Examine each sentence carefully to determine under which of the above four options it is best classified. Then, in the space to the right, print the capital letter preceding the option which is the BEST of the four suggested above. (Note that each faulty sentence contains but one type of error. Consider a sentence to be correct if it contains none of the types of errors mentioned, even though there may be other correct ways of expressing the same thought.)

1. Shall we go to the park. 1.____
2. They are, alike, in this particular way. 2.____
3. They gave the poor man sume food when he knocked on the door. 3.____
4. I regret the loss caused by the error. 4.____
5. The students' will have a new teacher. 5.____
6. They sweared to bring out all the facts. 6.____
7. He decided to open a branch store on 33rd street. 7.____
8. His speed is equal and more than that of a racehorse. 8.____
9. He felt very warm on that Summer day. 9.____
10. He was assisted by his friend, who lives in the next house. 10.____

KEY (CORRECT ANSWERS)

1.	B	6.	A
2.	B	7.	C
3.	C	8.	A
4.	D	9.	C
5.	B	10.	D

TEST 6

DIRECTIONS: Each of the sentences in this test may be classified under one of the following four categories:
- A. Faulty because of incorrect grammar or word usage
- B. Faulty because of incorrect punctuation
- C. Faulty because of incorrect capitalization or incorrect spelling
- D. Correct

Examine each sentence carefully to determine under which of the above four options it is best classified. Then, in the space to the right, print the capital letter preceding the option which is the BEST of the four suggested above. (Note that each faulty sentence contains but one type of error. Consider a sentence to be correct if it contains none of the types of errors mentioned, even though there may be other correct ways of expressing the same thought.)

1. The climate of New York is colder than California. 1.____
2. I shall wait for you on the corner. 2.____
3. Did we see the boy who, we think, is the leader. 3.____
4. Being a modest person, John seldom talks about his invention. 4.____
5. The gang is called the smith street bos. 5.____
6. He seen the man break into the store. 6.____
7. We expected to lay still there for quite a while. 7.____
8. He is considered to be the Leader of his organization. 8.____
9. Although I recieved an invitation, I won't go. 9.____
10. The letter must be here some place. 10.____

KEY (CORRECT ANSWERS)

1.	A	6.	A
2.	D	7.	A
3.	B	8.	C
4.	D	9.	C
5.	C	10.	A

TEST 7

DIRECTIONS: Each of the sentences in this test may be classified under one of the following four categories:
- A. Faulty because of incorrect grammar or word usage
- B. Faulty because of incorrect punctuation
- C. Faulty because of incorrect capitalization or incorrect spelling
- D. Correct

Examine each sentence carefully to determine under which of the above four options it is best classified. Then, in the space to the right, print the capital letter preceding the option which is the BEST of the four suggested above. (Note that each faulty sentence contains but one type of error. Consider a sentence to be correct if it contains none of the types of errors mentioned, even though there may be other correct ways of expressing the same thought.)

1. I though it to be he.   1.____
2. We expect to remain here for a long time.   2.____
3. The committee was agreed.   3.____
4. Two-thirds of the building are finished.   4.____
5. The water was froze.   5.____
6. Everyone of the salesmen must supply their own car.   6.____
7. Who is the author of Gone With the Wind?   7.____
8. He marched on and declaring that he would never surrender.   8.____
9. Who shall I say called?   9.____
10. Everyone has left but they.   10.____

KEY (CORRECT ANSWERS)

1. A   6. A
2. D   7. B
3. D   8. A
4. A   9. D
5. A   10. D

TEST 8

DIRECTIONS: Each of the sentences in this test may be classified under one of the following four categories:
- A. Faulty because of incorrect grammar or word usage
- B. Faulty because of incorrect punctuation
- C. Faulty because of incorrect capitalization or incorrect spelling
- D. Correct

Examine each sentence carefully to determine under which of the above four options it is best classified. Then, in the space to the right, print the capital letter preceding the option which is the BEST of the four suggested above. (Note that each faulty sentence contains but one type of error. Consider a sentence to be correct if it contains none of the types of errors mentioned, even though there may be other correct ways of expressing the same thought.)

1. Who did we give the order to? 1.____
2. Send your order in immediately. 2.____
3. I believe I paid the Bill. 3.____
4. I have not met but one person. 4.____
5. Why aren't Tom, and Fred, going to the dance? 5.____
6. What reason is there for him not going? 6.____
7. The seige of Malta was a tremendous event. 7.____
8. I was there yesterday I assure you 8.____
9. Your ukulele is better than mine. 9.____
10. No one was there only Mary. 10.____

KEY (CORRECT ANSWERS)

1.	A	6.	A
2.	D	7.	C
3.	C	8.	B
4.	A	9.	C
5.	B	10.	A

TEST 9

DIRECTIONS: In each of the following groups of sentences, one of the four sentences is faulty in grammar, punctuation, or capitalization. Select the INCORRECT sentence in each case.

1. A. If you had stood at home and done your homework, you would not have failed in arithmetic.
   B. Her affected manner annoyed every member of the audience.
   C. How will the new law affect our income taxes?
   D. The plants were not affected by the long, cold winter, but they succumbed to the drought of summer.

   1.____

2. A. He is one of the most able men who have been in the Senate.
   B. It is he who is to blame for the lamentable mistake.
   C. Haven't you a helpful suggestion to make at this time?
   D. The money was robbed from the blind man's cup.

   2.____

3. A. The amount of children in this school is steadily increasing.
   B. After taking an apple from the table, she went out to play.
   C. He borrowed a dollar from me.
   D. I had hoped my brother would arrive before me.

   3.____

4. A. Whom do you think I hear from every week?
   B. Who do you think is the right man for the job?
   C. Who do you think I found in the room?
   D. He is the man whom we considered a good candidate for the presidency.

   4.____

5. A. Quietly the puppy laid down before the fireplace.
   B. You have made your bed; now lie in it.
   C. I was badly sunburned because I had lain too long in the sun.
   D. I laid the doll on the bed and left the room.

   5.____

KEY (CORRECT ANSWERS)

1. A
2. D
3. A
4. C
5. A

PREPARING WRITTEN MATERIALS
EXAMINATION SECTION
TEST 1

DIRECTIONS: Each question or incomplete statement is followed by several suggested answers or completions. Select the one that BEST answers the question or completes the statement. *PRINT THE LETTER OF THE CORRECT ANSWER IN THE SPACE AT THE RIGHT.*

Questions 1-21.

DIRECTIONS: In each of the following sentences, which were taken from students' transcripts, there may be an error. Indicate the appropriate correction in the space at the right. If the sentence is correct as is, indicate this choice. Unnecessary changes will be considered incorrect.

1. In that building there seemed to be representatives of Teachers College, the Veterans Bureau, and the Businessmen's Association.
   A. Teacher's College
   B. Veterans' Bureau
   C. Businessmens Association
   D. Correct as is

   1.____

2. In his travels, he visited St. Paul, San Francisco, Springfield, Ohio, and Washington, D.C.
   A. Ohio and
   B. Saint Paul
   C. Washington, D.C.
   D. Correct as is

   2.____

3. As a result of their purchasing a controlling interest in the syndicate, it was well-known that the Bureau of Labor Statistics' calculations would be unimportant.
   A. of them purchasing
   B. well known
   C. Statistics
   D. Correct as is

   3.____

4. Walter Scott, Jr.'s, attempt to emulate his father's success was doomed to failure.
   A. Junior's,
   B. Scott's, Jr.
   C. Scott, Jr.'s attempt
   D. Correct as is

   4.____

5. About B.C. 250 the Romans invaded Great Britain, and remains of their highly developed civilization can still be seen.
   A. 250 B.C.
   B. Britain and
   C. highly-developed
   D. Correct as is

   5.____

6. The two boss's sons visited the children's department.
   A. bosses   B. bosses'   C. childrens'   D. Correct as is

   6.____

7. Miss Amex not only approved the report, but also decided that it needed no revision.
   A. report; but   B. report but   C. report. But   D. Correct as is

8. Here's brain food in a jiffy—economical, too!
   A. economical too!   B. "brain food"
   C. jiffy-economical   D. Correct as is

9. She said, "He likes the "Gatsby Look" very much."
   A. said "He   B. "he
   C. 'Gatsby Look'   D. Correct as is

10. We anticipate that we will be able to visit them briefly in Los Angeles on Wednesday after a five day visit.
    A. Wednes-   B. 5 day   C. five-day   D. Correct as is

11. She passed all her tests, and, she now has a good position.
    A. tests, and she   B. past
    C. tests;   D. Correct as is

12. The billing clerk said, "I will send the bill today"; however, that was a week ago, and it hasn't arrived yet!
    A. today;"   B. today,"   C. ago and   D. Correct as is

13. "She types at more-than-average speed," Miss Smith said, "but I feel that it is a result of marvelous concentration and self control on her part."
    A. more than average   B. "But
    C. self-control   D. Correct as is

14. The state of Alaska, the largest state in the union, is also the northernmost state.
    A. Union   B. Northernmost State
    C. State of Alaska   D. Correct as is

15. The memoirs of Ex-President Nixon, according to figures, sold more copies than Six Crises, the book he wrote in the '60s.
    A. Six Crises   B. ex-President
    C. 60s   D. Correct as is

16. "There are three principal elements, determining the hazard of buildings: the contents hazard, the fire resistance of the structure, and the character of the interior finish," concluded the speaker.
    The one of the following statements that is MOST acceptable is that, in the above passage,
    A. the comma following the word *elements* is incorrect
    B. the colon following the word *buildings* is incorrect
    C. the comma following the word *finish* is incorrect
    D. there is no error in the punctuation of the sentence

17. He spoke on his favorite topic, "Why We Will Win." (How could I stop him?)   17.____
    A. Win".   B. him?).   C. him)?   C. Correct as is

18. "All any insurance policy is, is a contract for services," said my insurance   18.____
    agent, Mr. Newton.
    A. Insurance Policy   B. Insurance Agent
    C. policy is is a   D. Correct as is

19. Inasmuch as the price list has now been up dated, we should sent it to the   19.____
    printer.
    A. In as much   B. updated
    C. pricelist   D. Correct as is

20. We feel that "Our know-how" is responsible for the improvement in technical   20.____
    developments.
    A. "our   B. know how   C. that,   D. Correct as is

21. Did Cortez conquer the Incas? the Aztecs? the South American Indians?   21.____
    A. Incas, the Aztecs, the South American Indians?
    B. Incas; the Aztecs; the South American Indians?
    C. south American Indians?
    D. Correct as is

22. Which one of the following forms for the typed name of the dictator in the closing   22.____
    lines of a letter is generally MOST acceptable in the United States?
    A. (Dr.) James F. Farley   B. Dr. James F. Farley
    C. Me. James J. Farley, Ph.D. D. James F. Farley

23. The plural of   23.____
    A. turkey is turkies   B. cargo is cargoes
    C. bankruptcy is bankruptcys   D. son-in-law is son-in-laws

24. The abbreviation viz. means MOST NEARLY   24.____
    A. namely   B. for example
    C. the following   D. see

25. In the sentence, *A man in a light-gray suit waited thirty-five minutes in the*   25.____
    ante-room for the all-important document, the word IMPROPERLY hyphenated
    is
    A. light-gray   B. thirty-five   C. ante-room   D. all-important

KEY (CORRECT ANSWERS)

1.	D	11.	A
2.	C	12.	D
3.	B	13.	D
4.	D	14.	A
5.	A	15.	B
6.	B	16.	A
7.	B	17.	D
8.	D	18.	D
9.	C	19.	B
10.	C	20.	A

21. D
22. D
23. B
24. A
25. C

TEST 2

DIRECTIONS: Each question or incomplete statement is followed by several suggested answers or completions. Select the one that BEST answers the question or completes the statement. *PRINT THE LETTER OF THE CORRECT ANSWER IN THE SPACE AT THE RIGHT.*

Questions 1-10.

DIRECTIONS: In each of the following groups of four sentences, one sentence contains an error in sentence structure, grammar, usage, diction, or punctuation. Indicate the INCORRECT sentence.

1. A. The lecture finished, the audience began asking questions.
   B. Any man who could accomplish that task the world would regard as a hero.
   C. Our respect and admiration are mutual.
   D. George did like his mother told him, despite the importunities of his playmates.

2. A. I cannot but help admiring you for your dedication to your job.
   B. Because they had insisted upon showing us films of their travels, we have lost many friends whom we once cherished.
   C. I am constrained to admit that your remarks made me feel bad.
   D. My brother having been notified of his acceptance by the university of his choice, my father immediately made plans for a vacation.

3. A. In no other country is freedom of speech and assembly so jealously guarded.
   B. Being a beatnik, he felt that it would be a betrayal of his cause to wear shoes and socks at the same time.
   C. Riding over the Brooklyn Bridge gave us an opportunity to see the Manhattan skyline.
   D. In 1961, flaunting SEATO, the North Vietnamese crossed the line of demarcation.

4. A. I have enjoyed the study of the Spanish language not only because of its beauty and the opportunity it offers to understand the Hispanic culture but also to make use of it in the business associations I have in South America.
   B. The opinions he expressed were decidedly different from those he had held in his youth.
   C. Had he actually studied, he certainly would have passed.
   D. A supervisor should be patient, tactful, and firm.

5. A. At this point we were faced with only three alternatives: to push on, to remain where we were, or to return to the village.
   B. We had no choice but to forgive so venial a sin.
   C. In their new picture, the Warners are flouting tradition.
   D. Photographs taken revealed that 2.5 square miles had been burned.

227

6. A. He asked whether he might write to his friends. 6.____
   B. There are many problems which must be solved before we can be assured of world peace.
   C. Each person with whom I talked expressed his opinion freely.
   D. Holding on to my saddle with all my strength the horse galloped down the road at a terrifying pace.

7. A. After graduating high school, he obtained a position as a runner in Wall Street. 7.____
   B. Last night, in a radio address, the President urged us to subscribe to the Red Cross.
   C. In the evening, light spring rain cooled the streets.
   D. "Un-American" is a word which has been used even by those whose sympathies may well have been pro-Nazi.

8. A. It is hard to conceive of their not doing good work. 8.____
   B. Who won—you or I?
   C. He having read the speech caused much comment.
   D. Their finishing the work proves that it can be done.

9. A. Our course of study should not be different now than it was five years ago. 9.____
   B. I cannot deny myself the pleasure of publicly thanking the mayor for his actions.
   C. The article on "Morale" has appeared in the Times Literary Supplement.
   D. He died of tuberculosis contracted during service with the Allied Forces.

10. A. If it wasn't for a lucky accident, he would still be an office-clerk. 10.____
    B. It is evident that teachers need help.
    C. Rolls of postage stamps may be bought at stationery stores.
    D. Addressing machines are used by firms that publish magazines.

11. The one of the following sentences which contains NO error in usage is: 11.____
    A. After the robbers left, the proprietor stood tied in his chair for about two hours before help arrived.
    B. In the cellar I found the watchmans' hat and coat.
    C. The persons living in adjacent apartments stated that they had heard no unusual noises.
    D. Neither a knife or any firearms were found in the room.

12. The one of the following sentences which contains NO error in usage is: 12.____
    A. The policeman lay a firm hand on the suspect's shoulder.
    B. It is true that neither strength nor agility are the most important requirement for a good patrolman.
    C. Good citizens constantly strive to do more than merely comply the restraints imposed by society.
    D. Twenty years is considered a severe sentence for a felony.

13. Select the sentence containing an adverbial objective, 13.____
    A. Concepts can only acquire content when they are connected, however indirectly, with sensible experience.
    B. The cloth was several shades too light to match the skirt which she had discarded.
    C. The Gargantuan Hall of Commons became a tri-daily horror to Kurt, because two youths discerned that he had a beard and courageously told the world about it.
    D. Brooding morbidly over the event, Elsie found herself incapable of engaging in normal activity.

14. Select the sentence containing a verb in the subjunctive mood. 14.____
    A. Had he known of the new experiments with penicillin dust for the cure of colds, he might have been tempted to try them in his own office.
    B. I should be very much honored by your visit.
    C. Though he has one of the highest intelligence quotients in his group, he seems far below the average in actual achievement.
    D. Long had I known that he would be the man finally selected for such signal honors.

15. Select the sentence containing one (or more) passive perfect participle(s). 15.____
    A. Having been apprised of the consequences of his refusal to answer, the witness finally revealed the source of his information.
    B. To have been placed in such an uncomfortable position was perhaps unfair to a journalist of his reputation.
    C. When deprived of special immunity he had, of course, no alternative but to speak.
    D. Having been obdurate until now, he was reluctant to surrender under this final pressure exerted upon him.

16. Select the sentence containing a predicate nominative. 16.____
    A. His dying wish, which he expressed almost with his last breath, was to see that justice was done toward his estranged wife.
    B. So long as we continue to elect our officials in truly democratic fashion, we shall have the power to preserve our liberties.
    C. We could do nothing, at this juncture, but walk the five miles back to camp.
    D. There was the spaniel, wet and cold and miserable, waiting silently at the door.

17. Select the sentence containing exactly TWO adverbs. 17.____
    A. The gentlemen advanced with exasperating deliberateness, while his lonely partner waited.
    B. If you are well, will you come early?
    C. I think you have guessed right, though you were rather slow, I must say.
    D. The last hundred years have seen more change than a thousand years of the Roman Empire, than a hundred thousand years of the stone age.

Questions 18-24.

DIRECTIONS: Select the choice describing the error in the sentence.

18. If us seniors do not support school functions, who will?
    A. Unnecessary shift in tense
    B. Incomplete sentence
    C. Improper case of pronoun
    D. Lack of parallelism

    18.____

19. The principal has issued regulations which, in my opinion, I think are too harsh.
    A. Incorrect punctuation
    B. Faulty sentence structure
    C. Misspelling
    D. Redundant expression

    19.____

20. The freshmens' and sophomores' performances equaled those of the juniors and seniors.
    A. Ambiguous reference
    B. Incorrect placement of punctuation
    C. Misspelling of past tense
    D. Incomplete comparison

    20.____

21. Each of them, Anne and her, is an outstanding pianist I can't tell you which one is best.
    A. Lack of agreement
    B. Improper degree of comparison
    C. Incorrect case of pronoun
    D. Run-on sentence

    21.____

22. She wears clothes that are more expensive than my other friends.
    A. Misuse of *than*
    B. Incorrect relative pronoun
    C. Shift in tense
    D. Faulty comparison

    22.____

23. At the very end of the story it implies that the children's father died tragically.
    A. Misuse of *implies*
    B. Indefinite use of pronoun
    C. Incorrect spelling
    D. Incorrect possessive

    23.____

24. At the end of the game both of us, John and me, couldn't scarcely walk because we were so tired.
    A. Incorrect punctuation
    B. Run-on sentence
    C. Incorrect case of pronoun
    D. Double negative

    24.____

Questions 25-30.

DIRECTIONS: Questions 25 through 30 consist of a sentence lacking certain needed punctuation. Pick as your answer the description of punctuation which will CORRECTLY complete the sentence.

25. If you take the time to keep up your daily correspondence you will no doubt be most efficient.
    A. Comma only after *doubt*
    B. Comma only after *correspondence*
    C. Commas after *correspondence*, *will*, and *be*
    D. Commas after *if*, *correspondence*, and *will*

    25.____

26. Because he did not send the application soon enough he did not receive the up to date copy of the book.
    A. Commas after *application* and *enough*, and quotation marks before *up* and after *date*
    B. Commas after *application* and *enough*, and hyphens between *to* and *date*
    C. Comma after *enough*, and hyphens between *up* and *to* and between *to* and *date*
    D. Comma after *application*, and quotation marks before *up* and after *date*

27. The coordinator requested from the department the following items a letter each week summarizing progress personal forms and completed applications for tests.
    A. Commas after *items* and *completed*
    B. Semi-colon after *items* and *progress*, comma after *forms*
    C. Colon after *items*, commas after *progress* and *forms*
    D. Colon after *items*, commas after *forms* and *applications*

28. The supervisor asked Who will attend the conference next month.
    A. Comma after *asked*, period after *month*
    B. Period after *asked*, question mark after *month*
    C. Comma after *asked*, quotation marks before *Who*, quotation marks after *month*, and question mark after the quotation marks
    D. Comma after *asked*, quotation marks before *Who*, question mark after *month*, and quotation marks after the question mark

29. When the statistics are collected, we will forward the results to you as soon as possible.
    A. Comma after *you*
    B. Commas after *forward* and *you*
    C. Commas after *collected*, *results* and *you*
    D. Comma after *collected*

30. The ecology of our environment is concerned with mans pollution of the atmosphere.
    A. Comma after *ecology*
    B. Apostrophe after *n* and before *s* in *mans*
    C. Commas after *ecology* and *environment*
    D. Apostrophe after *s* in *mans*

KEY (CORRECT ANSWERS)

1.	D	11.	C	21.	B
2.	A	12.	D	22.	D
3.	D	13.	B	23.	B
4.	A	14.	A	24.	D
5.	B	15.	A	25.	B
6.	D	16.	A	26.	C
7.	A	17.	C	27.	C
8.	C	18.	C	28.	D
9.	A	19.	D	29.	D
10.	A	20.	B	30.	B

TEST 3

DIRECTIONS: Each question or incomplete statement is followed by several suggested answers or completions. Select the one that BEST answers the question or completes the statement. *PRINT THE LETTER OF THE CORRECT ANSWER IN THE SPACE AT THE RIGHT.*

Questions 1-6.

DIRECTIONS: From the four choices offered in Questions 1 through 6, select the one which is INCORRECT.

1.
   A. Before we try to extricate ourselves from this struggle in which we are now engaged in, we must be sure that we are not severing ties of honor and duty.
   B. Besides being an outstanding student, he is also a leader in school government and a trophy-winner in school sports.
   C. If the framers of the Constitution were to return to life for a day, their opinion of our amendments would be interesting.
   D. Since there are three m's in the word, it is frequently misspelled.

   1.____

2.
   A. It was a college with an excellance beyond question.
   B. The coach will accompany the winners, whomever they may be.
   C. The dean, together with some other faculty members, is planning a conference.
   D. The jury are arguing among themselves.

   2.____

3.
   A. This box is less nearly square than that one.
   B. Wagner is many persons' choice as the world's greatest composer.
   C. The habits of Copperheads are different from Diamond Backs.
   D. The teacher maintains that the child was insolent.

   3.____

4.
   A. There was a time when the Far North was unknown territory. Now American soldiers manning radar stations there wave to Boeing jet planes zooming by overhead.
   B. Exodus, the psalms, and Deuteronomy are all books of the Old Testament.
   C. Linda identified her china dishes by marking their bottoms with india ink.
   D. Harry S. Truman, former president of the United States, served as a captain in the American army during World War I.

   4.____

5.
   A. The sequel of their marriage was a divorce.
   B. We bought our car secondhand.
   C. His whereabouts is unknown.
   D. Jones offered to use his own car, providing the company would pay for gasoline, oil, and repairs,

   5.____

233

6. A. I read Golding's "Lord of the Flies".
    B. The orator at the civil rights rally thrilled the audience when he said, "I quote Robert Burns's line, 'A man's a man for a' that."
    C. The phrase "producer to consumer" is commonly used by market analysts.
    D. The lawyer shouted, "Is not this evidence illegal?"

Questions 7-9.

DIRECTIONS: In answering Questions 7 through 9, mark the letter A if faulty because of incorrect grammar, mark the letter B if faulty because of incorrect punctuation, mark the letter C if correct.

7. Mr. Brown our accountant, will audit the accounts next week.

8. Give the assignment to whomever is able to do it most efficiently.

9. The supervisor expected either your or I to file these reports.

Questions 10-14.

DIRECTIONS: In each of the following groups of four sentences, one sentence contains an error in sentence structure, grammar, usage, diction, or punctuation. Indicate the INCORRECT sentence.

10. A. The agent asked, "Did you say, 'Never again?'"
    B. Kindly let me know whether you can visit us on the 17th.
    C. "I cannot accept that!" he exploded. "Please show me something else.
    D. Ed, will you please lend me your grass shears for an hour or so.

11. A. Recalcitrant though he may have been, Alexander was willfully destructive.
    B. Everybody should look out for himself.
    C. John is one of those students who usually spends most of his time in the principal's office.
    D. She seems to feel that what is theirs is hers.

12. A. Be he ever so much in the wrong, I'll support the man while deploring his actions.
    B. The schools' lack of interest in consumer education is shortsighted.
    C. I think that Fitzgerald's finest stanza is one which includes the reference to youth's "sweet-scented manuscript.
    D. I never would agree to Anderson having full control of the company's policies.

13. A. We had to walk about five miles before finding a gas station.
    B. The willful sending of a false alarm has, and may, result in homicide.
    C. Please bring that book to me at once.
    D. Neither my sister nor I am interested in bowling.

14. A. He is one of the very few football players who doesn't wear a helmet with a face guard.
    B. But three volunteers appeared at the recruiting office.
    C. Such consideration as you can give us will be appreciated.
    D. When I left them, the group were disagreeing about the proposed legislation.

14.____

Question 15.

DIRECTIONS: Question 15 contains two sentences concerning criminal law. The sentences could contain errors in English grammar or usage. A sentence does not contain an error simply because it could be written in a different manner. In answering this question, choose answer
A. if only sentence I is correct
B. if only sentence II is correct
C. if both sentences are correct
D. if neither sentence is correct

15. I. The use of fire or explosives to destroy tangible property is proscribed by the criminal mischief provisions of the Revised Penal Law.
    II. The defendant's taking of a taxicab for the immediate purpose of affecting his escape did not constitute grand larceny.

15.____

KEY (CORRECT ANSWERS)

1.	A	6.	A	11.	C
2.	B	7.	B	12.	D
3.	C	8.	A	13.	B
4.	B	9.	A	14.	A
5.	D	10	A	15.	A